225 COOKIES

225 COOKIES

TO MAKE AND DECORATE FOR EVERY OCCASION

Contributing editor: Catherine Atkinson

This edition is published by Southwater,
an imprint of Anness Publishing Ltd, Hermes House,
88–89 Blackfriars Road, London SE1 8HA
tel. 020 7401 2077; fax 020 7633 9499
www.southwaterbooks.com; www.annesspublishing.com

If you like the images in this book and would like to investigate using them for publishing, promotions or advertising, please visit our website www.practicalpictures.com for more information.

UK distributor: Book Trade Services; tel. 0116 2759086;
fax 0116 2759090; uksales@booktradeservices.com;
exportsales@booktradeservices.com
North American distributor: National Book Network;
tel. 301 459 3366; fax 301 429 5746; www.nbnbooks.com
Australian distributor: Pan Macmillan Australia; tel. 1300 135 113; fax 1300 135 103; customer.service@macmillan.com.au
New Zealand distributor: David Bateman Ltd;
tel. (09) 415 7664; fax (09) 415 8892

Publisher: Joanna Lorenz
Senior Editorial Director: Helen Sudell
Editor: Simona Hill
Editorial Reader: Molly Perham
Production Controller: Christine Ni
Recipes: Pepita Aris, Catherine Atkinson, Alex Barker, Ghillie Basan, Angela Boggiano, Carol Bowen, Georgina Campbell, Carla Capalbo, Maxine Clark, Carole Clements, Matthew Drennan, Tessa Evelegh, Joanna Farrow, Christine France, Brian Glover, Nicola Graimes, Carole Handslip, Biddy White Lennon, Sara Lewis, Gilly Love, Lesley Mackley, Norma MacMillan, Sue Maggs, Sally Mansfield, Jane Milton, Sallie Morris, Anna Mosesson, Janice Murfitt, Rena Salaman, Anne Sheasby, Young Jin Song, Marlena Spieler, Christopher Trotter, Laura Washburn, Kate Whiteman, Judy Williams, Carol Wilson, Elizabeth Wolf-Cohen, Jeni Wright, Annette Yates.
Photographers: Karl Adamson, Edward Allwright, Martin Brigdale, James Duncan, John Freeman, Michelle Garrett, Amanda Heywood, David Jordan, William Lingwood, Debbie Patterson, Sam Stowell.

ETHICAL TRADING POLICY
Because of our ongoing ecological investment programme, you, as our customer, can have the pleasure and reassurance of knowing that a tree is being cultivated on your behalf to naturally replace the materials used to make the book you are holding.
For further information about this scheme, go to www.annesspublishing.com/trees

Previously published as part of a larger volume, *500 Cookies, Biscuits & Bakes*.

PUBLISHER'S NOTE
Although the advice and information in this book are believed to be accurate and true at the time of going to press, neither the authors nor the publisher can accept any legal responsibility or liability for any errors or omissions that may have been made nor for any inaccuracies nor for any loss, harm or injury that comes about from following instructions or advice in this book.

Notes

Bracketed terms are intended for American readers.

For all recipes, quantities are given in both metric and imperial measures and, where appropriate, in standard cups and spoons. Follow one set of measures, but not a mixture, because they are not interchangeable.

Standard spoon and cup measures are level. 1 tsp = 5ml, 1 tbsp = 15ml, 1 cup = 250ml/8fl oz. Australian standard tablespoons are 20ml. Australian readers should use 3 tsp in place of 1 tbsp for measuring small quantities.

American pints are 16fl oz/2 cups. American readers should use 20fl oz/2.5 cups in place of 1 pint when measuring liquids. Electric oven temperatures in this book are for conventional ovens. When using a fan oven, the temperature will probably need to be reduced by about 10–20°C/20–40°F. Since ovens vary, you should check with your manufacturer's instruction book for guidance. The nutritional analysis given for each recipe is calculated per cookie, unless otherwise stated. Measurements for sodium do not include salt added to taste.
Medium (US large) eggs are used unless otherwise stated.
Granulated (white) sugar is used unless otherwise stated.
Main front cover image shows Chocolate Chip and Walnut Cookies – for recipe, see page 62

Contents

Introduction

The satisfaction of home baking is immense, and the only culinary skill that can produce fabulous results in such a short time and with so few ingredients. Commercial cake mixes, or shop-bought cookies are no match for home-made varieties in either texture or flavour. The delicious aroma and sweet wafts of baking that permeate the kitchen, stimulate the appetite and offer the enticing promise of a sweet treat are part of the appeal of home-baking for many cooks, especially those with a sweet tooth.

Baking gives the cook complete control of the choice of ingredients, so you can make sure that everything is of the best quality, and avoid the additives that are often present in commercial products. All the family can enjoy baking, and it offers a great opportunity to get children interested in making the food that they will eat. It's a therapeutic activity too, and sharing the results is a sociable and pleasing way to spend time with family and friends. Above all, everyone is sure to love the finished results and their appreciation is guaranteed. There is pride, too, in being the provider of such fare.

Below: *Fourth of July blueberry softbakes are perfect for a celebration.*

Above: *Crunchy chocolate chip cookies are everybody's favourites.*

Whether you're looking for a mid-morning or mid-afternoon snack to share with friends, feeding ravenous schoolchildren returning home, or are in need of a sweet taste to signal the finale of a meal, this fabulous book is guaranteed to contain the ideal solution.

There are recipes for every kind of sweet and savoury cookie and cracker, including plenty of innovative ideas using ingredients that were once only available from specialist outlets but are now more standard fare, such as finely ground cornmeal for chewy sultana cornmeal cookies, or poppy seeds for the festival cookies oznei hamam. There are recipes suitable for baking in batches to satisfy the needs of the cake stall such as peanut butter cookies, or orange oaties, as well as lavishly decorated confections for birthday parties for both children and adults. Indulgent recipes for special events include black Russian party cookies and the tipsy tiramisù special occasion cookies. Recipes from many countries are featured, and a special chapter is devoted to baking cookies for annual festivals and events, such as Christmas, Easter and New Year.

Above: *Savoury crackers can be eaten plain or served with cheese.*

Baking, in general, is an exact science and needs to be approached in an ordered way to achieve the best results, but cookie making is easier than cake baking, so it's a good choice for beginner cooks to achieve good results in a relatively short time. First read the recipe through from beginning to end to ensure that you understand the cooking method. Set out all the required ingredients and equipment before you begin, just to make sure that you have everything in stock. Eggs and butter should be at room temperature for best results, unless otherwise stated. Sift the flour after you have measured it. If you sift the flour from a fair height, it will have more chance to aerate and lighten.

No two ovens are alike. Buy a reliable oven thermometer and test the temperature of your oven. When possible bake the cookies in the centre of the oven where the heat is more likely to be constant. If you are using a fan-assisted oven, follow the manufacturer's guidelines. Choose good quality baking sheets. They can improve your results, as they conduct heat efficiently. Finally, if you are baking cookies on shelves at differing heights, swap the baking sheets midway through baking to ensure even cooking.

There are many ways of making cookie dough, but most cookies are made according to just a few methods: beating, melting and rubbing in, all of which are simple to master. Once the batter is thoroughly mixed, the cookies are either rolled out, shaped using a piping (pastry) bag, dropped from a teaspoon on to a baking sheet, piped and/or pressed into a mould, depending on the consistency of the batter. The quantity of each ingredient in the recipe, the combination of ingredients and the length and temperature of baking determine whether the cookie is soft-centred and chewy, hard and crunchy, or flaky with a melt-in-the-mouth consistency.

Everyday cookies may be left plain or lightly dusted with icing (confectioners') sugar or cocoa powder, while those for special occasions may be decorated with an assortment of toppings before baking, or sandwiched together with a sweet and creamy filling, and then drizzled with icing.

Whatever your baking requirements, with more than 225 tried-and-tested delicious recipes to choose from and comprehensive step-by-step instructions, this book contains the only cookie selection you'll ever need.

Below: *Macaroons contain no fat, so are a healthy choice for those watching their diet.*

Measuring Ingredients

Cooks with years of experience may not need to measure ingredients, but if you are a beginner or are trying a new recipe for the first time, it is best to follow instructions carefully. Also, measuring ingredients precisely will ensure consistent results. Always use the best quality ingredients that are within their "use-by" date.

1 For liquids measured in pints or litres, use a glass or clear plastic measuring jug (cup). Put it on a flat surface and pour in the liquid. Check that the liquid is level with the marking specified in the recipe.

2 For liquids measured in spoons, pour the liquid into the measuring spoon, to the brim, and then pour it into the mixing bowl. Do not measure it over the mixing bowl in case of spillages.

3 For measuring dry ingredients in a spoon, fill the spoon, scooping up the ingredients. Level the surface with the straight edge of a knife.

4 For measuring dry ingredients by weight, scoop or pour on to the scales, watching the dial and reading carefully. Balance scales give more accurate readings than spring scales.

5 For measuring syrups, set the mixing bowl on the scales and turn the gauge to zero, or make a note of the weight. Pour in the required weight of syrup.

6 For measuring butter, cut with a sharp knife and weigh, or cut off the specified amount following the markings on the wrapping paper.

Rubbing-in Method

Plain cookies are usually made by rubbing the fat into the flour. For this, the fat, whether butter, margarine or lard, should not be rock hard or too warm. It is first chopped into small pieces, then added to the dry ingredients. The mixture is lifted high and the lumps of fat rubbed between the fingertips as the mixture is allowed to fall back into the bowl.

1 Sift the flour into a bowl from a height, adding the raising agents, salt and any sugar or spices. Mix the dry ingredients evenly together. Sift in any other dry ingredients.

2 Add the diced butter, and use your fingertips to rub the fat into the flour. Cold fingertips produce the best results, rubbing in the fat without melting it. Sprinkle on any liquid ingredients.

3 Mix with a fork and then gather the ingredients together with your fingertips until the dough forms a ball. If it is too dry add more liquid. Turn on to a lightly floured surface and knead lightly.

Beating Method

To make cookies by the beating method, the fat and sugar are beaten together before the eggs and dry ingredients are added. The fat (usually butter) should be soft enough to be beaten so, if necessary, remove it from the refrigerator and leave for at least 30 minutes. For best results, the egg should be at room temperature too.

1 Sift the flour with the salt, raising agent and any other dry ingredients, such as spices or unsweetened cocoa powder, into a bowl. Set aside.

2 Put the fat in a bowl and beat with an electric mixer or a wooden spoon until soft and pliable. Add the sugar and beat until the mixture is pale and fluffy.

3 Add the eggs or egg yolks, one at a time, beating well after each addition. Scrape the bowl often so all the ingredients are evenly combined.

4 Add the sifted dry ingredients to the mixture. Beat at low speed just until smoothly combined, or fold in with a large metal spoon.

5 If the recipe calls for any liquid, add it in small portions, alternately with portions of the dry ingredients.

6 Drop spoonfuls of the ingredients on to the prepared baking sheet and bake as directed for the recipe.

Melting Method

Cookies such as flapjacks and gingernuts are made by first melting the fat and sugar or syrup together. The dry ingredients are then stirred in to make a soft dough that firms as it cools. The baked cookies become crisp as they cool, so should be quickly shaped or left on the baking sheets for a few minutes before transferring to a wire rack.

1 Put the butter, any syrup, milk and sugar in a heavy pan and heat gently over a low heat until the butter has just melted. The heat should be low so that the sugar does not burn, but melts instead into the butter. If the mixture boils it will alter the proportions.

2 Remove the pan from the heat and leave the mixture to cool for a few minutes. This is particularly important if you are going to add eggs to the mixture. Sift over the flour and any flavourings, salt and raising agents and stir well until the mixture is smooth.

3 Add the sifted dry ingredients to the mixture. Beat at low speed just until smoothly combined, or fold in with a large spoon. Shape the cookie dough as soon as possible before the raising agents start to work. Bake as directed for the recipe.

Butter Cookies

These crunchy, buttery cookies make a delicious afternoon treat served with a cup of tea or a glass of milk. The dough can be made in advance, wrapped in foil, and chilled in the refrigerator until you are ready to bake the cookies.

Makes 25–30
175g/6oz/³⁄₄ cup unsalted butter, at room temperature, diced
90g/3¹⁄₂oz/¹⁄₂ cup golden caster (superfine) sugar
250g/9oz/2¹⁄₄ cups plain (all-purpose) flour
demerara (raw) sugar, for coating

1 Put the butter and sugar in a bowl and beat until light and fluffy.

2 Add the flour, mix in, then, using your hands, gradually work in the crumbs until the mixture forms a smooth dough. Roll into a sausage shape about 30cm/12in long, then pat the sides flat to form a square log.

3 Sprinkle a thick layer of demerara sugar on a piece of baking parchment. Press each side of the dough into the sugar to coat. Wrap and chill for 30 minutes until firm.

4 Preheat the oven to 160°C/325°F/Gas 3.

5 Remove the dough from the refrigerator and unwrap. Cut it into thick slices and place slightly apart on lightly greased baking sheets. Bake for 20 minutes until just beginning to turn brown. Transfer to a wire rack to cool.

> **Variations**
> • To flavour the cookies, add ground cinnamon, grated lemon or orange rind, or vanilla or almond extract to the butter mixture, or add whole glacé (candied) cherries, chocolate chips, chopped nuts or dried fruit such as chopped apricots to the dough.
> • As an alternative, coat the outside in chopped nuts or sesame seeds.

Orange Buttery Cookies

These rich, buttery cookies with a smooth and crisp texture can be scented with rose water or vanilla instead of orange flower water and are delicious served with tea.

Makes 20–25
200g/7oz/scant 1 cup butter
130g/4¹⁄₂oz/generous 1 cup icing (confectioners') sugar, sifted
5–10ml/1–2 tsp orange flower water
250g/9oz/2¹⁄₄ cups plain (all-purpose) flour, sifted
handful of blanched almonds

1 Melt the butter in a pan and leave to cool until lukewarm.

2 Stir the icing sugar and orange flower water into the melted butter, then gradually beat in the flour to form a smooth, stiff dough. Wrap in clear film (plastic wrap) and chill for 15 minutes.

3 Preheat the oven to 180°C/350°F/Gas 4. Lightly grease a baking sheet.

4 Break off walnut-size pieces of dough and roll into balls. Place on the baking sheet and flatten slightly. Press a nut into the centre of each.

5 Bake for 20 minutes, or until golden. Allow to cool slightly on the baking sheet; when firm, transfer to a wire rack.

Chocolate-tipped Cookies

Wrap cold winter hands around a mug of steaming hot chocolate and dunk these cookies in for a special treat. The sweet taste and crunchy texture make these a moreish addition to the cookie jar.

Makes 14–16
115g/4oz/¹⁄₂ cup butter, softened
45ml/3 tbsp icing (confectioners') sugar, sifted
150g/9oz/2¹⁄₄ cups plain (all-purpose) flour
few drops vanilla extract
75g/3oz plain (semisweet) chocolate

1 Preheat the oven to 180°C/350°F/Gas 4. Lightly grease two baking sheets.

2 In a large bowl, beat together the butter and icing sugar until very soft. Mix in the flour and vanilla extract. The mixture should be quite stiff.

3 Put the mixture in a large piping (pastry) bag fitted with a large star nozzle and pipe 10–13cm/4–5in straight lines on the prepared baking sheets.

4 Bake for 15–20 minutes until pale golden brown. Allow to cool slightly before lifting on to a wire rack. Leave to cool completely.

5 Put the chocolate in a small heatproof bowl and set over a pan of gently simmering water. Heat gently, stirring frequently until melted. Dip both ends of each cookie in the chocolate. Place the dipped cookies on a wire rack and leave to set.

Butter Cookies Energy 84kcal/350kJ; Protein 0.8g; Carbohydrate 9.6g, of which sugars 3.3g; Fat 4.9g, of which saturates 3.1g; Cholesterol 12mg; Calcium 14mg; Fibre 0.3g; Sodium 36mg.
Orange Buttery Cookies Energy 131kcal/546kJ; Protein 2.3g; Carbohydrate 9.5g, of which sugars 3.5g; Fat 9.6g, of which saturates 2.9g; Cholesterol 16mg; Calcium 28mg; Fibre 0.7g; Sodium 5mg.
Chocalate-tipped Cookies Energy 120kcal/503kJ; Protein 1.2g; Carbohydrate 13.2g, of which sugars 6.1g; Fat 7.3g, of which saturates 4.6g; Cholesterol 16mg; Calcium 17mg; Fibre 0.4g; Sodium 44mg.

Buttery Vanilla Cookies

These crisp, buttery cookies are perfect with strawberries and cream. They are known as refrigerator cookies as the mixture is chilled until it is firm enough to cut neatly into thin slices. The dough can be frozen and when thawed enough to slice, can be freshly baked, but do allow a little extra baking time.

Makes 28–30
275g/10oz/2½ cups plain (all-purpose) flour
200g/7oz/scant 1 cup unsalted butter
90g/3½oz/scant 1 cup icing (confectioners') sugar, plus extra for dusting
10ml/2 tsp vanilla extract

1 Put the flour in a food processor. Add the butter and process until the mixture resembles coarse breadcrumbs.

2 Add the icing sugar and vanilla, and process until the mixture comes together to form a dough. Knead lightly and shape into a thick sausage, 30cm/12in long and 5cm/2in in diameter.

3 Wrap and chill for at least 1 hour, until firm.

4 Preheat the oven to 200°C/400°F/Gas 6. Lightly grease two baking sheets.

5 Using a sharp knife, cut 5mm/¼in thick slices from the dough and space them slightly apart on the baking sheet.

6 Bake for 8–10 minutes. Leave for 5 minutes, then transfer to a wire rack to cool. Serve dusted with icing sugar.

Cook's Tip
Alternate the position of the baking sheets in the oven halfway through cooking, if necessary, until the cookies are cooked evenly and have just turned pale golden around the edges.

Brittany Butter Cookies

These lightly glazed little cookies are similar to shortbread, but are richer. Traditionally, they are made with lightly salted butter.

Makes 18–20
6 egg yolks, lightly beaten
15ml/1 tbsp milk
250g/9oz/2¼ cups plain (all-purpose) flour
175g/6oz/¾ cup caster (superfine) sugar
200g/7oz/scant 1 cup butter at room temperature, diced

1 Preheat the oven to 180°C/350°F/Gas 4. Lightly grease two heavy baking sheets.

2 Mix 15ml/1 tbsp of the egg yolks with the milk to make a glaze. Set aside.

3 In a bowl, beat together the sugar and butter until light and creamy. Add the egg yolks and mix to combine. Add the flour in batches and stir well. Use your fingertips until it is all incorporated and the mixture forms a slightly sticky dough. Gather it together.

4 Using floured hands, pat out the dough to about 5mm/¼in thick and stamp out rounds using a 7.5cm/3in cutter. Transfer the rounds to the prepared baking sheet, brush each with a little of the reserved egg and milk glaze, then, using the back of a knife, score gently with lines to create a lattice pattern.

5 Bake for about 12 minutes or until golden. Cool on the baking sheet to firm up, then transfer to a wire rack and leave to cool completely.

Variation
To make a large Brittany butter cake, pat the dough with well-floured hands into a 23cm/9in loose-based cake tin (pan). Brush with the glaze and score the lattice pattern on top. Bake for 45–60 minutes until firm to the touch and golden brown.

Buttery Vanilla Cookies Energy 84kcal/350kJ; Protein 0.8g; Carbohydrate 9.6g, of which sugars 3.3g; Fat 4.9g, of which saturates 3.1g; Cholesterol 12mg; Calcium 14mg; Fibre 0.3g; Sodium 36mg.
Brittany Butter Cookies Energy 170kcal/711kJ; Protein 2.2g; Carbohydrate 19g, of which sugars 9.4g; Fat 10g, of which saturates 5.7g; Cholesterol 82mg; Calcium 32mg; Fibre 0.4g; Sodium 65mg.

Sugar-crusted Shortbread Rounds

Shortbread should melt in the mouth, taste buttery but never greasy. It tastes best when eaten freshly made with a cup of tea.

Makes about 24
450g/1lb/2 cups butter
225g/8oz/1 heaped cup caster (superfine) sugar

450g/1lb/4 cups plain (all-purpose) flour
225g/8oz/scant 1½ cups ground rice or rice flour
5ml/1 tsp salt
demerara (raw) sugar, to decorate
golden caster (superfine) sugar, for dusting

1 Preheat the oven to 190°C/375°F/Gas 5.

2 Make sure all the ingredients are at room temperature. Put the butter and sugar in a bowl and beat together until light, pale and fluffy.

3 Sift together the flour, ground rice or rice flour and salt and stir into the butter and sugar with a wooden spoon, until the mixture resembles fine breadcrumbs.

4 Gather the dough together with your hands, then put it on a clean work surface. Knead lightly until it forms a ball but do not over-knead or the shortbread will be tough and greasy. Roll into a sausage, about 7.5cm/3in thick. Wrap in clear film (plastic wrap) and chill until firm.

5 Pour the demerara sugar on to a sheet of baking parchment. Unwrap the dough and roll in the sugar until evenly coated. Slice the roll into discs about 1cm/½in thick.

6 Place the discs on to two lightly greased baking sheets lined with baking parchment, spacing them well apart to allow for spreading. Bake for 20–25 minutes until very pale gold.

7 Remove the cookies from the oven and sprinkle immediately with the golden caster sugar. Allow to cool on the baking sheet for 10 minutes before transferring to a wire rack to cool completely.

Shortbread Shells

These interesting shaped cookies are made by pressing the dough into a queen scallop shell prior to baking. If you don't have shells you could stamp out rounds with a cookie cutter instead.

Makes 12
100g/3½oz/½ cup butter, softened
50g/2oz/¼ cup caster (superfine) sugar, plus extra for sprinkling
150g/5½oz/1¼ cups plain (all-purpose) flour

1 Preheat the oven to 200°C/400°F/Gas 6. Lightly grease one large baking sheet and line with baking parchment.

2 Put the butter and sugar into a bowl and beat until light and fluffy. Sift the flour over and stir it in until the mixture can be gathered into a ball of soft dough.

3 Divide the dough into 12 and with your hands form into equal-sized balls.

4 Sprinkle the inside of a scallop shell with sugar, gently press a ball of dough into it, spreading it evenly so the shell is filled. Invert on to the prepared baking sheets, pressing it down to flatten the base and to mark it with the impression of the shell. Lift the shell off, carefully prising out the dough. Alternatively, press or roll the dough balls into plain round cookies measuring about 5cm/2in in diameter.

5 Bake for about 10 minutes until set. Traditionally, they should not be allowed to brown, but should have crisp golden edges.

6 Sprinkle with a little extra sugar, transfer to a wire rack and leave to cool completely.

> **Cook's Tip**
> *Although shaping the first shell-shape biscuit may seen tricky, the shell will coat with sugar and the rest will slip out easily. You could flavour the mixture with vanilla or spices in step 2.*

Sugar-crusted Shortbread Rounds Energy 275kcal/1147kJ; Protein 2.5g; Carbohydrate 32g, of which sugars 10.2g; Fat 15.7g, of which saturates 9.8g; Cholesterol 40mg; Calcium 37mg; Fibre 0.8g; Sodium 197mg.
Shortbread Shells Energy 121kcal/506kJ; Protein 1.2g; Carbohydrate 14.1g, of which sugars 4.6g; Fat 7g, of which saturates 4.4g; Cholesterol 18mg; Calcium 21mg; Fibre 0.4g; Sodium 51mg.

Almond Shortbread Fingers

This easy all-in-one recipe makes a very light, crisp shortbread with an excellent flavour, and it keeps well. Serve with tea or coffee, or to accompany light desserts.

Makes about 48
225g/8oz/1 cup butter, softened
*75g/3oz/6 tbsp caster
  (superfine) sugar*
*275g/10oz/2½ cups plain
  (all-purpose) flour*
25g/1oz/¼ cup ground almonds
grated rind of ½ lemon

1 Preheat the oven to 180°C/350°F/Gas 4. Lightly grease a large Swiss roll tin (jelly roll pan).

2 Beat the butter and sugar together in a mixing bowl until light and fluffy. Set aside.

3 Sift the flour and almonds into a clean mixing bowl. Turn the creamed mixture on to the flour and almonds, then work it together first using a wooden spoon and then using your fingers to make a smooth dough.

4 Turn the mixture out on the prepared tray and flatten it out to the edges with the back of a wooden spoon until it is an even thickness all over.

5 Bake for 20 minutes, or until pale golden brown. Remove from the oven and immediately mark the shortbread into fingers or squares with a sharp knife, while the mixture is soft.

6 Leave the shortbread in the tin to cool for a few minutes, and then transfer to a wire rack and leave to cool completely.

7 If stored in an airtight container, the shortbread can be kept for up to two weeks.

Variation
Replace the lemon rind with the grated rind of two oranges, if you like.

Shrewsbury Cakes

These are crisp, lemony shortbread cookies with fluted edges, which have been made and sold in the town of Shrewsbury, in England, since the 17th century.

Makes about 20
115g/4oz/½ cup butter, softened
*140g/5oz/¾ cup caster
  (superfine) sugar*
2 egg yolks
*225g/8oz/2 cups plain
  (all-purpose) flour, plus extra
  for dusting*
finely grated rind of 1 lemon

1 Preheat the oven to 180°C/350°F/Gas 4. Lightly grease two baking sheets.

2 In a mixing bowl, beat together the butter and sugar until pale, light and fluffy. Beat in each egg yolk one at a time, beating thoroughly after each addition.

3 Sift the flour over the top and add the lemon rind. Stir in with a wooden spoon at first and then gather up the mixture with your fingertips to make a stiff dough. Knead the dough lightly on a floured surface then roll it out evenly to about 5mm/¼in thick.

4 Using a 7.5cm/3in fluted cookie cutter, stamp out rounds and arrange on the baking sheets. Gather up the trimmings and roll out again to make more cookies until all the dough has been used up.

5 Bake for about 15 minutes, until firm to the touch and lightly browned.

6 Transfer to a wire rack and leave to cool completely.

Variations
• *Omit the lemon rind and sift 5ml/1 tsp mixed (apple pie) spice with the flour in step 3.*
• *Add 25g/1oz/2 tbsp currants or raisins to the mixture in step 3.*

Almond Shortbread Fingers Energy 64kcal/266kJ; Protein 0.7g; Carbohydrate 6.1g, of which sugars 1.8g; Fat 4.2g, of which saturates 2.5g; Cholesterol 10mg; Calcium 11mg; Fibre 0.2g; Sodium 29mg.
Shrewsbury Cakes Energy 115kcal/482kJ; Protein 1.4g; Carbohydrate 16.1g, of which sugars 7.5g; Fat 5.4g, of which saturates 3.2g; Cholesterol 32mg; Calcium 023mg; Fibre 0.4g; Sodium 37mg.

Butter and Almond Shortbreads

Moist shortbread cookies, flavoured with almonds, are cut into shapes of your choice and given a generous dusting of sugar so that they are pure white.

Makes 20–22
225g/8oz/1 cup unsalted butter
150g/5oz/²⁄₃ cup caster (superfine) sugar
2 egg yolks

5ml/1 tsp vanilla extract
2.5ml/½ tsp bicarbonate of soda (baking soda)
45ml/3 tbsp brandy
500g/1¼lb/5 cups plain (all-purpose) flour, plus extra for dusting
pinch of salt
150g/5oz/1¼ cups blanched almonds, toasted and coarsely chopped
350g/12oz/3 cups icing (confectioners') sugar

1 Preheat the oven to 180°C/350°F/Gas 4. Lightly grease two large baking sheets.

2 In a large bowl, beat together the butter and caster sugar until light and fluffy. Beat in the egg yolks one at a time, then add the vanilla extract.

3 In a small bowl, mix the baking soda with the brandy and stir into the butter and sugar mixture.

4 Sift together the flour and salt over the mixture and mix to a firm dough. Knead lightly with your fingertips, add the almonds and knead again.

5 Roll out the dough to 2.5cm/1in thick on a lightly floured surface. Press out shapes, using cookie cutters. Place on the baking sheets and bake for 20–25 minutes, or until pale golden. Do not let the cookies become brown.

6 Sift a quarter of the icing sugar on to a plate. Set aside. As soon as the cookies come out of the oven, dust them generously with sifted icing sugar. Leave to cool for a few minutes, then place them on the sugar-coated plate. Sift the remaining icing sugar over them. The aim is to give them a generous coating, so they are pure white.

Sweet Almond Cookies

Serve these crisp cookies with ice cream or fruit fool, or more simply with fresh fruit salad, yogurt or a spoonful of thick cream. Make a batch in advance and keep them in an airtight tin.

Makes about 25
25g/1oz/2 tbsp butter
30ml/2 tbsp milk

1 egg yolk
225g/8oz/2 cups ground almonds, plus extra for rolling out
25g/1oz/2 tbsp caster (superfine) sugar
5ml/1 tsp baking powder
2.5ml/½ tsp vanilla extract

1 Preheat the oven to 190°C/375°F/Gas 5.

2 Melt the butter in a pan and leave to cool until lukewarm.

3 Blend together the milk and egg yolk.

4 Mix the ground almonds, sugar and baking powder in a bowl then stir in the melted butter, vanilla extract and milk and egg mixture.

5 Knead the mixture with your hands to form a moist dough and then roll out to about 5mm/¼in thick on a cool surface lightly dusted with extra ground almonds.

6 Cut the dough into rounds using a 6cm/2½in cookie cutter. Gather the trimmings together and keep rolling out and cutting more cookies until all the mixture has been used up.

7 Transfer the dough rounds to a non-stick baking sheet and bake for about 10 minutes until lightly browned. Transfer to a wire rack and leave to cool completely.

> **Variation**
> The egg yolk is not essential but helps to bind the mixture together. If preferred, use an extra 15ml/1 tbsp milk.

Butter and Almond Shortbreads Energy 325kcal/1363kJ; Protein 4.4g; Carbohydrate 46.1g, of which sugars 26.9g; Fat 14.3g, of which saturates 6.4g; Cholesterol 44mg; Calcium 71mg; Fibre 1.3g; Sodium 72mg. **Sweet Almond Cookies** Energy 69kcal/288kJ; Protein 2.1g; Carbohydrate 1.7g, of which sugars 1.5g; Fat 6.1g, of which saturates 1g; Cholesterol 10mg; Calcium 25mg; Fibre 0.7g; Sodium 8mg.

Almond Cookies

Fine sugar and butter combine to give these cookies a light, delicate texture. They can be made days ahead, and are delicious with desserts or coffee.

Makes about 25
115g/4oz/1 cup plain
   (all-purpose) flour, plus extra
   for dusting
175g/6oz/1½ cups icing
   (confectioners') sugar
pinch of salt
50g/2oz/½ cup chopped almonds
2.5ml/½ tsp almond extract
115g/4oz/½ cup unsalted
   butter, softened
icing (confectioners') sugar,
   for dusting
halved almonds, to decorate

1 Preheat the oven to 180°C/350°F/Gas 4. Lightly grease two large baking sheets.

2 Combine the flour, icing sugar, salt and chopped almonds in a bowl. Add the almond extract.

3 Put the softened butter in the centre of the flour mixture and use your fingertips to draw the dry ingredients into the butter until a dough is formed. Knead until smooth. Shape the dough into a ball.

4 Place the dough on a lightly floured surface and roll it out to a thickness of about 3mm/⅛in. Using a 7.5cm/3in cookie cutter, stamp out 25 rounds, re-rolling the dough as necessary to use up any trimmings. Place the rounds on the baking sheets, leaving a little space between them. Decorate the cookies halved almonds.

5 Bake for 25–30 minutes until pale golden. Leave for 10 minutes, then transfer to wire racks to cool. Dust thickly with icing sugar before serving.

Cook's Tip
Use fancy cookie cutters such as hearts and crescents to make these cookies look even more interesting.

Almond Tiles

These cookies are named after the French roof tiles they resemble. Making them is a little fiddly, so bake a few at a time until you get the knack.

Makes about 24
70g/2½oz/½ cup whole
   blanched almonds, lightly
   toasted
70g/2½oz/⅓ cup caster
   (superfine) sugar
40g/1½oz/3 tbsp unsalted
   butter, softened
2 egg whites
2.5ml/½ tsp almond extract
35g/1¼oz scant ¼ cup plain
   (all-purpose) flour, sifted
55g/2oz/⅔ cup flaked
   (sliced) almonds

1 Preheat the oven to 200°C/400°F/Gas 6. Generously grease two baking sheets.

2 Put the almonds and 30ml/2 tbsp of the sugar in a food processor fitted with the metal blade, and pulse until ground.

3 In a large bowl, beat the butter until creamy, then add the remaining sugar and beat until light and fluffy. Gradually beat in the egg whites until well blended, then add the almond extract. Sift in the flour and fold in, then fold in the ground almond mixture.

4 Drop tablespoons of mixture on to the baking sheets about 15cm/6in apart. With the back of a wet spoon, spread each mound into a paper-thin 7.5cm/3in round. Sprinkle each round with a few flaked almonds.

5 Bake one sheet at a time, for 5–6 minutes until the edges are golden and the centres still pale. Working quickly, use a thin metal spatula to loosen the edges of each cookie. Lift on the spatula and place over a rolling pin, then press down the sides of the cookie to curve it.

6 Continue shaping the cookies, transferring them to a wire rack as they cool and crisp. If the cookies become too crisp to shape, return the baking sheet to the oven for 15–30 seconds to soften them, then continue as above.

Almond Cookies Energy 188kcal/788kJ; Protein 3.5g; Carbohydrate 22.5g, of which sugars 10.9g; Fat 10g, of which saturates 4.4g; Cholesterol 45mg; Calcium 44mg; Fibre 0.8g; Sodium 58mg.
Almond Tiles Energy 59kcal/246kJ; Protein 1.4g; Carbohydrate 4.5g, of which sugars 3.1g; Fat 4.1g, of which saturates 1.1g; Cholesterol 4mg; Calcium 16mg; Fibre 0.4g; Sodium 16mg.

Iced Almond Cookies

Crisp and crunchy, these small cookies are flavoured with ground almonds. They are delicious served with a bowl of vanilla ice cream.

Makes about 25
115g/4oz/¹/₂ cup butter
115g/4oz/generous ¹/₂ cup caster (superfine) sugar
1 egg, separated
5ml/1tsp vanilla extract
115g/4oz/1 cup ground almonds
115g/4oz/1 cup plain (all-purpose) flour

To decorate
50g/2oz/¹/₂ cup icing (confectioners') sugar
75–100 crystallized alpine pink petals (rose petals, primroses or violets could also be used)

1 Preheat the oven to 180°C/350°F/Gas 4. Lightly grease two large baking sheets.

2 In a large bowl, beat together the butter and sugar until light and fluffy. Add the egg yolk and vanilla extract and mix together. Stir in the ground almonds. Sift the flour over the mixture, stir in with a wooden spoon at first, and then knead together with your fingertips until the dough forms a ball.

3 With your hands, roll the dough into small balls about 2.5cm/1in diameter, then place on the prepared baking sheet. Flatten slightly with the back of a spoon.

4 Lightly beat the egg white and brush over the cookies. Bake for about 15 minutes. Using a metal spatula, transfer the cookies to a wire rack and leave to cool.

5 To decorate the cookies, sift the icing sugar into a bowl. Add about 1 tsp of hot water and stir until the mixture is smooth and thick enough to coat the back of a wooden spoon.

6 Spoon the icing on top of each cookie and while still wet secure the crystallized alpine pink petals to the top. Leave to set for about 30 minutes before serving. Store in an airtight container for 2–3 days.

Big Macs

These giant macaroons are crisp on the outside, chewy in the middle and naturally free from gluten and cow's milk. Ground almonds are a great alternative to the flour used in most cookies, and macaroons don't need butter for their deliciously moist, rich taste.

Makes 9
2 egg whites
5ml/1 tsp almond extract
115g/4oz/1 cup ground almonds
130g/4¹/₂oz/generous 1 cup light muscovado (brown) sugar

1 Preheat the oven to 180°C/350°F/Gas 4. Line a large baking sheet with baking parchment.

2 Put the egg whites in a large, clean bowl and whisk until they form stiff peaks.

3 Add the almond extract to the egg whites and whisk to combine. Sprinkle over the ground almonds and sugar and gently fold in using a large metal spoon.

4 Place nine tablespoonfuls of the mixture, spacing them well apart to allow room for spreading, on to the prepared baking sheet and flatten slightly with the back of a spoon. Bake for 15 minutes until risen, deep golden and beginning to turn crisp.

5 Leave the macaroons on the baking sheet for 5 minutes, then transfer to a wire rack and leave to crisp up and cool completely.

> **Cook's Tips**
> • These macaroons will store well in an airtight container; do not store in the refrigerator because they'll turn soft and lose their lovely crisp and chewy texture.
> • To make a macaroon with a milder flavour, use caster (superfine) sugar in place of the light muscovado sugar.

Iced Almond Cookies Energy 115kcal/481kJ; Protein 1.5g; Carbohydrate 15g, of which sugars 10.1g; Fat 5.8g, of which saturates 2.4g; Cholesterol 9mg; Calcium 24mg; Fibre 0.5g; Sodium 27mg.
Big Macs Energy 138kcal/577kJ; Protein 3.4g; Carbohydrate 16g, of which sugars 15.6g; Fat 7.1g, of which saturates 0.6g; Cholesterol 0mg; Calcium 39mg; Fibre 0.9g; Sodium 16mg.

Microwave Almond Cookies

These cookies are great to make if you want a sweet treat and are short of time. They look paler than conventionally baked cookies, but are just as delicious. Store in an airtight container once cool and eat within 24 hours.

Makes 12
50g/2oz/¼ cup butter
50g/2oz/¼ cup soft light
  brown sugar
1 egg yolk
75g/3oz/⅔ cup plain
  (all-purpose) flour
25g/1oz/¼ cup ground almonds

1 In a large bowl, beat the butter and sugar together until light and fluffy. Beat in the egg yolk.

2 Sift over the flour and gently fold into the butter mixture together with the ground almonds.

3 Place six tablespoonsfuls of the mixture in a circle on a microwave-proof dish or a piece of baking parchment. Cook for 1¾–2½ minutes on full (100 per cent) power or until the surface of the cookies is dry.

4 Remove the cookies carefully from the microwave as the edges will be soft. Leave to stand for 1 minute before lifting them on to a wire rack. They will finish cooking and become firmer as they cool.

Double Peanut Cookies

Packing up a party picnic? Got another birthday party coming up? Make sure that some of these fabulous nutty cookies are on the menu.

Makes 25
225g/8oz/1 cup butter
30ml/2 tbsp smooth peanut
  butter
115g/4oz/1 cup icing
  (confectioners') sugar
50g/2oz/¼ cup cornflour
  (cornstarch)
225g/8oz/2 cups plain
  (all-purpose) flour
115g/4oz/1 cup unsalted peanuts

1 Preheat the oven to 180°C/350°F/Gas 4. Lightly grease two baking sheets.

2 Put the butter and peanut butter in a bowl and beat together. Add the icing sugar, cornflour and plain flour and mix together to make a soft dough.

3 Roll the mixture into 25 small balls, using the palms of your hands, and place on the baking sheets. Leave plenty of room for the cookies to spread.

4 Press the tops of the balls of dough flat, using the back of a fork. Press a few of the peanuts into each of the cookies.

5 Bake for about 15–20 minutes, until lightly browned. Leave to cool for a few minutes before lifting the cookies carefully on to a wire rack with a metal spatula to cool completely.

Almond Ice Cream Sandwiches

These crisp, nutty wafer cookies make perfect ice cream sandwiches for a summer-time treat.

Makes 6 sandwiches
50g/2oz/¼ cup unsalted
  butter
2 egg whites
75g/3oz/scant ½ cup caster
  (superfine) sugar

50g/2oz/½ cup plain
  (all-purpose) flour
40g/1½oz/scant ½ cup
  ground almonds
30ml/2 tbsp flaked (sliced)
  almonds (optional)
raspberry ripple or vanilla ice
  cream, to serve
icing (confectioners') sugar,
  for dusting

1 Preheat the oven to 200°C/400°F/Gas 6. Line two large baking sheets with baking parchment.

2 Put the butter in a small pan and melt over a very low heat.

3 Put the egg whites and sugar in a bowl and whisk lightly with a fork until the egg whites are broken up. Add the flour, melted butter and ground almonds and mix until evenly combined.

4 Drop 6 level tablespoonfuls of mixture on to each baking sheet, spacing them well apart. Spread each tablespoonful of mixture into circles about 7cm/2¾in in diameter. Sprinkle with almonds, if using, and bake for 10–12 minutes until golden around the edges.

5 Remove from the oven, peel away the paper and transfer to a wire rack to cool.

6 Place a scoop of slightly softened ice cream on to one cookie and top with another, gently pressing them together. Dust with sugar and serve.

> **Cook's Tip**
> Don't be tempted to use greaseproof (waxed) paper instead of baking parchment as the cookies may stick to it.

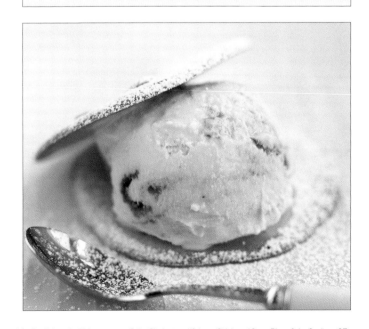

Microwave Almond Cookies Energy 87kcal/362kJ; Protein 1.3g; Carbohydrate 9.4g, of which sugars 4.6g; Fat 5.1g, of which saturates 2.4g; Cholesterol 26mg; Calcium 19mg; Fibre 0.4g; Sodium 27mg.
Double Peanut Cookies Energy 130kcal/543kJ; Protein 1.2g; Carbohydrate 13.9g, of which sugars 5.1g; Fat 8.2g, of which saturates 4.9g; Cholesterol 19mg; Calcium 17mg; Fibre 0.3g; Sodium 60mg.
Almond Ice Cream Sandwiches Energy 184kcal/771kJ; Protein 3.3g; Carbohydrate 20.1g, of which sugars 13.5g; Fat 10.7g, of which saturates 4.7g; Cholesterol 18mg; Calcium 36mg; Fibre 0.8g; Sodium 73mg.

Ladies' Kisses

These old-fashioned cookies are sweet, light and a moreish treat. With their delicious soft chocolate centre they are ideal for an elegant afternoon tea.

Makes 20

150g/5oz/10 tbsp butter, softened
115g/4oz/generous ½ cup caster (superfine) sugar
1 egg yolk
2.5ml/½ tsp almond extract
115g/4oz/1 cup ground almonds
175g/6oz/1½ cups plain (all-purpose) flour
50g/2oz plain (semisweet) chocolate

1 In a large bowl, beat the butter and sugar together until light and fluffy. Beat in the egg yolk, almond extract, ground almonds and flour until evenly mixed. Chill in the refrigerator for about 2 hours until firm.

2 Preheat the oven to 160°C/325°F/Gas 3. Line several baking sheets with baking parchment.

3 Break off small pieces of dough and roll into balls with your hands, making 40 altogether. Place the balls on the baking sheets and flatten slightly with the back of a spoon. Space them well apart as they will spread in the oven.

4 Bake for 20 minutes or until golden. Remove the baking sheets from the oven, lift off the parchment with the cookies still on it, then place on wire racks. Leave to cool. Repeat with the remaining mixture.

5 Lift the cooled cookies off the paper. Melt the chocolate in a bowl over a pan of hot water. Use to sandwich the cookies in pairs, then leave to cool and set before serving.

Cook's Tip
These cookies look dainty served in frilly petit fours cases.

Salted Peanut Cookies

The combination of salty and sweet flavours in these little cookies is delicious. The texture is delightfully crunchy and will appeal particularly to adult tastes.

Makes 70

250g/9oz/generous 1 cup soft light brown sugar, plus extra for dipping
350g/12oz/3 cups plain (all-purpose) flour
2.5ml/½ tsp bicarbonate of soda (baking soda)
115g/4oz/½ cup butter at room temperature, diced
115g/4oz/½ cup margarine
2 eggs
10ml/2 tsp vanilla extract
225g/8oz/2 cups salted peanuts

1 Preheat the oven to 190°C/375°F/Gas 5. Lightly grease two baking sheets. Grease the base of a small glass and dip in sugar. Set aside.

2 In a small bowl, sift together the flour and bicarbonate of soda and set aside.

3 In a large bowl, beat together the butter, margarine and sugar until the mixture is light and fluffy. Beat in the eggs, one at a time, and then the vanilla extract. Gently fold in the sifted flour mixture using a metal spoon.

4 Add the peanuts and gently stir them into the butter mixture until evenly combined.

5 On to the prepared baking sheets drop teaspoonfuls of the mixture, spaced 5cm/2in apart to allow room for spreading. Flatten each slightly with the prepared glass, dipping the base of the glass in the sugar after each use.

6 Bake the cookies in the oven for about 10 minutes, until lightly coloured. Remove from the oven and leave to set for a minute or two. With a metal spatula, carefully transfer the cookies to a wire rack and leave to cool completely before serving.

Ladies' Kisses Energy 159kcal/665kJ; Protein 2.4g; Carbohydrate 14.8g, of which sugars 8g; Fat 10.5g, of which saturates 4.7g; Cholesterol 26mg; Calcium 32mg; Fibre 0.8g; Sodium 47mg.
Salted Peanut Cookies Energy 77kcal/322kJ; Protein 1.5g; Carbohydrate 7.9g, of which sugars 4g; Fat 4.6g, of which saturates 1.2g; Cholesterol 9mg; Calcium 11mg; Fibre 0.3g; Sodium 38mg.

Peanut Butter Cookies

These cookies must be close to the top of the list of America's favourite cookies, ever since peanut butter was introduced at the 1904 St Louis, Missouri, World Fair.

Makes 24

115g/4oz/½ cup butter at room temperature, diced
125g/4½oz/¾ cup firmly packed soft light brown sugar
1 egg
5ml/1 tsp vanilla extract
225g/8oz/1 cup crunchy peanut butter
115g/4oz/1 cup plain (all-purpose) flour
2.5ml/½ tsp bicarbonate of soda (baking soda)
pinch of salt

1 In a large bowl, beat together the butter and sugar until light and fluffy.

2 In another bowl, mix the egg and vanilla extract, then gradually beat the liquid into the butter mixture.

3 Stir in the peanut butter and blend thoroughly.

4 Sift over the bowl the flour, bicarbonate of soda and salt and stir into the mixture to form a soft dough. Chill the dough for at least 30 minutes, until firm.

5 Preheat the oven to 180°C/350°F/Gas 4. Lightly grease two baking sheets.

6 Roll rounded teaspoonfuls of the dough into balls. Place on the baking sheets and press flat with a fork into rounds about 6cm/2½in in diameter, making a criss-cross pattern.

7 Bake for about 12 minutes or until lightly coloured. Transfer to a wire rack and leave to cool.

> **Variation**
> For extra crunch, add 50g/2oz/½ cup chopped peanuts with the peanut butter.

Lemony Peanut Pairs

These simple-to-make cookies are filled with peanut butter, but you could use buttercream or chocolate-and-nut spread instead. Make a selection with different fillings and let the kids choose.

Makes 8–10

40g/1½oz/3 tbsp soft light brown sugar
50g/2oz/¼ cup butter, softened
5ml/1 tsp grated lemon rind
75g/3oz/¾ cup wholemeal (whole-wheat) flour, plus extra for dusting
50g/2oz/¼ cup chopped crystallized (candied) pineapple
25g/1oz/2 tbsp smooth peanut butter
sifted icing (confectioners') sugar, for dusting

1 Preheat the oven to 190°C/375°F/Gas 3. Lightly grease a baking sheet.

2 In a large bowl, beat together the sugar, butter and lemon rind until light and fluffy. Beat in the flour, then knead until a smooth dough forms. On a lightly floured surface roll out the dough thinly.

3 Stamp out eight to 10 rounds using a cookie cutter. Space well apart on the baking sheet to allow room for spreading.

4 Press a piece of chopped pineapple on to each cookie. Bake for 20 minutes until golden brown. Transfer to a wire rack and leave to cool completely.

5 Sandwich two cookies together with the peanut butter. Serve lightly dusted with sifted sugar.

> **Variation**
> To make an alternative buttercream filling, beat 15g/½oz/1 tbsp butter until soft. Sift in 25g/1oz/2 tbsp icing (confectioners') sugar and beat together until smooth.

Peanut Butter Cookies Energy 154kcal/641kJ; Protein 3.4g; Carbohydrate 13.7g, of which sugars 8.3g; Fat 9.9g, of which saturates 4g; Cholesterol 18mg; Calcium 19mg; Fibre 0.8g; Sodium 71mg.
Lemony Peanut Pairs Energy 103kcal/431kJ; Protein 1.6g; Carbohydrate 12.3g, of which sugars 7.5g; Fat 5.6g, of which saturates 3g; Cholesterol 11mg; Calcium 13mg; Fibre 1.1g; Sodium 54mg.

Rich Peanut Crunch Cookies

These delicious sweet and nutty cookies are so easy to make. They puff up into lovely domed rounds during baking, giving them a really professional look. If you prefer cookies with a slightly less "nutty" texture, use smooth peanut butter rather than the crunchy variety.

Makes 25
150g/5oz/1¼ cups self-raising (self-rising) flour
2.5ml/ ½ tsp baking powder
115g/4oz/½ cup unsalted butter, at room temperature, diced
115g/4oz/generous ½ cup light muscovado (brown) sugar
1 egg
150g/5oz/generous ½ cup crunchy peanut butter
icing (confectioners') sugar, for dusting

1 Preheat the oven to 190°C/375°F/Gas 5. Lightly grease two baking sheets.

2 Sift the flour and baking powder together into a bowl.

3 Put the butter and sugar in a mixing bowl and beat until pale and creamy.

4 Beat in the egg, then add the sifted flour mixture and the peanut butter. Beat together until the ingredients are thoroughly mixed.

5 Place heaped teaspoonfuls of the mixture on to the baking sheets; space well apart to allow the cookies to spread while baking. (If necessary, spoon the dough on to the baking sheets in batches.)

6 Bake the cookies for about 20 minutes until risen; they will still be quite soft to the touch.

7 Leave the cookies on the baking sheets to set for about 5 minutes, then using a metal spatula carefully transfer them to a wire rack and leave to cool completely. To serve, lightly dust with icing sugar. Store in an airtight container for 2–3 days.

Hazelnut Cookies

Serve these sweet little nut cookies as petits fours with after-dinner coffee. As a healthy bonus, they are rich in vitamin E.

Makes about 25
115g/4oz/8 tbsp butter
75g/3oz/¾ cup icing (confectioners') sugar

115g/4oz/1 cup plain (all-purpose) flour
75g/3oz/¾ cup ground hazelnuts
1 egg yolk
blanched hazelnuts, to decorate
icing (confectioners') sugar, for dusting

1 Preheat the oven to 180°C/350°F/Gas 4. Lightly grease and then line three or four baking sheets with baking parchment.

2 In a large bowl, beat together the butter and sugar until light and fluffy.

3 Beat in the flour, ground hazelnuts and egg yolk until evenly mixed.

4 Take a teaspoonful of mixture at a time and shape it into a smooth ball with your fingers. Place the rounds well apart on the baking parchment, to allow room for spreading. Flatten slightly with your thumb and then press a whole hazelnut into the centre of each one to decorate.

5 Bake the cookies, one tray at a time, for about 10 minutes or until golden brown. Allow to set slightly for 1 or 2 minutes then transfer them to a wire rack using a metal spatula.

6 While still warm, sift icing sugar over each cookie to cover and then leave to cool completely before serving. Store in an airtight container interleaved with baking parchment.

Variation
Instead of the ground hazelnuts other ground nuts can be used, such as pecans, walnuts, macadamia and Brazil nuts.

Peanut Crunch Cookies Energy 112kcal/466kJ; Protein 2.1g; Carbohydrate 10.3g, of which sugars 5.3g; Fat 7.2g, of which saturates 3.2g; Cholesterol 18mg; Calcium 15mg; Fibre 0.5g; Sodium 50mg.
Hazelnut Cookies Energy 86kcal/359kJ; Protein 1.1g; Carbohydrate 6.9g, of which sugars 3.4g; Fat 6.2g, of which saturates 2.7g; Cholesterol 26mg; Calcium 15mg; Fibre 0.3g; Sodium 29mg.

Chocolate-dipped Hazelnut Crescents

Dipped in melted chocolate, these cookies look professionally made, yet they are surprisingly easy to make.

Makes about 35

285g/10oz/2 cups plain
  (all-purpose) flour
pinch of salt
225g/8oz/1 cup unsalted
  butter
55g/2oz/⅓ cup caster
  (superfine) sugar
15ml/1 tbsp hazelnut liqueur
  or water
5ml/1 tsp vanilla extract
175g/6oz milk chocolate, grated
85g/3oz/½ cup hazelnuts,
  toasted and finely chopped
icing (confectioners') sugar,
  for dusting
175g/6oz milk chocolate,
  for decorating

1 Preheat the oven to 160°C/325°F/Gas 3. Lightly grease two large baking sheets.

2 Sift the flour and salt into a bowl.

3 In another large bowl, beat the butter until creamy. Add the sugar and beat until fluffy, beat in the hazelnut liqueur and vanilla. Gently stir in the flour, until just blended, then fold in the grated chocolate and hazelnuts.

4 With floured hands, shape the dough into 5 ×1cm/2 × ½in crescents and place on the prepared baking sheets spaced widely apart to allow room for spreading.

5 Bake in the oven for 20–25 minutes until the edges are set and the biscuits slightly golden. Remove the crescents from the baking sheets and transfer to a wire rack to cool for 10 minutes.

6 Break the milk chocolate into a small heatproof bowl and set over a pan of gently simmering water. Heat gently, stirring frequently, until melted. Remove from the heat.

7 Dust the crescents with icing sugar. Dip half of each crescent into melted chocolate. Place on a baking sheet lined with baking parchment and leave to cool. Chill until the chocolate has set.

Cashew Nut Button Cookies

These light little cookies, flavoured with ground cashew nuts, are coated in toasted hazelnuts. You will need a food processor to grind the cashew nuts.

Makes about 20

150g/5oz/1¼ cups unroasted
  cashew nuts
1 egg white
25g/1oz/2 tbsp caster
  (superfine) sugar
50g/2oz/⅓ cup dates,
  finely chopped
5ml/1 tsp finely grated
  orange rind
30ml/2 tbsp pure maple or
  maple-flavoured syrup
90g/3½oz/scant 1 cup toasted
  hazelnuts, chopped

1 Preheat the oven to 190°C/375°F/Gas 5. Lightly grease two baking sheets.

2 Put the cashew nuts in a food processor, fitted with a metal blade, and process until finely ground.

3 In a large bowl, whisk the egg white until stiff. Whisk in the sugar. Stir in the ground cashews, dates, orange rind and syrup. Mix together well.

4 Put the chopped hazelnuts in a small bowl. Drop small spoonfuls of the cookie mixture into the hazelnuts and toss until well coated.

5 Place the coated cookies on the prepared baking sheets and bake in the oven for about 10 minutes until lightly browned. Leave the cookies on the baking sheets to firm up slightly, then using a metal spatula carefully transfer them to a wire rack and leave to cool completely.

Variation
You could buy ground almonds, rather than grinding your own, and use them to replace the ground cashew nuts. For coating the cookies substitute toasted almonds in place of the toasted hazelnuts.

Chocolate-dipped Hazelnut Crescents Energy 102kcal/427kJ; Protein 1.9g; Carbohydrate 13.8g, of which sugars 7.6g; Fat 4.7g, of which saturates 2g; Cholesterol 2mg; Calcium 38mg; Fibre 0.5g; Sodium 9mg. Cashew Nut Button Cookies Energy 92kcal/382kJ; Protein 2.4g; Carbohydrate 5.9g, of which sugars 4.8g; Fat 6.7g, of which saturates 1g; Cholesterol 0mg; Calcium 11mg; Fibre 0.6g; Sodium 29mg.

Mini Pecan Fudge Bites

These cute little cookies have the flavour of butterscotch and fudge and are topped with chopped pecan nuts for a delicious crunch – just the right size for an afternoon treat with tea or coffee.

Makes 30
200g/7oz/1¾ cups self-raising
 (self-rising) flour
115g/4oz/½ cup butter, at room
 temperature, diced
115g/4oz/generous ½ cup dark
 muscovado (molasses) sugar
75g/3oz vanilla cream
 fudge, diced
1 egg, beaten
25g/1oz/½ cup pecan nut halves,
 sliced widthways

1 Preheat the oven to 190°C/375°F/Gas 5. Lightly grease two or three baking sheets.

2 Put the flour in a bowl, and using your fingertips, rub in the butter until the mixture resembles fine breadcrumbs. Alternatively, put the flour and butter in a food processor and process until the mixture resembles breadcrumbs.

3 Add the muscovado sugar and diced vanilla cream fudge to the flour mixture and stir well until combined. Add the beaten egg and mix in well.

4 Bring the dough together with your hands, then knead gently on a lightly floured surface. It will be soft yet firm.

5 Roll the dough into two cylinders, 23cm/9in long. Cut into 1cm/½in slices and place on the baking sheets. Sprinkle over the pecan nuts and press in lightly.

6 Bake for about 12 minutes until browned at the edges. Transfer to a wire rack to cool.

Variation
Use walnut halves, sliced, instead of the pecan nuts.

Pecan Nut Puffs

As they don't keep very well, you have the perfect excuse to enjoy these melt-in-the-mouth, light-as-air cookies as freely as you like.

Makes 24
115g/4oz/1 cup plain
 (all-purpose) flour
pinch of salt
115g/4oz/½ cup unsalted butter
 at room temperature, diced
30ml/2 tbsp sugar
5ml/1 tsp vanilla extract
115g/4oz/1 cup pecan nuts
icing (confectioners') sugar,
 for dusting

1 Preheat the oven to 150°C/300°F/Gas 2. Lightly grease two baking sheets.

2 Sift the flour and salt together into a bowl.

3 In a large bowl, beat together the butter and sugar until light and fluffy. Stir in the vanilla extract.

4 Grind the pecan nuts in a food processor, blender or nut grinder. Stir several times to prevent the nuts from becoming oily.

5 Push the ground nuts through a sieve (strainer) set over a bowl to aerate them. Any pieces that are too large to go through the sieve can be ground again.

6 Stir the nuts and sifted flour into the butter mixture to make a dough. Roll the dough into marble-size balls between the palms of your hands.

7 Place the balls on the prepared baking sheets, spaced well apart to allow room for spreading. Bake in the oven for 45 minutes.

8 Leave the puffs to cool slightly, then, while they are still hot, roll them in icing sugar. Leave to cool completely on a wire rack, then roll once more in icing sugar.

Min Pecan Fudge Bites Energy 86kcal/359kJ; Protein 1g; Carbohydrate 11.3g, of which sugars 6.2g; Fat 4.4g, of which saturates 2.3g; Cholesterol 15mg; Calcium 17mg; Fibre 0.2g; Sodium 29mg.
Pecan Nut Puffs Energy 90kcal/373kJ; Protein 0.9g; Carbohydrate 5.3g, of which sugars 1.6g; Fat 7.4g, of which saturates 2.8g; Cholesterol 10mg; Calcium 11mg; Fibre 0.4g; Sodium 29mg.

Walnut Cookies

These cookies are for lovers of walnuts, but the same recipe can be used for pecan nut lovers too.

Makes 60
115g/4oz/½ cup butter
175g/6oz/scant 1 cup caster
   (superfine) sugar
115g/4oz/1 cup plain
   (all-purpose) flour
10ml/2 tsp vanilla extract
115g/4oz/⅔ cup walnuts,
   finely chopped

1 Preheat the oven to 150°C/300°F/ Gas 2. Lightly grease two baking sheets.

2 In a mixing bowl, beat the butter until soft. Add 100g/4oz/ ½ cup of the sugar and continue beating until light and fluffy. Stir in the flour, vanilla extract and walnuts.

3 Drop teaspoonfuls of the batter 5cm/2in apart on the prepared baking sheets and flatten slightly. Bake for about 25 minutes.

4 Transfer to a wire rack set over a baking sheet and sprinkle with the remaining sugar.

Walnut Crescents

Although delicious just as they are, these cookies are also good when one end is dipped and coated in melted chocolate.

Makes 9
115g/4oz/⅔ cup walnuts
225g/8oz/1 cup unsalted
   butter
115g/4oz/generous ½ cup sugar
2.5ml/½ tsp vanilla extract
225g/8oz/2 cups plain
   (all-purpose) flour
pinch of salt
icing (confectioners') sugar,
   for dusting

1 Preheat the oven to 180°C/350F/Gas 4.

2 Grind the walnuts in a food processor, blender or nut grinder until they are almost a paste. Transfer to a bowl.

3 Add the butter to the walnuts and mix with a wooden spoon until blended. Add the sugar and vanilla, and stir to blend.

4 Sift the flour and salt into the walnut mixture. Work into a dough.

5 Shape the dough into small cylinders about 4cm/1½in long. Bend into crescents and place evenly spaced on an ungreased baking sheet.

6 Bake for about 15 minutes until lightly browned. Transfer to a rack to cool slightly. Set the rack over a baking sheet and dust lightly with icing sugar. Leave to cool completely. Store in an airtight container.

Pecan Tassies

These cookies are made in two parts, a rich cream cheese base is filled with a sweet and nutty filling.

Makes 24
115g/4oz/½ cup cream cheese
115g/4oz/½ cup butter, diced
115g/4oz/1 cup plain
   (all-purpose) flour, plus extra
   for dusting

For the filling
2 eggs
115g/4oz/½ cup soft dark
   brown sugar
5ml/1 tsp vanilla extract
pinch of salt
25g/1oz/2 tbsp butter, melted
115g/4oz/⅔ cup pecan nuts

1 Place a baking sheet in the oven and preheat to 180°C/ 350°F/Gas 4. Lightly grease 24 mini-muffin tins (pans).

2 Put the cream cheese and butter in a mixing bowl. Sift over the flour in two batches and mix well to a smooth paste after each addition.

3 Roll out the dough thinly on a lightly floured surface. Try not to add too much flour to the rolling pin. With a floured cookie cutter, stamp out 24 6cm/2½in rounds. Gather the trimmings together and continue to roll and stamp out rounds. Line the mini-muffin tins with the rounds and chill for 30 minutes.

4 To make the filling, lightly whisk the eggs in a bowl. Gradually whisk in the brown sugar, and add the vanilla extract, salt and melted butter. Set aside.

5 Reserve 24 pecan halves and chop the rest coarsely with a sharp knife.

6 Place a spoonful of chopped nuts in each muffin tin and cover with the filling. Set a pecan half on the top of each.

7 Place the muffin tins on top of the hot baking sheet and bake in the oven for about 20 minutes until puffed and set. Using a metal spatula, carefully transfer the tassies to a wire rack to cool. Serve at room temperature.

Walnut Cookies Energy 107kcal/449kJ; Protein 1.7g; Carbohydrate 16.2g, of which sugars 16.1g; Fat 4.4g, of which saturates 0.4g; Cholesterol 0mg; Calcium 14mg; Fibre 0.2g; Sodium 15mg.
Walnut Crescents Energy 51kcal/212kJ; Protein 0.5g; Carbohydrate 3.7g, of which sugars 1.6g; Fat 3.9g, of which saturates 1.9g; Cholesterol 7.5mg; Calcium 6.7mg; Fibre 0.1g; Sodium 28mg.
Pecan Tassies Energy 139kcal/576kJ; Protein 1.6g; Carbohydrate 9g, of which sugars 5.3g; Fat 10.9g, of which saturates 4.9g; Cholesterol 33mg; Calcium 20mg; Fibre 0.4g; Sodium 56mg.

Walnut Biscotti

These light crunchy cookies with toasted walnuts are flavoured with orange and coriander seeds.

Makes about 40
115g/4oz/½ cup unsalted
   butter, diced
200g/7oz/1 cup sugar
2 eggs
15ml/1 tbsp walnut or olive oil
finely grated rind of 1 large
   orange
350g/12oz/3 cups plain
   (all-purpose) flour
7.5ml/1½ tsp baking powder
75g/3oz/¾ cup cornmeal
115g/4oz/1 cup walnuts, toasted
   and chopped
10ml/2 tsp coriander seeds,
   crushed

1 Preheat the oven to 160°C/325°F/Gas 3.

2 Put the butter and sugar in a large bowl and beat together until light and fluffy. Add the eggs, walnut or olive oil and orange rind and mix well.

3 Sift the flour and baking powder over the mixture and add the cornmeal, walnuts and coriander seeds. Mix thoroughly and with your hands bring together to form a soft but not sticky dough.

4 Shape the dough into four logs, each measuring about 18cm/7in long and 5cm/2in in diameter. Place slightly apart on non-stick baking sheets. Bake in the oven for 35 minutes until lightly golden.

5 Transfer to wire racks and leave the logs for 10 minutes to cool slightly, then slice diagonally into 1cm/½in slices. Return the slices to the baking sheets and bake for 10 minutes. Transfer to wire racks to cool completely.

> **Cook's Tip**
> *To toast the nuts, spread them on a baking sheet and place in the oven at 160°C/325°F/Gas 3 for 5–7 minutes until just beginning to brown.*

Almond Biscotti

This Italian speciality is a traditional recipe. It does not contain butter or oil but uses the eggs to bind the mixture together.

Makes 48
200g/7oz/generous 1 cup whole
   unblanched almonds
215g/7½oz/scant 2 cups plain
   (all-purpose) flour
90g/3½oz/½ cup caster
   (superfine) sugar
pinch of salt
pinch of saffron threads
2.5ml/½ tsp bicarbonate of soda
   (baking soda)
2 eggs
1 egg white, lightly beaten

1 Preheat the oven to 190°C/375°F/Gas 5. Lightly grease and sift flour over two baking sheets.

2 Spread the almonds in a baking tray and bake for about 15 minutes until lightly browned. When cool, put 50g/2oz/⅓ cup of the almonds in a food processor, blender, or nut grinder and process until finely ground. Coarsely chop the remaining almonds into two or three pieces each. Set aside.

3 Combine the flour, sugar, salt, saffron, bicarbonate of soda and ground almonds in a bowl and mix to blend. Make a well in the centre and add the eggs. Stir to form a rough dough. Transfer to a floured surface and knead until well blended. Knead in the chopped almonds.

4 Divide the dough into three equal parts. Roll into logs about 2.5cm/1in in diameter. Place on one of the prepared sheets, brush with the egg white and bake for 20 minutes.

5 Slice each log at an angle, making 1cm/½in slices. Return the slices to the baking sheets and bake at 140°C/275°F/Gas 1 for 25 minutes more. Transfer to a rack to cool.

> **Cook's Tip**
> *Dunk biscotti in sweet white wine, such as an Italian Vin Santo.*

Walnut Biscotti Energy 104kcal/434kJ; Protein 1.8g; Carbohydrate 13.5g, of which sugars 5.4g; Fat 5g, of which saturates 1.8g; Cholesterol 16mg; Calcium 20mg; Fibre 0.4g; Sodium 22mg.
Almond Biscotti Energy 51kcal/216kJ; Protein 1.6g; Carbohydrate 5.7g, of which sugars 2.2g; Fat 2.6g, of which saturates 0.3g; Cholesterol 8mg; Calcium 18mg; Fibre 0.4g; Sodium 5mg.

Coffee Biscotti

These crisp cookies are made twice as delicious with both freshly roasted ground coffee beans and strong aromatic brewed coffee in the mixture.

Makes about 30

25g/1oz/⅓ cup espresso-roasted coffee beans
115g/4oz/⅔ cup blanched almonds
200g/7oz/scant 2 cups plain (all-purpose) flour

7.5ml/1½ tsp baking powder
pinch of salt
75g/3oz/6 tbsp unsalted butter, cubed
150g/5oz/¾ cup caster (superfine) sugar
2 eggs, beaten
25–30ml/1½–2 tbsp strong brewed coffee
5ml/1 tsp ground cinnamon, for dusting

1 Preheat the oven to 180°C/350°F/Gas 4. Lightly grease two baking sheets.

2 Put the espresso coffee beans in a single layer on one side of a large baking sheet and the almonds on the other. Roast in the oven for 10 minutes. Leave to cool.

3 Put the coffee beans in a blender or food processor and process until fairly fine. Tip out and set aside. Process the almonds until finely ground.

4 Sift the flour, baking powder and salt into a bowl. Rub in the butter until the mixture resembles fine breadcrumbs. Stir in the caster sugar, ground coffee and almonds. Add the beaten eggs and enough brewed coffee to make a fairly firm dough.

5 Lightly knead for a few seconds until smooth and shape into two rolls about 7.5cm/3in in diameter. Place on the baking sheet and dust with cinnamon. Bake for 20 minutes.

6 Using a sharp knife, cut the rolls into 4cm/1½in slices on the diagonal. Arrange the slices on the baking tray and bake for another 10 minutes, or until lightly browned. Transfer to a wire rack and leave to cool.

Orange Biscotti

These crisp, crunchy cookies are based on a traditional Italian recipe in which the cookies are packed with nuts and twice baked. This version is flavoured with orange instead of nuts and shaped into long, thin sticks. They are a little softer than the classic biscotti, which are very hard.

Makes about 20

50g/2oz/¼ cup unsalted butter, at room temperature, diced
90g/3½oz/½ cup light muscovado (brown) sugar
1 egg
finely grated rind of 1 small orange, plus 10ml/2 tsp juice
175g/6oz/1½ cups self-raising (self-rising) flour
7.5ml/1½ tsp baking powder
good pinch of ground cinnamon
50g/2oz/½ cup polenta
icing (confectioners') sugar, for dusting

1 Preheat the oven to 160°C/325°F/Gas 3. Lightly grease a large baking sheet.

2 In a large bowl, beat together the butter and sugar until smooth and creamy. Beat in the egg, then the orange rind and juice, flour, baking powder, cinnamon and polenta.

3 Tip the mixture on to a lightly floured surface and knead until well blended. Place the dough on the baking sheet and flatten out with the palm of your hand to make a rectangle about 25 x 18cm/10 x 7in.

4 Bake the dough for 25 minutes, then remove from the oven and leave to stand for about 5 minutes until slightly cooled.

5 Using a sharp knife, cut the mixture widthways into thin sticks, about 1cm/½in wide.

6 Space the cookies out slightly on the baking sheet so there's a gap between each one, then return to the oven and bake for another 20 minutes until crisp. Transfer the biscotti to a wire rack and leave to cool. Serve dusted with a little icing sugar.

Coffee Biscotti Energy 97kcal/409kJ; Protein 2g; Carbohydrate 12.9g, of which sugars 5.7g; Fat 4.4g, of which saturates 1.4g; Cholesterol 12mg; Calcium 37mg; Fibre 0.6g; Sodium 54mg.
Orange Biscotti Energy 80kcal/337kJ; Protein 1.4g; Carbohydrate 13.6g, of which sugars 5.1g; Fat 2.5g, of which saturates 1.4g; Cholesterol 15mg; Calcium 17mg; Fibre 0.3g; Sodium 19mg.

Mandelbrot

These crisp, twice-baked cookies, studded with almonds, are similar to biscotti. Serve them with coffee, tea or a glass of schnapps.

Makes 24–36
375g/13oz/3¼ cups plain
  (all-purpose) flour
115g/4oz/1 cup ground almonds
5ml/1 tsp bicarbonate of soda
  (baking soda)
pinch of salt
3 eggs
250g/9oz/1¼ cups caster
  (superfine) sugar
grated rind of 1 lemon
5ml/1 tsp almond extract
5ml/1 tsp vanilla extract
130g/4½oz/1 cup blanched
  almonds, roughly chopped

1 Preheat the oven to 180°C/350°F/Gas 4. Lightly grease two baking sheets.

2 Sift together the plain flour, ground almonds, bicarbonate of soda and salt.

3 Using a whisk, beat together the eggs and sugar until light and fluffy, then beat in the lemon rind and almond and vanilla extracts. Slowly add the flour and ground almonds, a little at a time, mixing until well blended. Add the chopped almonds and mix well.

4 Turn the mixture on to a floured surface and knead gently for about 5 minutes. Divide the dough into two pieces and form each into a long, flat loaf. Place on the baking sheets and bake for 35 minutes, or until golden brown.

5 Remove the loaves from the oven and leave for 15 minutes to cool slightly. Cut them into 1cm/½in diagonal slices, taking care not to break or crush the soft insides of the loaves.

6 Arrange the slices on clean baking sheets (working in batches). Bake for 6–7 minutes until the undersides are golden and flecked with brown. Turn the slices over and bake for another 6–7 minutes. Transfer to wire racks to cool.

Amaretti

These moreish cookies are great with afternoon tea, although they are equally delicious served with a sweet white dessert wine later in the day.

Makes 36
200g/7oz/1¾ cups almonds
plain (all-purpose) flour,
  for dusting
225g/8oz/generous 1 cup caster
  (superfine) sugar
2 egg whites
2.5ml/½ tsp almond extract or
  5ml/1 tsp vanilla extract
icing (confectioners') sugar,
  for dusting

1 Preheat the oven to 160°C/325°F/Gas 3.

2 Skin the almonds by dropping them into a pan of boiling water for 1–2 minutes. Drain well, then rub the almonds in a clean dish towel to remove the skins.

3 Spread out the almonds on a baking sheet and let them dry out in the oven for 10–15 minutes but do not allow them to turn brown. Remove them from the oven and leave to cool. Dust the almonds with a little flour. Increase the oven temperature to 180°C/350°F/Gas 4.

4 Put the almonds and half of the sugar in a food processor and process until finely ground.

5 Whisk the egg whites in a grease-free bowl until they form soft peaks. Gradually add half the remaining sugar and whisk until stiff peaks form. With a metal spoon, gently fold in the remaining sugar, the almond or vanilla extract and the almonds.

6 Spoon the almond mixture into a piping (pastry) bag and, using a plain nozzle, pipe the mixture in walnut-size rounds on to a baking sheet. Sprinkle lightly with the icing sugar and leave to stand for 2 hours.

7 Bake for 15 minutes, until pale golden brown. Transfer to a wire rack and leave to cool.

Mandelbrot Energy 111kcal/466kJ; Protein 3g; Carbohydrate 15.8g, of which sugars 7.7g; Fat 4.4g, of which saturates 0.5g; Cholesterol 16mg; Calcium 37mg; Fibre 0.8g; Sodium 8mg.
Amaretti Energy 37kcal/155kJ; Protein 1.1g; Carbohydrate 3.2g, of which sugars 3.1g; Fat 2.3g, of which saturates 0.2g; Cholesterol 0mg; Calcium 12mg; Fibre 0.3g; Sodium 4mg.

Nut Lace Wafers

These cookies look so pretty, it almost seems a shame to eat them, but if you didn't, you would certainly be missing out on a treat. Serve them with smooth and creamy desserts.

Makes 18

50g/2oz/½ cup blanched
    almonds
50g/2oz/¼ cup butter
45ml/3 tbsp plain
    (all-purpose) flour
115g/4oz/½ cup sugar
30ml/2 tbsp double (heavy)
    cream
2.5ml/½ tsp vanilla extract

1 Preheat the oven to 190°C/375°F/Gas 5. Thoroughly grease two baking sheets.

2 With a sharp knife, chop the almonds as finely as possible, or put them in a food processor or blender fitted with a metal blade and process until finely ground.

3 Melt the butter in a small pan over a low heat. Remove from the heat and stir in the ground almonds, plain flour, sugar, double cream and vanilla extract until well combined.

4 Drop teaspoonfuls of the mixture 6cm/2½in apart on the prepared baking sheets, to allow room for spreading during baking.

5 Bake in the oven for about 5 minutes, or until golden brown. Allow to cool on the sheets briefly, until the cookies are just firm.

6 With a metal spatula, transfer the cookies to a wire rack and leave to cool completely. These cookies have a soft and chewy texture, but will harden.

Variation
Add 40g/1½oz/¼ cup finely chopped candied orange peel to the mixture with the almonds in step 3.

Oatmeal Lace Rounds

Any-time-of-day cookies, these are delicious with morning coffee or as a great after-school treat for hungry children. These cookies can also be served with ice cream as an unusual alternative to wafers, and makes for a more substantial dessert.

Makes 14

150g/5½oz/⅔ cup butter at
    room temperature, diced
125g/4½oz/¾ cup rolled oats
165g/5¾oz/¾ cup dark
    brown sugar
150g/5¼oz/¾ cup caster
    (superfine) sugar
45g/1½oz/⅓ cup plain
    (all-purpose) flour
pinch of salt
1 egg, lightly beaten
5ml/1tsp vanilla extract
70g/2½oz/½ cup pecans or
    walnuts, finely chopped

1 Preheat the oven to 180°C/359°F/Gas 4. Lightly grease two baking sheets.

2 Melt the butter in a pan over a low heat, stirring occasionally. Remove from the heat and set aside.

3 Put the oats in a large bowl. Sift over the brown sugar, caster sugar, flour and salt. Mix well to combine.

4 Make a well in the centre and add the melted butter, egg and vanilla extract. Mix until blended, using a wooden spoon, then stir in the chopped nuts.

5 Drop rounded teaspoonfuls of the mixture about 2in/5cm apart on the prepared baking sheets, to allow room for spreading during baking.

6 Bake in the oven for 5–8 minutes until lightly browned around the edges and bubbling. Allow to cool on the baking sheet for 2 minutes.

7 With a metal spatula, transfer the cookies to a wire rack and leave to cool completely.

Nut Lace Wafers Energy 78kcal/327kJ; Protein 1g; Carbohydrate 7.2g, of which sugars 5.5g; Fat 5.2g, of which saturates 2.2g; Cholesterol 8mg; Calcium 16mg; Fibre 0.3g; Sodium 18mg.
Oatmeal Lace Rounds Energy 103kcal/431kJ; Protein 1g; Carbohydrate 13.2g, of which sugars 9.7g; Fat 5.5g, of which saturates 2.5g; Cholesterol 15mg; Calcium 11mg; Fibre 0.4g; Sodium 32mg.

Spiced Lace Cookies

Very pretty, delicate and crisp, these lacy cookies are ideal for serving with elegant creamy or iced desserts, or to be eaten with a cup of coffee mid morning. Don't be tempted to bake more than four on a sheet.

115g/4oz/generous ½ cup golden caster (superfine) sugar
1 egg, beaten
10ml/2 tsp plain (all-purpose) flour
5ml/1 tsp baking powder
2.5ml/½ tsp mixed (apple pie) spice

Makes about 14
75g/3oz/6 tbsp butter, diced
75g/3oz/¾ cup rolled oats

1 Preheat the oven to 180°C/350°F/Gas 4. Lightly grease and then line three or four baking sheets with baking parchment.

2 Put the butter in a medium pan and set over a low heat until just melted. Remove from the heat.

3 Stir the rolled oats into the melted butter. Add the sugar, egg, flour, baking powder and mixed spice and mix well to combine.

4 Place only 3 or 4 heaped teaspoonfuls of the mixture, spaced well apart, on each of the lined baking sheets.

5 Bake in the oven for about 5–7 minutes, or until a deepish golden brown all over. Leave the cookies on the baking sheets for about 1–2 minutes to firm up slightly.

6 Carefully cut the parchment so you can lift each cookie singly using a metal spatula. Invert on to a wire rack and remove the parchment. Leave to cool completely, while you cook the remaining batches.

Variation
Replace the mixed (apple pie) spice with ground cinnamon.

Oaty Biscuits

In England oats have been one of the principal crops since the days of the Anglo-Saxons and King Alfred the Great. By the 14th century, the grain had become a major export. Nutritious and delicious, oats are a major ingredient in these biscuits.

Makes about 18
115g/4oz/½ cup butter
115g/4oz/½ cup soft brown sugar
115g/4oz/½ cup golden (light corn) syrup
150g/5oz/1¼ cups self-raising (self-rising) flour
150g/5oz rolled oats

1 Preheat the oven to 180°C/350°F/Gas 4. Lightly grease two or three baking sheets with butter.

2 Gently heat the butter, sugar and golden syrup in a pan, stirring occasionally until the butter has melted and the sugar has dissolved. Remove from the heat and leave to cool slightly.

3 Sift the flour over the mixture in the pan and stir well to combine. Add the oats, to make a soft dough.

4 With your hands, roll small pieces of the dough into small balls and arrange them on the prepared baking sheets, leaving plenty of room for them to spread. Flatten each ball slightly with a metal spatula.

5 Put one tray into the oven and cook for 12–15 minutes until golden brown and cooked through.

6 Leave to cool on the baking sheet for 1–2 minutes, then carefully transfer to a wire rack to crisp up and cool completely, while you cook the remaining batches.

Variation
Add 25g/1oz/¼ cup finely chopped toasted almonds or walnuts, or a small handful of dried fruit such as raisins or sultanas (golden raisins) in step 3.

Spiced Lace Cookies Energy 101kcal/425kJ; Protein 1.3g; Carbohydrate 13.1g, of which sugars 8.6g; Fat 5.3g, of which saturates 2.9g; Cholesterol 25mg; Calcium 11mg; Fibre 0.4g; Sodium 40mg.
Oaty Biscuits Energy 151kcal/637kJ; Protein 1.8g; Carbohydrate 23.9g, of which sugars 11.9g; Fat 6g, of which saturates 3.3g; Cholesterol 14mg; Calcium 22mg; Fibre 0.8g; Sodium 59mg.

Oaty Coconut Cookies

Toasting the oats and coconut before mixing them with the other ingredients is the secret of both the delicious flavour and the lovely crunchy texture of these cookies. You'll need to keep an eye on the oats and coconut and give them the occasional stir, as they will burn if cooked too long.

Makes 18
115g/4oz/½ cup sugar
175g/6oz/2 cups rolled oats
75g/3oz/1 cup desiccated (dry unsweetened shredded) coconut
225g/8oz/1 cup butter, at room temperature, diced
40g/1½oz/¼ cup firmly packed soft dark brown sugar
2 eggs
60ml/4 tbsp milk
7.5ml/1½ tsp vanilla extract
115g/4oz/1 cup plain (all-purpose) flour
2.5ml/½ tsp bicarbonate of soda (baking soda)
pinch of salt
5ml/1 tsp ground cinnamon

1 Preheat the oven to 200°C/400°F/Gas 6. Lightly grease two baking sheets. Grease the base of a small glass and dip it in some sugar.

2 Spread the oats and coconut on an ungreased baking sheet. Bake in the oven for 8–10 minutes until golden brown, stirring occasionally.

3 In a large bowl, beat the butter and sugars together until light and fluffy. Beat in the eggs, then add the milk and vanilla extract. Sift the flour, bicarbonate of soda, salt and cinnamon together and fold into the creamed mixture. Stir in the oat and coconut mixture.

4 Drop spoonfuls of the mixture on to the baking sheets, spaced well apart to allow for spreading while baking. Flatten each with the sugared glass. Bake for 8–10 minutes until golden brown.

5 Transfer the cookies to a wire rack and leave to firm up and cool completely. The cookies will keep stored in an airtight container for 3–4 days.

Melting Moments

As the name suggests, these crisp cookies really do melt in the mouth. They have a texture like shortbread but are covered in rolled oats to give a crunchy surface and extra flavour, and are traditionally topped with a nugget of glacé cherry.

Makes 16–20
40g/1½oz/3 tbsp butter, softened
65g/2½oz/5 tbsp lard
85g/3oz/6 tbsp caster (superfine) sugar
1 egg yolk, beaten
few drops of vanilla or almond extract
150g/5oz/1¼ cups self-raising (self-rising) flour
rolled oats, for coating
4–5 glacé (candied) cherries

1 Preheat the oven to 180°C/350°F/Gas 4.

2 In a large bowl, beat together the butter, lard and sugar until light and fluffy, then gradually beat in the egg yolk and vanilla or almond extract.

3 Sift the flour over the creamed mixture and stir together to make a soft dough. With your hands, gently roll into 16–20 small balls.

4 Spread the rolled oats on to a sheet of baking parchment and roll the dough balls in them until evenly coated.

5 Place the balls, spaced slightly apart, on two baking sheets. Flatten each ball a little with your thumb.

6 Cut the cherries into quarters and place a piece of cherry on top of each cookie.

7 Bake in the oven for 15–20 minutes, until the cookies are lightly browned.

8 Allow the cookies to set slightly for 1–2 minutes on the baking sheets. With a metal spatula, transfer the cookies to a wire rack and leave to cool completely. Store in an airtight container for 2–3 days.

Oaty Coconut Cookies Energy 84kcal/352kJ; Protein 1.1g; Carbohydrate 8.3g, of which sugars 3.8g; Fat 5.4g, of which saturates 3.4g; Cholesterol 18mg; Calcium 11mg; Fibre 0.5g; Sodium 34mg.
Melting Moments Energy 88kcal/370kJ; Protein 0.7g; Carbohydrate 10.9g, of which sugars 5.4g; Fat 5g, of which saturates 2.4g; Cholesterol 7mg; Calcium 30mg; Fibre 0.3g; Sodium 40mg.

Tea Swirls

These cookies are very quick and easy to make. If you don't want to pipe the mixture, simply spoon it on to the baking parchment and press it down with a fork.

Makes 20

150g/5oz/⅔ cup butter, softened
75g/3oz/¾ cup caster (superfine) sugar, sifted
1 egg, beaten
a few drops almond extract
225g/8oz/2 cups plain (all-purpose) flour
2–3 large pieces candied peel, cut into small diamond shapes

1 Preheat the oven to 230°C/450°F/Gas 8. Line two baking sheets with baking parchment.

2 Beat together the butter and sugar in a large bowl until light and fluffy, then beat in the egg yolk and almond extract.

3 Sift the flour over the mixture in batches and beat well until smooth.

4 Spoon the mixture into a piping (pastry) bag fitted with a large star nozzle and pipe 10 rosette shapes on each of the baking sheets, spacing them slightly apart. It is best to work with cold hands so that the consistency of the mixture is not affected by heat.

5 Press a piece of candied peel diamond gently into the centre of each cookie. Bake in the oven for 5 minutes until golden brown.

6 Leave to cool for a few minutes, then using a metal spatula, transfer the cookies to a wire rack to cool completely. These cookies can be stored in an airtight container for several days.

Variation
Use 10 halved glacé (candied) cherries instead of the candied peel and cut each in half.

Crunchy Jumbles

Making up your mind about whether you prefer milk or plain chocolate chips is the perfect excuse for baking another batch of these tasty cookies.

Makes 36

115g/4oz/½ cup butter at room temperature, diced
225g/8oz/1 cup sugar
1 egg
5ml/1 tsp vanilla extract
175g/6oz/1¼ cups plain (all-purpose) flour
2.5ml/½ tsp bicarbonate of soda (baking soda)
pinch of salt
115g/4oz/2 cups crisped rice cereal
175g/6oz/1 cup chocolate chips

1 Preheat the oven to 180°C/350°F/Gas 4. Lightly grease two or three large baking sheets.

2 In a large bowl, beat together the butter and sugar until light and fluffy. Beat in the egg and vanilla extract.

3 Sift the flour, bicarbonate of soda and salt over the mixture and fold in until just mixed.

4 Add the cereal and chocolate chips to the mixture and stir thoroughly to mix. Drop spoonfuls of the dough on to the baking sheets, spacing them well apart to allow room for spreading during baking.

5 Bake the cookies in the oven for 10–12 minutes until golden brown. Leave to firm up slightly on the baking sheet for 1–2 minutes. Use a metal spatula to transfer the cookies to a wire rack to cool completely.

Variation
To make Crunchy Walnut Jumbles, add 50g/2oz/½ cup walnuts, coarsely chopped, with the cereal and chocolate. Alternatively you could try adding different breakfast cereals for different textures and tastes.

Tea Swirls Energy 113kcal/471kJ; Protein 1.4g; Carbohydrate 12.7g, of which sugars 4.1g; Fat 6.6g, of which saturates 4g; Cholesterol 26mg; Calcium 21mg; Fibre 0.4g; Sodium 50mg.
Crunchy Jumbles Energy 95kcal/398kJ; Protein 0.9g; Carbohydrate 14.2g, of which sugars 9.8g; Fat 4.2g, of which saturates 2.5g; Cholesterol 12mg; Calcium 18mg; Fibre 0.3g; Sodium 31mg.

Farmhouse Cookies

Packed with cereal, these are true farmhouse cookies that your grandmother would have made but with the addition of peanut butter. With the muesli, and peanut butter, these cookies are high in fibre and children will love them as much as the adults.

Makes 18

115g/4oz/¹/2 cup butter, at room temperature
90g/3¹/2oz/generous 1 cup light brown sugar
65g/2¹/2oz/¹/4 cup crunchy peanut butter
1 egg
50g/2oz/¹/2 cup plain (all-purpose) flour
2.5ml/¹/2 tsp baking powder
2.5ml/¹/2 tsp ground cinnamon
pinch of salt
175g/6oz/1¹/2 cups muesli (granola)
50g/2oz/¹/3 cup raisins
50g/2oz/¹/2 cup chopped walnuts

1 Preheat the oven to 180°C/350°F/Gas 4. Lightly grease one or two baking sheets.

2 In a large bowl, beat together the butter and sugar until light and fluffy. Beat in the peanut butter, until mixed, then beat in the egg.

3 Sift the flour, baking powder, cinnamon and salt over the peanut butter mixture in batches and stir well after each addition. Stir in the muesli, raisins and walnuts. (Taste the mixture to see if it needs more sugar, as muesli varies.)

4 Drop rounded tablespoonfuls of the mixture on to the prepared baking sheet about 2.5cm/1in apart to allow room for spreading during baking. Press each gently with the back of a spoon to spread each mound into a circle.

5 Bake in the oven for about 15 minutes until lightly coloured. Leave to firm up slightly on the baking sheets, then with a metal spatula, transfer the cookies to a wire rack and leave to cool completely. Store the cookies in an airtight container.

Crunchy Oatmeal Cookies

This combination of crunchy cereal and oats is highly nutritious, providing protein, carbohydrate, vitamins and minerals – and the cookies taste wonderful.

Makes 14

175g/6oz/³/4 cup butter, at room temperature, diced
125g/4¹/2oz/³/4 cup caster (superfine) sugar
1 egg yolk

175g/6oz/1¹/2 cups plain (all-purpose) flour, plus extra for dusting
5ml/1 tsp bicarbonate of soda (baking soda)
pinch of salt
40g/1¹/2oz/¹/2 cup rolled oats
40g/1¹/2oz/¹/2 cup crunchy nugget cereal

1 In a large bowl, beat together the butter and sugar until light and fluffy. Mix in the egg yolk.

2 Sift over the flour, bicarbonate of soda and salt, then stir into the butter mixture. Add the oats and cereal and stir to blend. Chill for at least 20 minutes.

3 Preheat the oven to 190°C/375°F/Gas 5. Lightly grease a baking sheet. Flour the base of a wide, heavy glass.

4 Using two spoons, drop teaspoons of the dough on to the prepared baking sheet, spaced well apart. Gently flatten them with the floured base of the glass, dusting it with more flour if necessary.

5 Bake for 10–12 minutes until golden. With a metal spatula, transfer the cookies to a wire rack. Allow to cool completely before serving or storing.

> **Variation**
> To make nutty oatmeal cookies, substitute an equal quantity of chopped walnuts or pecan nuts for the cereal, and prepare as described in the recipe.

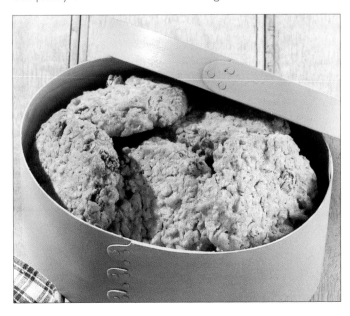

Crunchy Oatmeal Cookies Energy 220kcal/923kJ; Protein 2.3g; Carbohydrate 27.6g, of which sugars 14.3g; Fat 11.9g, of which saturates 6.8g; Cholesterol 41mg; Calcium 33mg; Fibre 0.8g; Sodium 81mg.
Farmhouse Cookies Energy 165kcal/688kJ; Protein 2.9g; Carbohydrate 16.9g, of which sugars 10.1g; Fat 10g, of which saturates 4.1g; Cholesterol 24mg; Calcium 25mg; Fibre 1.1g; Sodium 94mg.

Luxury Muesli Cookies

It is best to use a "luxury" muesli for this recipe, preferably one with 50 per cent mixed cereal and 50 per cent fruit, nuts and seeds. These buttery, crunchy cookies are ideal for a snack at any time.

Makes about 20

115g/4oz/¹/₂ cup unsalted butter
15ml/3 tbsp golden (light corn) syrup
115g/4oz/generous ¹/₂ cup demerara (raw) sugar
175g/6oz/1¹/₂ cups "luxury" muesli (granola)
90g/3¹/₂oz/³/₄ cup self-raising (self-rising) flour
5ml/1 tsp ground cinnamon

1 Preheat the oven to 160°C/325°F/Gas 3. Line two or three baking sheets with baking parchment.

2 Put the butter, syrup and sugar in a large pan and heat gently. Stir constantly until the butter has completely melted.

3 Remove the pan from the heat, then stir in the muesli, flour and cinnamon and mix together until well combined. Set aside to cool slightly.

4 Place spoonfuls of the mixture, slightly apart, on the baking sheets to allow room for spreading during baking.

5 Bake for 15 minutes until the cookies are just beginning to brown around the edges. Leave to cool for a few minutes on the baking sheets.

6 With a metal spatula, carefully transfer the cookies to a wire rack and leave to cool completely before serving or storing.

> **Variation**
> Tropical muesli containing coconut and dried tropical fruits makes an interesting alternative to regular luxury muesli. Try different versions using your favourite muesli flavours.

Fruit and Nut Cookies

The mixture for these cookies can be made ahead of time and stored in the refrigerator. The muscovado sugar lends a rich addition to these flavoursome chocolate chip, fruit and nut cookies.

Makes about 20 cookies

115g/4oz/¹/₂ cup unsalted butter, at room temperature, diced
115g/4oz/generous ¹/₂ cup sugar
115g/4oz/generous ¹/₂ cup light muscovado (brown) sugar
1 large (US extra large) egg
5ml/1 tsp vanilla extract
200g/7oz/1³/₄ cups self-raising (self-rising) flour
150g/5oz/scant 1 cup chocolate chips
50g/2oz/¹/₂ cup hazelnuts or walnuts, chopped and toasted
50g/2oz/scant ¹/₂ cup raisins

1 Preheat the oven to 180°C/350°F/Gas 4. Line two baking sheets with baking parchment.

2 Put the butter and sugars in a mixing bowl and beat together until light and fluffy. Add the egg and vanilla extract and beat to combine.

3 Add the flour, chocolate chips, chopped toasted hazelnuts or walnuts, and raisins and mix together. The dough will now have a crumbly texture.

4 Place teaspoonfuls of the mixture, spaced well apart, on the baking sheets. Bake for 15 minutes until golden. Leave for 5 minutes, then use a metal spatula to transfer to a wire rack to cool.

> **Cook's Tip**
> If you don't want to bake the mixture all at once, spoon it into a plastic container, cover the surface tightly with clear film (plastic wrap) and replace the lid. Keep in the refrigerator for up to 1 week. When required, remove the dough from the refrigerator 15 minutes before you want to bake the cookies, and stir well.

Malted Oat Cookies

This recipe is packed with oats, which produces a crisp, chewy cookie. Flavoured with malt, they are hard to resist.

Makes 18

175g/6oz/1½ cups rolled oats
75g/3oz/½ cup light muscovado
   (brown) sugar
1 egg
60ml/4 tbsp sunflower or
   vegetable oil
30ml/2 tbsp malt extract

1 Preheat the oven to 190°C/375°F/Gas 5. Lightly grease two baking sheets.

2 Mix the rolled oats and brown sugar in a bowl, breaking up any lumps in the sugar.

3 Beat the egg in a small bowl and add it together with the sunflower oil and malt extract to the oats and sugar mixture. Set the mixture aside to soak for 15 minutes, then beat together to combine thoroughly.

4 Using a teaspoon, place small heaps of the mixture well apart to allow room for spreading on the prepared baking sheets. Press the heaps into 7.5cm/3in rounds with the back of a dampened fork.

5 Bake the cookies in the oven for 10–15 minutes, until golden brown. Leave on the baking sheets for 1 minute to cool slightly.

6 With a metal spatula, transfer the cookies to a wire rack and leave to cool completely.

> **Variation**
> *Try replacing 25g/1oz/¼ cup of the rolled oats with ground Brazil nuts. This will provide a healthy dose of selenium and make a cookie with a slightly different texture as well as a strong nutty taste.*

Ker-runch Cookies

An unusual coating of bran flakes covers these small cookies – a painless way of making sure that you have plenty of fibre in your diet. Children will find them fun to make, too.

Makes about 18
175g/6oz/¾ cup butter
175g/6oz/¾ cup light muscovado
   (brown) sugar
1 egg
175g/6oz/1½ cups self-raising
   (self-rising) wholemeal
   (whole-wheat) flour
115g/4oz/generous 1 cup
   rolled oats
115g/4oz/⅔ cup mixed
   dried fruit
50g/2oz/2 cups bran flakes
   breakfast cereal

1 Preheat the oven to 160°C/325°F/Gas 3. Line two baking sheets with baking parchment.

2 Put the butter and sugar in a large bowl and beat together until pale and creamy.

3 Add the egg to the butter mixture and beat in until thoroughly combined. Stir in the flour, oats and fruit.

4 Roll the mixture into walnut-size balls between the palms of your hands.

5 Spread out the bran flakes on a shallow plate and roll the balls in them to coat. Place on the prepared baking sheets and flatten each one gently with your hand.

6 Bake the cookies in the oven for about 20 minutes until firm and golden brown. Remove from the baking sheets while still hot as these cookies firm up very quickly.

7 Transfer to a wire rack and leave to cool completely.

> **Variation**
> *Coat the cookies in oats instead of bran flakes.*

Malted Oat Cookies Energy 86kcal/364kJ; Protein 1.6g; Carbohydrate 12.8g, of which sugars 5.7g; Fat 3.6g, of which saturates 0.4g; Cholesterol 11mg; Calcium 9mg; Fibre 0.7g; Sodium 12mg.
Ker-runch Cookies Energy 196kcal/825kJ; Protein 2.9g; Carbohydrate 27.5g, of which sugars 15.4g; Fat 9.1g, of which saturates 3.6g; Cholesterol 12mg; Calcium 20mg; Fibre 1.8g; Sodium 110mg.

Florentine Cookies

These are not traditional Florentines but an utterly yummy version with a soft crumbly base and a wonderfully chewy topping.

Makes 24
115g/4oz/½ cup unsalted
   butter, at room temperature,
   diced
115g/4oz/generous ½ cup caster
   (superfine) sugar
1 egg
a few drops of almond extract
   (optional)
225g/8oz/2 cups self-raising
   (self-rising) flour, plus extra
   for dusting

For the topping
175g/6oz/1½ cups ready-to-eat
   dried apricots, chopped
50g/2oz/½ cup dried mango
   pieces, chopped
100g/3½oz/scant 1 cup flaked
   (sliced) almonds
60ml/4 tbsp plain (all-purpose)
   flour
50g/2oz/¼ cup unsalted
   butter
50g/2oz/¼ cup golden caster
   (superfine) sugar
60ml/4 tbsp golden (light
   corn) syrup

1 Preheat the oven to 190°C/375°F/Gas 5. Lightly grease two baking sheets.

2 In a large bowl, beat together the butter and sugar until the mixture is light and fluffy, then beat in the egg. Stir in the almond extract, if using, and the flour, using a wooden spoon and then your hands to make a firm soft dough.

3 Roll the dough out on a floured surface and, using a 7.5cm/3in round cookie cutter, stamp out 24 rounds. Place them on the baking sheets, spaced slightly apart.

4 To make the topping, combine the apricots, mango, almonds and flour in a bowl. Put the butter, sugar and syrup in a small pan and heat gently until the butter has melted and the mixture is combined. Pour over the fruit and nuts and mix together.

5 Spoon the mixture on top of the cookies. Bake for 12–14 minutes until golden and crisp. Leave the cookies on the baking sheets for 5 minutes, then transfer to a wire rack to cool.

Microwave Fruit and Nut Cookies

These irresistible cookies make the best of familiar flapjacks and old-fashioned, chocolate-coated Florentines.

Makes 16
75g/3oz/6 tbsp butter
45ml/3 tbsp/¼ cup golden (light
   corn) syrup

115g/4oz/1¼ cups rolled oats
25g/1oz/2 tbsp soft brown sugar
25g/1oz/2 tbsp chopped mixed
   candied peel
25g/1oz/2 tbsp glacé (candied)
   cherries, coarsely chopped
25g/1oz/¼ cup hazelnuts,
   coarsely chopped
115g/4oz/⅔ cup plain
   (semisweet) chocolate

1 Lightly grease a 20cm/8in square microwave-proof shallow dish and line the base with a sheet of rice paper.

2 Place the butter and golden syrup in a microwave-proof bowl and microwave on full (100 per cent) power for 1½ minutes until melted. Stir well together.

3 Add the oats, sugar, peel, cherries and hazelnuts and mix well.

4 Spoon the mixture into the dish and level the surface with the back of a spoon. Microwave on full (100 per cent) power for 6 minutes, giving the dish a half turn every 2 minutes. Allow to cool slightly, then cut into 16 fingers and place on a wire rack to cool.

5 Break the chocolate into pieces and put in a microwave-proof bowl. Microwave on full (100 per cent) power for 2–3 minutes, stirring twice, until melted and smooth.

6 Spread the chocolate over the tops of the cookies and mark in a zig-zag pattern with the prongs of a fork. Leave to set.

Cook's Tip
Rice paper is used for cooking in traditional recipes as well as in microwave methods. It prevents mixtures, such as this sweet oat base, from sticking by cooking on to them. When cooked, the rice paper can be eaten with the biscuits or other items.

Florentine Cookies Energy 167kcal/699kJ; Protein 2.5g; Carbohydrate 22.1g, of which sugars 13g; Fat 8.2g, of which saturates 3.8g; Cholesterol 15mg; Calcium 39mg; Fibre 1.3g; Sodium 51mg.
Microwave Fruit and Nut Cookies Energy 133kcal/555kJ; Protein 1.5g; Carbohydrate 15.7g, of which sugars 10.4g; Fat 7.5g, of which saturates 3.7g; Cholesterol 10mg; Calcium 14mg; Fibre 0.9g; Sodium 44mg.

Fruit and Millet Treacle Cookies

These little cookies are quick to make, and will no doubt disappear just as quickly when they come out of the oven. However, if you are not fond of treacle then golden syrup can be used equally successfully as an alternative.

Makes about 25–30
90g/3¹/₂oz/7 tbsp butter
150g/5oz/²/₃ cup light muscovado (brown) sugar
30ml/2 tbsp black treacle (molasses)
1 egg
150g/5oz/1¹/₄ cups plain (all-purpose) flour
50g/2oz/¹/₂ cup millet flakes
50g/2oz/¹/₂ cup almonds, chopped
200g/7oz/generous 1 cup luxury mixed dried fruit

1 Preheat the oven to 190°C/375°F/Gas 5. Lightly grease two large baking sheets.

2 Put the butter, muscovado sugar, treacle and egg in a large bowl and beat together until well combined and the mixture is light and fluffy.

3 Stir in the flour and millet flakes, the almonds and dried fruit. Put tablespoonfuls of the mixture on to the prepared baking sheets, spaced well apart to allow room for spreading during baking.

4 Bake in the oven for about 15 minutes until golden brown.

5 Leave the cookies on the baking sheets to firm up for a few minutes, then use a metal spatula to transfer them to a wire rack and leave to cool completely.

> **Cook's Tip**
> *Make sure that you use millet flakes for these cookies rather than millet grains. The grains will swell too much during cooking and spoil the cookies.*

Candied Peel Crumble Cookies

Crumbly, melt-in-the-mouth cookies, these incorporate candied peel, walnuts and white chocolate chips and are coated with a zingy lemon glaze.

Makes about 24
175g/6oz/³/₄ cup unsalted butter, at room temperature, diced
90g/3¹/₂oz/¹/₂ cup caster (superfine) sugar
1 egg, beaten
finely grated rind of 1 lemon

200g/7oz/1³/₄ cups self-raising (self-rising) flour
90g/3¹/₂oz/generous ¹/₂ cup candied peel, chopped
75g/3oz/³/₄ cup chopped walnuts
50g/2oz/¹/₃ cup white chocolate chips

For the glaze
50g/2oz/¹/₂ cup icing (confectioners') sugar, sifted
15ml/1 tbsp lemon juice
thin strips of candied peel, to decorate (optional)

1 Preheat the oven to 180°C/350°F/Gas 4. Lightly grease two baking sheets.

2 Put the butter and sugar in a large bowl and beat together until light and fluffy. Add the egg and beat well together.

3 Add the lemon rind and flour and stir together gently. Fold the candied peel, walnuts and chocolate chips into the mixture.

4 Place tablespoonfuls of the mixture, spaced slightly apart, on the baking sheets and bake in the oven for 12–15 minutes, until cooked but still pale in colour. Transfer the cookies to a wire rack using a metal spatula and to leave to cool completely.

5 For the glaze, put the icing sugar in a bowl and stir in the lemon juice. Spoon some glaze over each cookie. Decorate with candied peel, if using.

> **Variation**
> *Replace the candied peel in the cookies with glacé (candied) cherries and decorate with a small piece of cherry on top.*

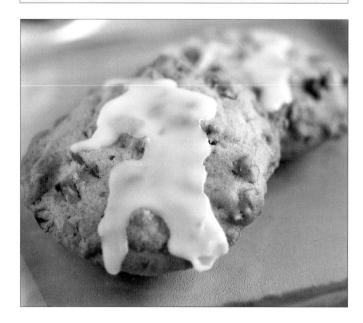

Fruit and Millet Treacle Cookies Energy 99kcal/416kJ; Protein 1.2g; Carbohydrate 15.8g, of which sugars 10.5g; Fat 3.7g, of which saturates 1.2g; Cholesterol 7mg; Calcium 20mg; Fibre 0.4g, Sodium 32mg. **Candied Peel Crumble Cookies** Energy 150kcal/626kJ; Protein 1.8g; Carbohydrate 16.2g, of which sugars 9.8g; Fat 9.2g, of which saturates 4.4g; Cholesterol 23mg; Calcium 31mg; Fibre 0.5g; Sodium 61mg

Toffee Apple and Oat Crunchies

An unashamedly addictive mixture of chewy oats, soft apple and wonderfully crunchy toffee, this cookie won't win large prizes in the looks department but is top of the class for flavour.

Makes about 16
150g/5oz/10 tbsp unsalted butter
175g/6oz/scant 1 cup light muscovado (brown) sugar
90g/3½oz/½ cup sugar
1 large (US extra large) egg, beaten
75g/3oz/⅔ cup plain (all-purpose) flour
2.5ml/½ tsp bicarbonate of soda (baking soda)
pinch of salt
250g/9oz/2½ cups rolled oats
50g/2oz/scant ½ cup sultanas (golden raisins)
50g/2oz dried apple rings, coarsely chopped
50g/2oz chewy toffees, coarsely chopped

1 Preheat the oven to 180°C/350°F/Gas 4. Line two or three baking sheets with baking parchment.

2 In a large bowl, beat together the butter and both sugars until light and creamy. Add the beaten egg and beat well until thoroughly combined.

3 Sift together the flour, bicarbonate of soda and salt. Add to the butter, sugar and egg mixture and mix in well. Finally add the oats, sultanas, chopped apple rings and toffee pieces and stir gently until just combined.

4 Using a large tablespoon, place heaps of the mixture well apart on the prepared baking sheets to allow room for spreading during baking. Bake for about 10–12 minutes, or until lightly set in the centre and just beginning to brown at the edges.

5 Remove the cookies from the oven and leave to firm up on the baking sheets for a few minutes.

6 Using a metal spatula, transfer the cookies to a wire rack and leave to cool completely. Store in an airtight container for 3–4 days.

Apple and Elderflower Stars

These delicious, crumbly apple cookies are topped with a sweet yet very sharp icing. Packaged in a pretty box, they would make a delightful gift for someone special.

Makes about 18
115g/4oz/½ cup unsalted butter, at room temperature, diced
75g/3oz/scant ½ cup caster (superfine) sugar
2.5ml/½ tsp mixed (apple pie) spice
1 large (US extra large) egg yolk
25g/1oz dried apple rings, finely chopped
200g/7oz/1¾ cups self-raising (self-rising) flour
5–10ml/1–2 tsp milk, if necessary

For the topping
200g/7oz/1¾ cups icing (confectioners') sugar, sifted
60–90ml/4–6 tbsp elderflower cordial
sugar, for sprinkling

1 Preheat the oven to 190°C/375°F/Gas 5. Lightly grease two baking sheets.

2 Beat together the butter and sugar until light and fluffy. Beat in the mixed spice and egg yolk. Add the chopped apple and flour and stir together well. The mixture should form a stiff dough but if it is too dry, add some milk.

3 Roll the dough out on a floured surface to 5mm/¼in thick. Using a star cookie cutter, stamp out the cookies.

4 Place on the baking sheets and bake for about 10–15 minutes, or until beginning to brown around the edges. Using a metal spatula, transfer the cookies to a wire rack to cool.

5 To make the topping, sift the icing sugar into a bowl and add just enough elderflower cordial to mix to a fairly thick but still pourable consistency.

6 When the cookies are completely cool, trickle the icing randomly over the stars. Immediately sprinkle with sugar and leave to set.

Toffee Apple and Oat Crunchies Energy 249kcal/1047kJ; Protein 3.1g; Carbohydrate 38.8g, of which sugars 23.2g; Fat 10.1g, of which saturates 5.3g; Cholesterol 32mg; Calcium 34mg; Fibre 1.3g; Sodium 79mg.
Apple and Elderflower Stars Energy 157kcal/659kJ; Protein 1.4g; Carbohydrate 26.6g, of which sugars 18.1g; Fat 5.7g, of which saturates 3.4g; Cholesterol 25mg; Calcium 27mg; Fibre 0.4g; Sodium 42mg.

Apricot and Hazelnut Oat Cookies

These cookie-cum-flapjacks have a chewy, crumbly texture. They are sprinkled with apricots and toasted hazelnuts, but any combination of dried fruit and nuts can be used.

Makes 9
115g/4oz/1 cup self-raising
  (self-rising) flour, sifted
115g/4oz/1 cup rolled oats
75g/3oz/scant ½ cup chopped
  ready-to-eat dried apricots
115g/4oz/½ cup unsalted
  butter

75g/3oz/scant ½ cup golden
  caster (superfine) sugar
15ml/1 tbsp clear honey

For the topping
25g/1oz/2 tbsp chopped
  ready-to-eat dried apricots
25g/1oz/¼ cup toasted and
  chopped hazelnuts

1 Preheat the oven to 160°C/325°F/Gas 3. Lightly grease a large baking sheet.

2 Put the flour, oats and chopped apricots in a large mixing bowl.

3 Put the butter, sugar and honey in a pan and cook over a gentle heat until the butter melts and the sugar dissolves, stirring the mixture occasionally. Remove the pan from the heat.

4 Pour the honey and sugar mixture into the bowl containing the flour, oats and apricots. Mix with a wooden spoon to form a sticky dough.

5 Divide the dough into nine pieces and place on the prepared baking sheet. Press into 1cm/½in thick rounds.

6 Scatter over the topping of apricots and hazelnuts and press into the dough. Bake the cookies for about 15 minutes, until they are golden and slightly crisp. Leave to cool on the baking sheet for 5 minutes, then transfer to a wire rack to cool completely.

Date and Orange Oat Cookies

The fragrant aroma of orange permeates the kitchen when these cookies are baking. Orange is a classic partner with dates and both add a richness to these healthy crumbly oat cookies.

Makes 25
150g/5oz/¾ cup soft dark
  brown sugar
150g/5oz/10 tbsp butter
finely grated rind of 1 unwaxed
  orange
150g/5oz/1¼ cups self-raising
  (self-rising) wholemeal
  (whole-wheat) flour
5ml/1 tsp baking powder
75g/3oz/⅔ cup medium oatmeal
75g/3oz/½ cup dried dates,
  roughly chopped

1 Preheat the oven to 180°C/350°F/Gas 4. Lightly grease two baking sheets.

2 Put the sugar and butter in a large bowl and beat together until light and fluffy. Stir in the orange rind.

3 In a separate bowl, sift the flour with the baking powder. Fold the flour mixture and then the oatmeal in to the butter and sugar mixture until well combined. Add the dates and mix well.

4 Place heaped tablespoonfuls of the mixture on to the prepared baking sheets, spacing them well apart to allow the mixture room for spreading. Bake in the oven for 15–20 minutes, until golden.

5 Leave the cookies to firm up slightly on the baking sheet for 1–2 minutes. Use a metal spatula to carefully transfer the cookies to wire racks and leave to cool completely. Store in an airtight container for 3–4 days.

Variation
Replace the dates with dried chopped apricots, raisins, sultanas (golden raisins) or figs.

Date and Orange Oat Cookies Energy 121kcal/508kJ; Protein 1.5g; Carbohydrate 17.4g, of which sugars 8.4g; Fat 5.5g, of which saturates 3.1g; Cholesterol 13mg; Calcium 17mg; Fibre 0.7g; Sodium 39mg. **Apricot and Hazelnut Oat Cookies** Energy 262kcal/1098kJ; Protein 3.7g; Carbohydrate 33.2g, of which sugars 14.4g; Fat 13.6g, of which saturates 6.8g; Cholesterol 27mg; Calcium 71mg; Fibre 2.1g; Sodium 130mg.

Sultana Cornmeal Cookies

These little yellow biscuits come from Italy, where cornmeal is produced in the North of the country and Marsala is produced in Sicily.

Makes 48
75g/3oz/½ cup sultanas (golden raisins)
115g/4oz/1 cup finely ground yellow cornmeal
175g/6oz/1½ cups plain (all-purpose) flour
7.5ml/1½ tsp baking powder
pinch of salt
225g/8oz/1 cup butter
225g/8oz/1 cup sugar
2 eggs
15ml/1 tbsp Marsala or 5ml/1 tsp vanilla extract

1 Soak the sultanas in a small bowl of warm water for 15 minutes. Drain.

2 Preheat the oven to 180°C/350°F/Gas 4. Lightly grease two or three baking sheets.

3 Sift the cornmeal, flour, baking powder and salt together into a mixing bowl. Set aside.

4 Put the butter and sugar in a large bowl and beat together until light and fluffy. Beat in the eggs, one at a time. Beat in the Marsala or vanilla extract. Add the dry ingredients to the butter mixture, beating until well blended. Stir in the sultanas.

5 Drop heaped teaspoons of the mixture on to the prepared baking sheet in rows about 5cm/2in apart to allow room for spreading while baking.

6 Bake in the oven for 7–8 minutes, until the cookies are golden brown at the edges.

7 Leave to firm up slightly on the baking sheets for 1–2 minutes before carefully transferring the cookies to a wire rack using a metal spatula.

8 Leave to cool completely before serving. Store the cookies in an airtight container for up to 5 days.

Prune and Peel Rock Buns

These buns are quick and easy to make and taste absolutely wonderful.

Makes 12
225g/8oz/2 cups plain (all-purpose) flour
10ml/2 tsp baking powder
75g/3oz/⅔ cup demerara (raw) sugar
50g/2oz/½ cup chopped ready-to-eat dried prunes
50g/2oz/⅓ cup chopped mixed (candied) peel
finely grated rind of 1 lemon
60ml/4 tbsp sunflower oil
75ml/5 tbsp milk

1 Preheat the oven to 200°C/400°F/Gas 6. Lightly grease a large baking sheet.

2 Sift the flour and baking powder, then stir in the sugar, prunes, peel and lemon rind.

3 Mix the oil and milk, then stir into the mixture, to make a dough which just binds together.

4 Spoon into rocky heaps on the baking sheet and bake for about 20 minutes, until golden. Transfer to a wire rack and leave to cool completely.

Lemon and Raisin Rock Cakes

These lightly spiced, fruity rock buns are easy to make, and delicious to eat.

Makes 16
225g/8oz/2 cups self-raising (self-rising) wholemeal (whole-wheat) flour
pinch of salt
115g/4oz/½ cup butter
115g/4oz/ generous ½ cup golden caster (superfine) sugar
5ml/1 tsp ground mixed (apple pie) spice
finely grated rind of 1 lemon
115g/4oz/⅔ cup raisins
1 egg, beaten
milk, to mix
pared lemon rind, to decorate

1 Preheat the oven to 200°C/400°F/Gas 6. Lightly grease two baking sheets.

2 Put the flour and salt in a bowl and lightly rub in the butter until the mixture resembles breadcrumbs.

3 Add the sugar, spice, lemon rind and raisins to the flour mixture and mix together.

4 Stir in the egg and enough milk to make a stiff, but crumbly mixture.

5 Using two spoons, put rough heaps of the mixture on to the prepared baking sheets. Bake for 15–20 minutes, until lightly browned and firm to the touch. Leave to firm up on the baking sheet for 1–2 minutes.

6 Using a metal spatula, transfer the rock cakes to a wire rack and leave to cool completely. Serve the cookies decorated with lemon rind.

Sultana Cornmeal Cookies Energy 60kcal/254kJ; Protein 1.1g; Carbohydrate 9.6g, of which sugars 3.3g; Fat 2.1g, of which saturates 1.2g; Cholesterol 12mg; Calcium 10mg; Fibre 0.3g; Sodium 17mg.
Prune and Peel Rock Buns Energy 132kcal/559kJ; Protein 2.1g; Carbohydrate 25.3g, of which sugars 11g; Fat 3.2g, of which saturates 0.4g; Cholesterol 0mg; Calcium 44mg; Fibre 1g; Sodium 16mg.
Lemon and Raisin Rock Cakes Energy 147kcal/617kJ; Protein 1.9g; Carbohydrate 21.6g, of which sugars 10.9g; Fat 6.5g, of which saturates 3.9g; Cholesterol 27mg; Calcium 27mg; Fibre 0.6g; Sodium 72mg.

Cinnamon Treats

These simple cookies really are a treat and there's no better accompaniment than a large pot of tea.

Makes 50

250g/9oz/2¼ cups plain (all-purpose) flour
pinch of salt
10ml/2 tsp ground cinnamon
225g/8oz/1 cup unsalted butter, at room temperature
225g/8oz/generous 1 cup caster (superfine) sugar
2 eggs
5ml/1 tsp vanilla extract

1 In a large bowl, sift together the flour, salt and cinnamon. Set aside.

2 In a large bowl, beat the butter until soft. Add the sugar and continue beating together until the mixture is light and fluffy.

3 Beat the eggs and vanilla, then gradually stir into the butter mixture. Stir in the dry ingredients.

4 Divide the mixture into four equal parts, then roll each into 5cm/2in diameter logs. Wrap tightly in foil and chill in the refrigerator until firm.

5 Preheat the oven to 190°C/375°F/Gas 5. Lightly grease two baking sheets.

6 With a sharp knife, cut the logs into 5mm/¼in slices. Place the rounds on the prepared sheets, spaced slightly apart, and bake for about 10 minutes, until lightly coloured. Leave on the baking sheet for 1–2 minutes until the cookies firm up slightly.

7 With a metal spatula, transfer the cookies to a wire rack and leave to cool completely.

Variation
Replace the ground cinnamon with mixed (apple pie) spice, if you like.

Cinnamon-coated Cookies

The aroma that fills the kitchen while these cookies are baking is mouthwatering. They are too good to resist.

Makes 30

115g/4oz/½ cup butter, at room temperature
350g/12oz/1¾ cups caster (superfine) sugar
5ml/1 tsp vanilla extract
2 eggs
50ml/2fl oz/¼ cup milk
400g/14oz/3½ cups plain (all-purpose) flour
5ml/1 tsp bicarbonate of soda (baking soda)
50g/2oz/½ cup finely chopped walnuts

For the coating
65g/2½oz/5 tbsp sugar
30ml/2 tbsp ground cinnamon

1 Preheat the oven to 190°C/375°F/Gas 5. Lightly grease two baking sheets.

2 In a large bowl, beat the butter until light. Add the sugar and vanilla extract and continue mixing until pale and fluffy. Add one egg at a time, beating well after each addition, then add the milk and mix well together.

3 Sift the flour and bicarbonate of soda over the butter mixture and stir in until combined. Stir in the chopped walnuts. Put in the refrigerator to chill for 15 minutes.

4 For the coating, mix the sugar and cinnamon. Roll tablespoonfuls of the dough mixture into walnut-size balls. Roll the balls in the sugar mixture.

5 Place the cookies 5cm/2in apart on the prepared sheets to allow for spreading during baking and flatten slightly with the back of a spoon. Bake in the oven until golden brown, about 10 minutes.

6 Leave to firm up slightly on the baking sheets for a few minutes, then using a metal spatula carefully transfer the cookies to a wire rack. Leave to cool completely before serving.

Cinnamon Treats Energy 71kcal/298kJ; Protein 0.8g; Carbohydrate 8.6g, of which sugars 4.8g; Fat 4g, of which saturates 2.4g; Cholesterol 17mg; Calcium 11mg; Fibre 0.2g; Sodium 31mg.
Cinnamon-coated Cookies Energy 65kcal/773kJ; Protein 0.9g; Carbohydrate 7.8g, of which sugars 3.1g; Fat 3.6g, of which saturates 2.2g; Cholesterol 14mg; Calcium 15mg; Fibre 0.2g; Sodium 28mg.

Clementine Shortbread Fingers

Light and mouthwatering, these citrus shortbreads are a real tea-time treat. Made with clementines, they are subtly sweet.

Makes 18
115g/4oz/½ cup unsalted butter
50g/2oz/¼ cup caster (superfine) sugar, plus extra for sprinkling
finely grated rind of 4 clementines
175g/6oz/1½ cups plain (all-purpose) flour, plus extra for dusting

1 Preheat the oven to 190°C/375°F/Gas 5. Lightly grease a large baking sheet.

2 Beat together the butter and sugar until soft and creamy, then add the grated clementine rind and beat well until it is fully incorporated.

3 Gradually add the flour, using a wooden spoon at first, and then with your hands gently pull the dough together to form a soft ball. Roll out the dough on a lightly floured surface to about 1cm/½in thick.

4 Cut into fingers, sprinkle over a little extra sugar and put on to the baking sheet spaced well apart. Prick lightly with a fork.

5 Bake for 20 minutes, or until light golden brown. Carefully lift the cookies on to a wire rack with a metal spatula and leave to cool completely.

> **Cook's Tip**
> *The shortbread fingers will keep in an airtight container.*

> **Variation**
> *Substitute the grated rind of one Ugli fruit for the clementine rind and sprinkle the shortbread fingers well with sugar before baking.*

Five-spice Fingers

These light, crumbly cookies have an unusual Chinese five-spice flavouring. Pipe them into finger shapes.

Makes 28
115g/4oz/½ cup butter, at room temperature, diced, plus extra for greasing
50g/2oz/½ cup icing (confectioners') sugar
115g/4oz/1 cup plain (all-purpose) flour
10ml/2 tsp Chinese five-spice powder
grated rind and juice of ½ orange

1 Preheat the oven to 180°C/350°F/Gas 4. Lightly grease two baking sheets.

2 Put the butter and half the icing sugar in a bowl and beat well with a wooden spoon, until the mixture is smooth and creamy.

3 Add the flour and five-spice powder and beat again until thoroughly mixed. Spoon the mixture into a large piping (pastry) bag fitted with a large star nozzle.

4 Pipe short lines of mixture, about 7.5cm/3in long, on the prepared baking sheets. Leave enough room for them to spread.

5 Bake for 15 minutes, until lightly browned. Leave to cool slightly before transferring to a wire rack using a metal spatula.

6 Sift the remaining icing sugar into a small bowl and stir in the orange rind. Add enough juice to make a thin icing. Brush over the cookies while they are still warm.

> **Variation**
> *Substitute syrup from a jar of preserved stem ginger for the orange juice in the icing.*

Clementine Shortbread Fingers Energy 87kcal/362kJ; Protein 0.7g; Carbohydrate 9.5g, of which sugars 4.7g; Fat 5.4g, of which saturates 3.3g; Cholesterol 14mg; Calcium 15mg; Fibre 0.3g; Sodium 47mg.
Five-spice Fingers Energy 53kcal/221kJ; Protein 0.5g; Carbohydrate 5.3g, of which sugars 2g; Fat 3.5g, of which saturates 2.2g; Cholesterol 9mg; Calcium 8mg; Fibre 0.1g; Sodium 25mg.

Almond Orange Cookies

The combination of lard and almonds gives these traditional cookies a lovely short texture, so that they melt in the mouth, but you could use white cooking fat, if you like. Serve them whenever you have guests – they are perfect with coffee or hot chocolate.

Makes 36
250g/9oz/1½ cups lard, softened
125g/4½oz/generous ½ cup
   caster (superfine) sugar
2 eggs, beaten

grated rind and juice of
   1 small orange
300g/11oz/2¾ cups plain
   (all-purpose) flour, plus extra
   for dusting
5ml/1 tsp baking powder
200g/7oz/1¾ cups ground
   almonds

For dusting
50g/2oz/½ cup icing
   (confectioners') sugar
5ml/1 tsp ground cinnamon

1 Preheat the oven to 200°C/400°F/Gas 6. Lightly grease two or three large baking sheets.

2 Place the lard in a large bowl and beat until light and fluffy. Gradually beat in the caster sugar.

3 Beat in the eggs, orange rind and juice until well combined, then sift over the flour and baking powder in batches and stir in after each addition. Add the almonds and bring together to form a dough.

4 Roll out on a lightly floured surface to 1cm/½in thick. Stamp out 36 rounds with a cookie cutter.

5 Lift the rounds on to the prepared baking sheets and bake for about 10 minutes, until golden. Leave on the baking sheets for 10 minutes to cool and firm slightly before transferring with a metal spatula to a wire rack to cool.

6 Place the wire rack over the baking sheet. Combine the icing sugar with the cinnamon and sift evenly over the cookies. Leave to cool completely.

Orange Cookies

Easy to make and even easier to eat, these cookies are just perfect with a cup of steaming hot chocolate on a winter's afternoon or with ice cream on a warm summer's evening.

Makes 30
115g/4oz/½ cup butter, at room
   temperature

200g/7oz/1 cup sugar
2 egg yolks
15ml/1 tbsp fresh orange juice
grated rind of 1 large orange
200g/7oz/1¾ cups plain
   (all-purpose) flour
15ml/1 tbsp cornflour
   (cornstarch)
pinch of salt
5ml/1 tsp baking powder

1 In a large bowl, beat together the butter and sugar until light and fluffy. Add the egg yolks, orange juice and rind, and continue beating to blend. Set aside.

2 In another bowl, sift together the flour, cornflour, salt and baking powder. Add to the butter mixture and stir until it forms a dough.

3 Wrap the dough in baking parchment and chill in the refrigerator for 2 hours.

4 Preheat the oven to 375°F/190°C/Gas 5. Lightly grease two baking sheets.

5 Roll spoonfuls of the dough into balls and place 1–2in/ 2.5–5cm apart on the prepared sheets.

6 Press down with a fork to flatten. Bake for about 8–10 minutes, until golden brown. Leave to firm up slightly for 1–2 minutes. With a metal spatula, transfer the cookies to a wire rack and leave to cool completely.

Cook's Tip
When rolling the dough into balls, try not to handle it too much or it may become greasy.

Almond Orange Cookies Energy 148kcal/617kJ; Protein 2.3g; Carbohydrate 12.1g, of which sugars 5.6g; Fat 10.4g, of which saturates 3.1g; Cholesterol 17mg; Calcium 29mg; Fibre 0.7g; Sodium 5mg.
Orange Cookies Energy 83kcal/350kJ; Protein 0.9g; Carbohydrate 12.6g, of which sugars 7.1g; Fat 3.6g, of which saturates 2.1g; Cholesterol 22mg; Calcium 15mg; Fibre 0.2g; Sodium 25mg.

Citrus Drops

These soft, cake-like treats are deliciously tangy, with a zesty, crumbly base filled with sweet, sticky lemon or orange curd. The crunchy topping of almonds makes the perfect finish.

Makes about 20
175g/6oz/³⁄4 cup unsalted butter,
   at room temperature, diced
150g/5oz/³⁄4 cup caster
   (superfine) sugar
finely grated rind of 1 large lemon
finely grated rind of 1 orange
2 egg yolks
50g/2oz/¹⁄2 cup ground almonds
225g/8oz/2 cups self-raising
   (self-rising) flour
lemon and/or orange curd
milk, for brushing
flaked (sliced) almonds,
   for sprinkling

1 Preheat the oven to 160°C/325°F/Gas 3. Lightly grease two baking sheets

2 In a large bowl, beat the butter and sugar together until light and fluffy, then stir in the citrus rinds.

3 Stir the egg yolks into the mixture, then add the ground almonds and flour and mix well.

4 Divide the mixture into 20 pieces and shape each into a smooth ball with your hands. Place on the baking sheets. Using the handle of a wooden spoon, make a hole in the centre of each cookie.

5 Put about 2.5ml/¹⁄2 tsp lemon or orange curd into each hole and gently pinch the opening together with your fingers to semi-enclose the curd.

6 Brush the top of each cookie with milk and sprinkle with flaked almonds.

7 Bake for about 20 minutes, until pale golden brown. Leave to cool slightly on the baking sheets to firm up, then transfer to a wire rack using a metal spatula and leave to cool completely.

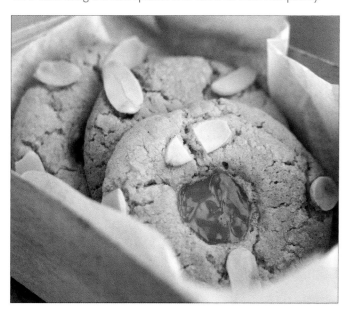

Raspberry Sandwich Cookies

Children will love these sweet, sticky treats. If you need to store them, layer with baking parchment in an airtight container.

Makes 32
115g/4oz/1 cup blanched
   almonds
175g/6oz/1¹⁄2 cups plain
   (all-purpose) flour, plus extra
   for dusting
175g/6oz/³⁄4 cup butter
115g/4oz/generous ¹⁄2 cup caster
   (superfine) sugar
grated rind of 1 lemon
5ml/1 tsp vanilla extract
1 egg white
pinch of salt
40g/1¹⁄2oz/¹⁄3 cup flaked (sliced)
   almonds, chopped
350g/12oz/1¹⁄4 cups raspberry
   jam (jelly)
15ml/1 tbsp lemon juice

1 Preheat the oven to 160°C/325°F/Gas 3. Lightly grease two baking sheets.

2 In a processor or nut grinder, finely grind the almonds with 45ml/3 tbsp of the flour.

3 Beat together the butter and sugar until light and fluffy. Stir in the lemon rind and vanilla.

4 Add the ground almonds and remaining flour and mix to form a dough. Gather it into a ball, wrap in baking parchment and chill for 1 hour.

5 Roll out on a lightly floured surface to 3mm/¹⁄8in thick. With a floured 6cm/2¹⁄2in cookie cutter, stamp out rounds, then stamp out the centres from half of them. Place them 1cm/¹⁄2in apart on the baking sheets.

6 Whisk the egg white with the salt until just frothy. Brush only the rings with the egg white, then sprinkle over the chopped almonds. Bake for 12–15 minutes, until lightly browned. Cool for 2–3 minutes on the sheets before transferring to a wire rack.

7 In a small, heavy pan, heat the jam with the lemon juice until it melts and comes to a simmer. Brush the jam over the cookie rounds and sandwich together with the rings.

Citrus Drops Energy 157kcal/658kJ; Protein 2.1g; Carbohydrate 16.8g, of which sugars 8.2g; Fat 9.6g, of which saturates 4.9g; Cholesterol 39mg; Calcium 31mg; Fibre 0.6g; Sodium 55mg.
Raspberry Sandwich Cookies Energy 133kcal/554kJ; Protein 2g; Carbohydrate 13.9g, of which sugars 9.5g; Fat 8.1g, of which saturates 3.1g; Cholesterol 12mg; Calcium 27mg; Fibre 0.6g; Sodium 39mg.

Apple Sauce Cookies

Apple sauce, nuts and cinnamon are the perfect combination for cookies for winter.

Makes 36
455g/1lb cooking apples, peeled, cored and chopped
45ml/3 tbsp water
115g/4oz/¼ cup sugar
115g/4oz/½ butter
175g/6oz/1 cup plain (all-purpose) flour
2.5ml/½ tsp baking powder
1.5ml/¼ tsp bicarbonate of soda (baking soda)
pinch of salt
2.5ml/½ tsp ground cinnamon
50g/2oz/½ cup chopped walnuts

1 Cook the apples with the water in a covered pan over a low heat until tender. Leave to cool slightly then purée in a blender or mash the apples with a fork. Measure out 175ml/6fl oz/ ¾ cup. Set aside and leave to cool.

2 Preheat the oven to 190°C/375°F/Gas 5. Lightly grease two or three baking sheets.

3 In a bowl, beat together the sugar and butter until pale and fluffy. Beat in the apple sauce.

4 Sift the flour, baking powder, bicarbonate of soda, salt and cinnamon into the mixture, and stir to blend. Fold in the chopped walnuts.

5 Drop teaspoonfuls of the dough on to the prepared baking sheets, spacing them well apart to allow room for spreading while baking.

6 Bake the cookies for 8–10 minutes, until they are golden brown. Using a metal spatula, transfer them to a wire rack and leave to cool before serving.

> **Cook's Tip**
> *If the apple sauce is too runny, put it in a sieve (strainer) over a bowl and let it drain for 10 minutes before measuring it out.*

Banana Cream Cookies

These delicious cookies are inspired by the classic childhood dessert bananas and cream. The warm banana cookies are coated in crisp sugar-frosted cornflakes and, for the ultimate indulgence, are delicious served warm drizzled with clear honey.

Makes about 24
2 eggs
250g/9oz/1¼ cups soft light brown sugar
5ml/1 tsp vanilla extract
100ml/3½fl oz/scant ½ cup sunflower oil
90g/3½oz/scant ½ cup crème fraîche
200g/7oz/1¾ cups plain (all-purpose) flour
200g/7oz/1¾ cups self-raising (self-rising) flour
50g/2oz/2½ cups frosted cornflakes
125g/4¼oz dried small bananas, chopped, or 2 bananas, peeled and chopped
icing (confectioners') sugar, sifted, for dredging

1 Put the eggs and sugar in a large bowl and whisk together until well blended. Stir in the vanilla extract.

2 Add the oil and crème fraîche and stir well to combine. Add the flours and mix well. (The mixture will be quite runny at this stage.) Cover with clear film (plastic wrap) and chill for about 30 minutes.

3 Preheat the oven to 180°C/350°F/Gas 4. Lightly grease two or three baking sheets.

4 Put the frosted cornflakes in a large bowl. Remove the cookie dough from the refrigerator and stir in the bananas.

5 Using a tablespoon, drop heaps of the cookie mixture into the cornflakes. Lightly toss so that each cookie is well coated, then remove and place on the prepared baking sheets. Flatten slightly with your fingertips.

6 Bake for 15–20 minutes, or until risen and golden brown and crispy. Transfer the cookies to a wire rack and dredge with sifted icing sugar. Serve while still warm.

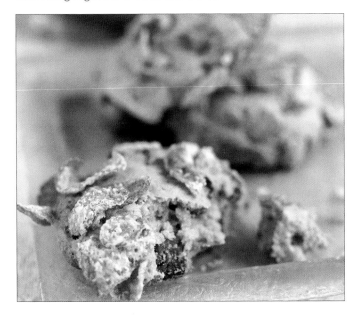

Apple Sauce Cookies Energy 54kcal/227kJ; Protein 0.7g; Carbohydrate 5g, of which sugars 1.3g; Fat 3.7g, of which saturates 1.8g; Cholesterol 7mg; Calcium 9mg; Fibre 0.4g; Sodium 20mg.
Banana Cream Cookies Energy 159kcal/669kJ; Protein 2.5g; Carbohydrate 27.7g, of which sugars 13.1g; Fat 5g, of which saturates 1.5g; Cholesterol 20mg; Calcium 34mg; Fibre 0.6g; Sodium 29mg.

Rose Water Biscuits

These light, crunchy cookies are easy to make. They are perfect served with mint tea – the two flavours are made for each other. The mixture makes about 60 cookies, so bake them in batches, two trays at a time.

Makes 60
225g/8oz/1 cup butter, softened at room temperature
225g/8oz/generous 1 cup caster (superfine) sugar
1 egg
15ml/1 tbsp single (light) cream
15ml/1 tbsp rose water
300g/11oz/2¾ cups plain (all-purpose) flour
pinch of salt
5ml/1 tsp baking powder
caster (superfine) sugar, for sprinkling

1 In a large bowl, beat together the butter and sugar until light and fluffy.

2 Break in the egg, pour in the cream and rose water and beat until well combined.

3 Sift over the flour, salt and baking powder a little at a time, combining well after each addition. Use your fingertips to combine to a firm dough.

4 Mould the mixture into an even roll and wrap in clear film (plastic wrap). Chill for 1–1½ hours.

5 Preheat the oven to 190°C/375°F/Gas 5. Lightly grease two large baking sheets.

6 Using a sharp knife, thinly slice the cookie dough into rounds. Arrange the cookies on the prepared baking sheets, allowing enough space for them to spread during cooking. Sprinkle with a little caster sugar and bake for about 10 minutes, until they are just turning brown at the edges.

7 Using a metal spatula, transfer the cookies to a wire rack and leave to cool completely.

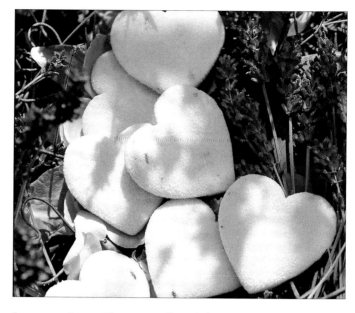

Lavender Heart Cookies

These delicate and fragrant cookies make an unusual treat and their pretty heart shape is sure to charm both family and friends.

Makes about 18
115g/4oz/½ cup unsalted butter at room temperature, diced
50g/2oz/¼ cup caster (superfine) sugar
175g/6oz/1½ cups plain (all-purpose) flour
30ml/2 tbsp fresh lavender florets or 15ml/1 tbsp dried culinary lavender, coarsely chopped
30ml/2 tbsp caster (superfine) sugar, for sprinkling

1 Preheat the oven to 200°C/400°F/Gas 6. Lightly grease a large baking sheet.

2 In a large bowl, beat together the butter and sugar until light and fluffy.

3 Stir in the flour and lavender and bring the mixture together in a soft ball. Cover with clear film (plastic wrap) and chill for about 15 minutes.

4 Roll out the dough on a lightly floured surface and stamp out about 18 cookies, using a 5cm/2in cookie cutter. Place on the baking sheet and bake for about 10 minutes, until golden.

5 Leave the cookies for 5 minutes to set. Using a metal spatula, transfer carefully from the baking sheet on to a wire rack to cool completely.

6 The cookies can be stored in an airtight container for up to 1 week.

> **Cook's Tip**
> If you are using fresh lavender, make sure that it has not been sprayed with any chemicals or subjected to traffic pollution.

Rose Water Biscuits Energy 61kcal/257kJ; Protein 0.6g; Carbohydrate 7.8g, of which sugars 4g; Fat 3.3g, of which saturates 2g; Cholesterol 11mg; Calcium 10mg; Fibre 0.2g; Sodium 24mg.
Lavender Heart Cookies Energy 97kcal/406kJ; Protein 1g; Carbohydrate 11.9g, of which sugars 4.5g; Fat 5.4g, of which saturates 3.4g; Cholesterol 14mg; Calcium 17mg; Fibre 0.3g; Sodium 39mg.

Oat and Apricot Clusters

Here is a variation on an old favourite, which children can easily make themselves, so have plenty of the dried fruits and nuts ready for them to add. No baking is involved with these cookies.

Makes 12
50g/2oz/¼ cup butter
50g/2oz/¼ cup clear honey
50g/2oz/½ cup medium rolled oats
50g/2oz/½ cup chopped ready-to-eat dried apricots
15ml/1 tbsp dried banana chips
15ml/1 tbsp shredded coconut or desiccated (dry unsweetened shredded) coconut
50–75g/2–3oz/2–3 cups cornflakes or crisped rice cereal

1 Place the butter and honey in a small pan and warm over a low heat, stirring until the butter melts. Remove the pan from the heat.

2 Add the oats, apricots, banana chips, coconut and cornflakes or crisped rice cereal and stir well with a wooden spoon until combined.

3 Spoon the mixture into 12 paper muffin cases, piling it up roughly. Transfer to a baking sheet and chill in the refrigerator until set and firm.

Variations
• *To make Oat and Cherry Clusters, use rinsed and chopped glacé (candied) cherries in place of the apricots.*
• *To make Chocolate Chip Clusters, substitute 75g/3oz/½ cup chocolate chips.*

Cook's Tip
The ingredients can be changed according to what you have in your store cupboard (pantry) – try peanuts, pecan nuts, raisins or dried dates.

Orange Oaties

These are so delicious that it is difficult to believe that they are healthy too. As they are packed with flavour and are wonderfully crunchy, the whole family will love them.

Makes about 16
175g/6oz/¾ cup clear honey
120ml/4fl oz/½ cup orange juice
90g/3½oz/1 cup rolled oats, lightly toasted
115g/4oz/1 cup plain (all-purpose) flour
115g/4oz/generous ½ cup golden caster (superfine) sugar
finely grated rind of 1 orange
5ml/1 tsp bicarbonate of soda (baking soda)

1 Preheat the oven to 180°C/350°F/Gas 4. Line two baking sheets with baking parchment.

2 Put the honey and orange juice in a small pan and simmer over a low heat for 8–10 minutes, stirring occasionally, until the mixture is thick and syrupy. Remove the pan from the heat and set aside to cool slightly.

3 Put the oats, flour, sugar and orange rind into a bowl. Mix the bicarbonate of soda with 15ml/1 tbsp boiling water and add to the flour mixture, together with the honey and orange syrup. Mix well with a wooden spoon.

4 Place spoonfuls of the mixture on to the prepared baking sheets, spaced slightly apart, and bake for 10–12 minutes, or until golden brown.

5 Leave to firm up slightly on the baking sheets for 5 minutes, then using a metal spatula, carefully transfer the cookies to a wire rack and leave to cool completely.

Variation
For additional flavour and aroma, use orange blossom honey for making the orange syrup in step 2.

Oat and Apricot Clusters Energy 97kcal/407kJ; Protein 1.2g; Carbohydrate 11.7g, of which sugars 5.2g; Fat 5.4g, of which saturates 3.5g; Cholesterol 9mg; Calcium 7mg; Fibre 0.9g; Sodium 70mg.
Orange Oaties Energy 110kcal/466kJ; Protein 1.5g; Carbohydrate 26.2g, of which sugars 16.6g; Fat 0.6g, of which saturates 0g; Cholesterol 0mg; Calcium 18mg; Fibre 0.6g; Sodium 4mg.

Rosemary-scented Citrus Tuiles

These delicious crisp cookies are flavoured with tangy orange and lemon rind, and made beautifully fragrant with fresh rosemary – an unusual but winning combination.

Makes 18–20

50g/2oz/¼ cup unsalted
   butter, diced
2 egg whites
115g/4oz/generous ½ cup caster
   (superfine) sugar
finely grated rind of ½ lemon
finely grated rind of ½ orange
10ml/2 tsp finely chopped
   fresh rosemary
50g/2oz/½ cup plain
   (all-purpose) flour

1 Preheat the oven to 190°C/375°F/Gas 5. Lightly grease two baking sheets.

2 Melt the butter in a pan over a low heat. Remove the pan from the heat and leave to cool.

3 Whisk the egg whites until stiff, then gradually whisk in the sugar.

4 Fold the lemon and orange rinds, rosemary, flour and then the melted butter into the egg white mixture.

5 Place two large tablespoonfuls of mixture on a baking sheet. Spread each to a thin disc about 9cm/3½in in diameter. Bake for 5–6 minutes until golden.

6 Remove from the oven and carefully lift the tuiles using a metal spatula and drape over a rolling pin. Transfer to a wire rack when set in a curved shape. Bake the rest of the mixture in the same way.

> **Cook's Tip**
> *Don't be tempted to bake more than two tuiles at a time or they will set firm before you have time to shape them.*

Honey Crunch Creams

Different types of honey lend a different character to the flavour of these cookies. Try using orange blossom or lavender honey.

finely grated rind of
   1 large orange
115g/4oz/½ cup clear honey
25g/1oz/¼ cup pine nuts or
   chopped walnuts

Makes 20

250g/9oz/2¼ cups self-raising
   (self-rising) flour
10ml/2 tsp bicarbonate of soda
   (baking soda)
50g/2oz/¼ cup caster
   (superfine) sugar
115g/4oz/½ cup unsalted
   butter, diced

For the filling

50g/2oz/¼ cup unsalted
   butter, at room temperature,
   diced
115g/4oz/1 cup icing
   (confectioners') sugar, sifted
15ml/1 tbsp clear honey

1 Preheat the oven to 200°C/400°F/Gas 6. Lightly grease three or four baking sheets.

2 Sift the flour, bicarbonate of soda and caster sugar into a bowl. Add the butter and rub in until the mixture resembles breadcrumbs. Stir in the orange rind.

3 Put the honey in a small pan and heat until just runny but not hot. Pour over the dry mixture and mix to a firm dough.

4 Shape half of the dough into 20 small balls. Place on the baking sheets, spaced well apart, and gently flatten. Bake for 6–8 minutes, until golden. Leave for a few minutes. Use a metal spatula to transfer the cookies to a wire rack to cool.

5 Shape the remaining dough into 20 balls and dip one side of each into the pine nuts or walnuts. Place the cookies, nut sides up, on the baking sheets, and bake as before.

6 To make the filling, put the butter, icing sugar and honey in a bowl and beat together. Use the mixture to sandwich the cookies together in pairs using a plain cookie for the base and a nut-coated one for the top.

Rosemary-scented Citrus Tuiles Energy 51kcal/214kJ; Protein 0.6g; Carbohydrate 8g, of which sugars 6.1g; Fat 2.1g, of which saturates 1.3g; Cholesterol 5mg; Calcium 7mg; Fibre 0.1g; Sodium 22mg.
Honey Crunch Creams Energy 164kcal/688kJ; Protein 1.5g; Carbohydrate 23.4g, of which sugars 13.9g; Fat 7.8g, of which saturates 4.4g; Cholesterol 18mg; Calcium 24mg; Fibre 0.4g; Sodium 52mg.

Tea Finger Cookies

The unusual ingredient in these cookies is Lady Grey tea – similar to Earl Grey but with the addition of Seville orange and lemon peel – which imparts a subtle flavour.

Makes about 36
150g/5oz/²⁄₃ cup unsalted butter, at room temperature, diced

115g/4oz/generous ¹⁄₂ cup light muscovado (brown) sugar
15–30ml/1–2 tbsp Lady Grey tea leaves
1 egg, beaten
200g/7oz/1¾ cups plain (all-purpose) flour, plus extra for dusting
demerara (raw) sugar, for sprinkling

1 Preheat the oven to 190°C/375°F/Gas 5. Lightly grease two or three baking sheets.

2 Beat the butter and sugar until light and creamy. Stir in the tea leaves until combined. Beat in the egg, then fold in the flour.

3 Using your hands, roll the dough on a lightly floured surface into a long cylinder, about 23cm/9in long. Gently press down on the cylinder to flatten slightly. Wrap the dough in clear film (plastic wrap) and chill for about 1 hour until the dough is firm enough to slice.

4 Cut the dough cylinder into 5mm/¹⁄₄in slices and place slightly apart on the prepared baking sheets.

5 Sprinkle the cookies with a little demerara sugar, then bake for 10–15 minutes, until lightly browned. Transfer the cookies to a wire rack with a metal spatula and leave to cool.

> **Variation**
> *You could use other exotic types of tea for making these cookies. Try Earl Grey, flavoured with bergamot, or aromatic flower or fruit teas, such as jasmine, rose congou or pouchong, chrysanthemum, passion fruit or strawberry.*

Apricot and Coconut Kisses

These tangy, fruity treats make a colourful addition to the tea table. Although they are easy to make and can be mixed and shaped in a matter of a few minutes, allow plenty of time for the apricots to soak and also for the cookies to chill before serving.

Makes 12
130g/4¹⁄₂oz/generous ¹⁄₂ cup dried apricots

100ml/3¹⁄₂fl oz/scant ¹⁄₂ cup orange juice
40g/1¹⁄₂oz/3 tbsp unsalted butter, at room temperature, diced
75g/3oz/³⁄₄ cup icing (confectioners') sugar, plus extra for dusting
90g/3¹⁄₂oz/generous 1 cup desiccated (dry unsweetened shredded) coconut, lightly toasted
2 glacé (candied) cherries, cut into wedges

1 Finely chop the dried apricots, then tip them into a bowl. Pour in the orange juice and leave to soak for about 1 hour, until all the juice has been absorbed.

2 In a large bowl, beat together the butter and sugar with a wooden spoon until pale and creamy. Gradually add the soaked apricots to the creamed butter and sugar mixture, beating well after each addition. Stir in the toasted coconut.

3 Lightly grease a small baking tray. Place teaspoonfuls of the coconut mixture on to the baking sheet, piling them up into little pyramids. Gently press the mixture together with your fingers to form neat shapes.

4 Top each cookie with a wedge of cherry. Chill in the refrigerator for about 1 hour until firm, then serve lightly dusted with icing sugar.

> **Cook's Tip**
> *It is essential that all the orange juice has been absorbed by the apricots before adding them to the butter mixture, otherwise the cookies will be too moist to set properly.*

Tea Finger Cookies Energy 65kcal/270kJ; Protein 0.7g; Carbohydrate 7.7g, of which sugars 3.4g; Fat 3.7g, of which saturates 2.2g; Cholesterol 14mg; Calcium 11mg; Fibre 0.2g; Sodium 28mg.
Apricot and Coconut Kisses Energy 115kcal/480kJ; Protein 1g; Carbohydrate 11.7g, of which sugars 11.7g; Fat 7.5g, of which saturates 5.7g; Cholesterol 7mg; Calcium 14mg; Fibre 1.7g; Sodium 25mg.

Coconut Pyramids

Deliciously moist and melt-in-the-mouth, these golden-topped cookies are great favourites with children. A special but strictly adult treat would be to serve them with a glass of rum.

Makes 15

225g/8oz/2²⁄₃ cups desiccated (dry unsweetened shredded) coconut
115g/4oz/½ cup caster (superfine) sugar
2 egg whites

1 Preheat the oven to 190°C/375°F/Gas 5. Lightly grease a large baking sheet.

2 Put the desiccated coconut and caster sugar into a bowl and mix well. Set aside.

3 In a grease-free bowl lightly whisk the egg whites. Fold enough egg white into the coconut and sugar to make a fairly firm mixture. You may not need all the egg whites.

4 Form the mixture into pyramids by taking a teaspoonful and rolling it first into a ball. Flatten the base and press the top into a point. Arrange the pyramids on the prepared baking sheet, spaced well apart.

5 Bake for 12–15 minutes on a low shelf. The tips should begin to turn golden and the pyramids should be just firm, but still soft inside.

6 Slide a metal spatula under the pyramids to loosen them and leave to cool before transferring to a wire rack.

> **Cook's Tips**
> • The heat in conventional ovens tends to be uneven, so, if necessary, turn the sheets around during baking for the pyramids to brown evenly. However, this is not necessary in a fan-assisted oven.
> • Keep an eye on the use-by date as desiccated coconut, like all nuts and nut products, can quickly become rancid.

Almond Macaroons

Freshly ground almonds that have been lightly toasted to intensify the flavour give these cookies their rich taste and texture. So, for best results, avoid using ready-ground almonds as a shortcut.

Makes 12

120g/4oz/1 cup blanched almonds, toasted
160g/5½oz/generous ¾ cup caster (superfine) sugar
2 egg whites
2.5ml/½ tsp almond or vanilla extract
icing (confectioners') sugar, for dusting

1 Preheat the oven to 180°C/350°F/Gas 5. Lightly grease a large baking sheet.

2 Reserve 12 almonds for decorating. In a food processor fitted with a metal blade, process the rest of the almonds and the sugar until finely ground.

3 With the machine running, slowly pour in enough of the egg whites to form a soft dough. Add the almond or vanilla extract and pulse to mix.

4 With moistened hands, shape the mixture into walnut-size balls and arrange on the baking sheet. Press a reserved almond on to each, flattening slightly, and dust lightly with icing sugar.

5 Bake the macaroons for about 10–12 minutes, until the tops are lightly golden and feel slightly firm. Transfer the baking sheet to a wire rack, leave to cool slightly, then transfer the cookies to a wire rack using a metal spatula and leave to cool completely.

Coconut Macaroons

These macaroons should be soft and chewy on the inside with a crisp texture on the outside.

Makes 24

40g/1½oz/⅓ cup plain (all-purpose) flour
pinch of salt

215g/7¼oz/2½ cups desiccated (dry unsweetened shredded) coconut
150ml/¼ pint/⅔ cup sweetened condensed milk
5ml/1 tsp vanilla extract

1 Preheat the oven to 180°C/350°F/Gas 4. Line two baking sheets with baking parchment and lightly grease the paper.

2 Sift the flour and salt into a large bowl. Add the desiccated coconut and stir to combine.

3 Pour in the sweetened condensed milk. Add the vanilla extract and stir together from the centre. Continue stirring until a very thick batter is formed.

4 Drop heaped tablespoonfuls of batter 2.5cm/1in apart on the prepared baking sheets. Bake for about 20 minutes, until golden brown. Transfer the macaroons to a wire rack using a metal spatula and leave to cool completely.

Coconut Pyramids Energy 122kcal/509kJ; Protein 1.3g; Carbohydrate 9g, of which sugars 9g; Fat 9.3g, of which saturates 8g; Cholesterol 0mg; Calcium 8mg; Fibre 2.1g; Sodium 13mg.
Almond Macaroons Energy 102kcal/426kJ; Protein 2.8g; Carbohydrate 7.8g, of which sugars 7.5g; Fat 6.9g, of which saturates 0.6g; Cholesterol 13mg; Calcium 33mg; Fibre 0.9g; Sodium 5mg.
Coconut Macaroons Energy 86kcal/358kJ; Protein 1.3g; Carbohydrate 5.8g, of which sugars 4.6g; Fat 6.6g, of which saturates 5.5g; Cholesterol 3mg; Calcium 25mg; Fibre 1.3g; Sodium 37mg.

Creamed Coconut Macaroons

Finely grated creamed coconut gives these soft-centred cookies a rich creaminess. Use coconut cream if creamed coconut is not available. For a tangy flavour, or to ring the changes, add the grated rind of one lime to the mixture in step 2. The cooked macaroons can be stored in an airtight container for up to 1 week.

Makes 16–18
50g/2oz creamed coconut, chilled, or 120ml/8 tbsp coconut cream
2 large (US extra large) egg whites
90g/3½oz/½ cup caster (superfine) sugar
75g/3oz/1 cup desiccated (dry unsweetened shredded) coconut

1 Preheat the oven to 180°C/350°F/Gas 4. Line a large baking sheet with baking parchment.

2 Finely grate the creamed coconut, if using.

3 Use an electric beater to whisk the egg whites in a large, grease-free bowl until stiff.

4 Whisk in the sugar, a little at a time, to make a stiff and glossy meringue. Fold in the grated creamed coconut, or coconut cream, and desiccated coconut, using a metal spoon.

5 Place dessertspoonfuls of the mixture, spaced slightly apart, on the baking sheet. Bake for 15–20 minutes, until slightly risen and golden brown. Leave to cool on the parchment, then transfer to an airtight container.

Variation
For very rich, sweet and tempting petits fours, make the macaroons smaller, and when cooked coat them in melted plain (semisweet) chocolate. Place on greaseproof (waxed) paper and leave until the chocolate is hard. Serve with small cups of strong, black coffee after a dinner party.

Coconut and Lime Macaroons

These pretty pistachio nut-topped cookies are crunchy on the outside and soft and gooey in the centre. The zesty lime topping contrasts wonderfully with the sweetness of the coconut.

Makes 12–14
4 large (US extra large) egg whites
250g/9oz/3 cups desiccated (dry unsweetened shredded) coconut
150g/5oz/¾ cup sugar
10ml/2 tsp vanilla extract
25g/1oz/¼ cup plain (all-purpose) flour
115g/4oz/1 cup icing (confectioners') sugar, sifted
grated rind of 1 lime
15–20ml/3–4 tsp lime juice
about 15g/½oz/1 tbsp pistachio nuts, chopped

1 Preheat the oven to 180°C/350°F/Gas 4. Line two baking sheets with baking parchment.

2 Put the egg whites, desiccated coconut, sugar, vanilla extract and flour in a large, heavy pan. Mix well. Place over a low heat and cook for 6–8 minutes, stirring constantly to ensure it does not stick. When the mixture becomes the consistency of thick porridge (oatmeal), remove from the heat.

3 Place spoonfuls of the mixture in rocky piles on the lined baking sheets. Bake for 12–13 minutes, until golden. Leave to cool completely on the baking sheets.

4 To make the topping, put the icing sugar and lime rind into a bowl and add enough lime juice to give a thick pouring consistency. Place a spoonful of icing on each macaroon and allow it to drip down the sides. Sprinkle over the pistachio nuts and serve.

Variation
If you prefer, make Coconut and Lemon Macaroons by substituting grated lemon rind and juice.

Creamed Coconut Macaroons Energy 65kcal/270kJ; Protein 0.7g; Carbohydrate 5.7g, of which sugars 5.7g; Fat 4.5g, of which saturates 3.9g; Cholesterol 0mg; Calcium 4mg; Fibre 0.6g; Sodium 9mg.
Coconut and Lime Macaroons Energy 198kcal/830kJ; Protein 2.3g; Carbohydrate 22.4g, of which sugars 21g; Fat 11.7g, of which saturates 9.6g; Cholesterol 0mg; Calcium 18mg; Fibre 2.6g; Sodium 29mg.

Coffee and Hazelnut Macaroons

Macaroons are traditionally made with ground almonds. This recipe uses hazelnuts, which are lightly roasted before grinding, but you can use walnuts instead.

Makes 20

edible rice paper
115g/4oz/1 cup skinned
  hazelnuts
225g/8oz/generous 1 cup
  caster (superfine) sugar
15ml/1 tbsp ground rice
10ml/2 tsp ground coffee
2 egg whites
caster (superfine) sugar,
  for sprinkling

1 Preheat the oven to 180°C/350°F/Gas 4. Line two baking sheets with rice paper.

2 Place the skinned hazelnuts on another baking sheet and cook in the oven for 5 minutes. Cool, then place in a food processor fitted with a metal blade and grind the nuts until fine.

3 Mix the ground nuts with the sugar, ground rice and coffee. Stir in the egg whites to make a fairly stiff paste.

4 Spoon into a piping (pastry) bag fitted with a 1cm/½in plain nozzle. Pipe rounds on the rice paper, leaving room for the cookies to spread.

5 Sprinkle each macaroon with a little caster sugar, then bake for 20 minutes, or until pale golden.

6 Using a metal spatula, transfer the macaroons to a wire rack and leave to cool completely. Remove the excess rice paper when completely cold.

> **Cook's Tip**
> Rice paper, traditionally used as a base for macaroons, is an edible, smooth, flavourless, glossy paper made from the pith of a tropical tree.

Cherry Coconut Munchies

You'll find it hard to stop at just one of these munchies, which make a wonderful morning or afternoon treat. If you like, drizzle 25–50g/1–2oz melted chocolate over the cold munchies and leave to set before serving.

Makes 20

2 egg whites
115g/4oz/1 cup icing
  (confectioners') sugar, sifted
115g/4oz/1 cup ground almonds
115g/4oz/generous 1 cup
  desiccated (dry unsweetened
  shredded) coconut
few drops of almond extract
75g/3oz/⅓ cup glacé (candied)
  cherries, finely chopped

1 Preheat the oven to 150°C/300°F/Gas 2. Line two baking sheets with baking parchment.

2 Place the egg whites in a grease-free bowl and whisk until stiff peaks form.

3 Gently fold in the icing sugar using a metal spoon and a figure-of-eight stirring motion. Fold in the ground almonds, coconut and almond extract to form a sticky dough. Finally, fold in the chopped glacé cherries.

4 Place mounds on the baking sheets. Bake for 25 minutes. Allow to cool and set briefly on the baking sheets, then transfer to a wire rack.

> **Cook's Tips**
> • These cookies are at their best when just baked, but may be stored in an airtight container for up to 3 days.
> • When whisking egg whites, avoid using a plastic bowl, as plastic scratches easily.

> **Variation**
> Use ground hazelnuts in place of the almonds and omit the almond extract.

Coffee and Hazelnut Macaroons Energy 64kcal/267kJ; Protein 1.2g; Carbohydrate 7g, of which sugars 6.2g; Fat 3.7g, of which saturates 0.3g; Cholesterol 0mg; Calcium 11mg; Fibre 0.4g; Sodium 7mg.
Cherry Coconut Munchies Energy 103kcal/431kJ; Protein 1.9g; Carbohydrate 9.3g, of which sugars 9.1g; Fat 6.8g, of which saturates 3.3g; Cholesterol 0mg; Calcium 20mg; Fibre 1.2g; Sodium 10mg.

Golden Ginger Macaroons

With their warm, spicy, ginger flavour, these slightly chewy little cookies are good served with ice cream and will go beautifully with mid-morning or after-dinner coffee.

Makes 18–20

1 egg white
75g/3oz/scant ¹/₂ cup soft
   light brown sugar
115g/4oz/1 cup ground almonds
5ml/1 tsp ground ginger

1 Preheat the oven to 180°C/350°F/Gas 4.

2 In a large, grease-free bowl, whisk the egg white until stiff and standing in peaks, but not crumbly, then whisk in the brown sugar.

3 Sprinkle the ground almonds and ginger over the whisked egg white and gently fold them together.

4 Using two teaspoons, place spoonfuls of the mixture on baking trays, leaving plenty of space between each.

5 Bake for about 20 minutes, until pale golden brown and just turning crisp.

6 Leave to cool slightly on the baking trays before using a metal spatula to transfer the cookies to a wire rack. Leave to cool completely.

Cook's Tip
Use non-stick baking trays or line trays with baking parchment to make sure the cookies don't stick.

Variation
You can substitute other ground nuts, such as hazelnuts or walnuts, for the almonds. Ground cinnamon or mixed (apple pie) spice could be added to the mixture instead of ginger for another variation.

Ginger Snaps

When these cookies are baked their tops craze and crack into an attractive pattern that is characteristic of this traditional family favourite cookie.

Makes about 24

115g/4oz/¹/₂ cup butter, diced
115g/4oz/generous ¹/₂ cup caster
   (superfine) sugar
115g/4oz/¹/₂ cup golden
   (light corn) syrup
225g/8oz/2 cups plain
   (all-purpose) flour
10ml/2 tsp ground ginger
5ml/1 tsp bicarbonate of soda
   (baking soda)

1 Preheat the oven to 180°C/350°F/Gas 4. Line two or three baking sheets with baking parchment.

2 Put the butter, sugar and syrup into a pan and heat gently, stirring occasionally, until the butter has melted and the sugar has dissolved. Remove the pan from the heat and leave to cool slightly.

3 Sift the flour, ginger and bicarbonate of soda and stir into the mixture in the pan to make a soft dough.

4 Shape the dough into about 24 balls and arrange them on the prepared baking sheets, well spaced out. Flatten each ball slightly with a metal spatula.

5 Put one tray into the hot oven and cook for about 12 minutes until golden brown (they burn easily). Leave to cool on the baking sheet for 1–2 minutes, then using a metal spatula, carefully transfer to a wire rack to crisp up and cool completely.

6 Cook the remaining cookies in the same way.

Cook's Tip
Measuring syrup is easier if you dip a metal spoon in very hot water first, then quickly dry it.

Golden Ginger Macaroons Energy 5kcal/21kJ; Protein 0.1g; Carbohydrate 0.4g, of which sugars 0.4g; Fat 0.3g, of which saturates 0g; Cholesterol 1mg; Calcium 2mg; Fibre 0g; Sodium 0mg.
Ginger Snaps Energy 101kcal/424kJ; Protein 1g; Carbohydrate 16.1g, of which sugars 9g; Fat 4.1g, of which saturates 2.5g; Cholesterol 10mg; Calcium 17mg; Fibre 0.3g; Sodium 43mg.

Double Ginger Cookies

These are a supreme treat for ginger lovers – richly spiced cookies packed with chunks of succulent preserved stem ginger. They are sure to give a boost when your energy flags.

Makes 20 large cookies

350g/12oz/3 cups self-raising (self-rising) flour
pinch of salt
200g/7oz/1 cup golden caster (superfine) sugar
15ml/1 tbsp ground ginger
5ml/1 tsp bicarbonate of soda (baking soda)
115g/4oz/½ cup unsalted (sweet) butter, diced
90g/3½oz/generous ¼ cup golden (light corn) syrup
1 large (US extra large) egg, beaten
150g/5oz preserved stem ginger in syrup, drained and coarsely chopped

1 Preheat the oven to 160°C/325°F/Gas 3. Lightly grease three baking sheets.

2 Sift the flour into a large bowl, add the salt, caster sugar, ground ginger and bicarbonate of soda and stir to combine.

3 Put the butter in a small pan with the syrup. Heat gently, stirring, until the butter has melted. Remove from the heat and set aside to cool until just warm.

4 Pour the butter mixture over the dry ingredients, then add the egg and two-thirds of the chopped ginger. Mix thoroughly, then use your hands to bring the dough together.

5 Shape the dough into 20 balls. Place them, spaced well apart, on the baking sheets and gently flatten them with your fingers or a metal spatula.

6 Press a few pieces of the remaining preserved stem ginger into the top of each of the cookies.

7 Bake for about 12–15 minutes, until golden. Leave to cool for 1 minute on the baking sheets to firm up. Using a metal spatula, transfer the cookies to a wire rack to cool completely.

Treacly Ginger Cookies

Packed with flavour and an extra hint of spice, these fabulous cookies will be a sure-fire hit with children and adults alike.

Makes 36

225g/8oz/generous 1 cup caster (superfine) sugar
90g/3½oz/generous 1 cup soft light brown sugar
115g/4oz/½ cup butter, at room temperature
115g/4oz/½ cup margarine, at room temperature
1 egg
90ml/6 tbsp black treacle (molasses)
250g/9oz/2¼ cups plain (all-purpose) flour
10ml/2 tsp ground ginger
2.5ml/½ tsp freshly grated nutmeg
5ml/1 tsp ground cinnamon
10ml/2 tsp bicarbonate of soda (baking soda)
pinch of salt

1 Preheat the oven to 170°C/325°F/Gas 3. Lightly grease two or three baking sheets.

2 In a large bowl, beat together half the caster sugar, the brown sugar, butter and margarine until light and fluffy. Add the egg and continue beating to blend well. Add the treacle and stir until fully incorporated.

3 Sift the flour, ginger, nutmeg, cinnamon, bicarbonate of soda and salt into the mixture and gently stir in. Cover with cling film (plastic wrap) and chill in the refrigerator for about 30 minutes.

4 Place the remaining sugar in a shallow dish. Roll tablespoonfuls of the cookie mixture into balls, then roll the balls in the sugar to coat.

5 Place the balls on the prepared baking sheets, spaced about 5cm/2in apart to allow for spreading during baking, and flatten slightly with your fingers or a metal spatula. Bake for 12–15 minutes, until golden brown around the edges but still soft in the middle. Leave to stand on the baking sheets for 5 minutes, then using a metal spatula, transfer to a wire rack to cool completely.

Double Ginger Cookies Energy 114kcal/479kJ; Protein 1.4g; Carbohydrate 20.4g, of which sugars 11.5g; Fat 3.5g, of which saturates 2.1g; Cholesterol 15mg; Calcium 23mg; Fibre 0.4g; Sodium 42mg.
Treacly Ginger Cookies Energy 57kcal/239kJ; Protein 0.6g; Carbohydrate 10.3g, of which sugars 6.8g; Fat 1.7g, of which saturates 1g; Cholesterol 7mg; Calcium 16mg; Fibre 0.1g; Sodium 15mg.

Ginger Bites

Delightfully crisp, these tasty cookies make a delicious accompaniment to rich desserts and ice cream. They are equally good with a cup of strong tea or coffee, and perfect for feeding large groups of people.

Makes about 50
150g/5¹/₂oz/1/₂ cup plus
   3 tbsp butter
400g/14oz/2 cups sugar
50ml/2fl oz/¹/₄ cup golden (light
   corn) syrup
15ml/1 tbsp black treacle
   (molasses)
15ml/1 tbsp ground ginger
30ml/2 tbsp ground cinnamon
15ml/1 tbsp ground cloves
5ml/1 tsp ground cardamom
5ml/1 tsp bicarbonate of soda
   (baking soda)
250ml/8fl oz/1 cup water
150g/5oz/1¹/₄ cups plain
   (all-purpose) flour, plus extra
   for dusting

1 Put the butter, sugar, syrup, treacle, ginger, cinnamon, cloves and cardamom in a heavy pan and heat gently, stirring frequently, until the butter has melted and the sugar has dissolved. Remove the pan from the heat.

2 Mix together the bicarbonate of soda and measured water in a large heatproof bowl. Pour in the warm spice mixture and stir well with a wooden spoon until thoroughly blended, then add the flour and stir in well. Cover the bowl with clear film (plastic wrap) and put it into the refrigerator overnight to rest.

3 Preheat the oven to 220°C/425°F/Gas 7. Line several baking sheets with baking parchment.

4 Briefly knead the dough, then roll out on a lightly floured surface as thinly as possible. Stamp out flower shapes with a cookie cutter or cut the dough into shapes of your choice. Place them on the baking sheets spaced well apart.

5 Bake the cookies in the oven for about 5 minutes until golden brown, cooking in batches until all the cookies are cooked. Leave to cool on the baking sheet. Store in an airtight container for 1–2 days.

Gingerbread Men

These perennially popular little figures are easy to make and a guaranteed success. They're surprisingly healthy too, as they're sweetened only with fruit.

Makes 8
115g/4oz/1 cup plain
   (all-purpose) flour, sifted, plus
   extra for dusting
7.5ml/1¹/₂ tsp ground ginger
   grated rind of 1 orange and
   1 lemon
75ml/5 tbsp unsweetened pear
   and apple spread or jam
25g/1oz/2 tbsp butter
16 currants and 8 raisins, to
   decorate (optional)

1 Preheat the oven to 180°C/350°F/Gas 4.

2 Mix the sifted flour, ginger and grated orange and lemon rind in a bowl.

3 Melt the pear and apple jam and the butter in a small pan over a low heat. Stir it into the dry ingredients. Mix to a firm dough, wrap in clear film (plastic wrap) and chill for 2–3 hours.

4 Roll out the dough on a lightly floured surface to a thickness of 5mm/¹/₄in. Cut out gingerbread men, using a cutter.

5 Give the gingerbread men currant eyes and raisin noses. Using the point of a knife, draw a mouth on each. Place the cookies on a lightly floured baking sheet and bake for 8–10 minutes. Using a metal spatula, transfer to a wire rack and leave to cool completely.

> **Cook's Tip**
> If you have time, you could add extra decoration to the cookies. For example, make a row of currant buttons down the front of each gingerbread man's body before baking, or pipe a colourful waistcoat (vest) with glacé icing afterwards. You could also add small sweets (candies) stuck on to the baked cookies with a dab of icing.

Ginger Bites Energy 31kcal/130kJ; Protein 0.2g; Carbohydrate 5.8g, of which sugars 4.2g; Fat 0.8g, of which saturates 0.5g; Cholesterol 2mg; Calcium 5mg; Fibre 0.1g; Sodium 13mg.
Gingerbread Men Energy 143kcal/600kJ; Protein 1.5g; Carbohydrate 17.7g, of which sugars 6.7g; Fat 7.9g, of which saturates 4.9g; Cholesterol 20mg; Calcium 23mg; Fibre 0.5g; Sodium 60mg.

Ginger Glass Cookies

As thin, delicate and elegant as fine glass, these ginger cookies are ideal served with creamy desserts, syllabubs, sorbets and luxury ice creams.

Makes about 18
50g/2oz/¹/₄ cup unsalted butter, diced
40g/1¹/₂oz/3 tbsp liquid glucose (clear corn syrup)
90g/3¹/₂oz/¹/₂ cup caster (superfine) sugar
40g/1¹/₂oz/¹/₃ cup plain (all-purpose) flour
5ml/1 tsp ground ginger

1 Put the butter and liquid glucose in a heatproof bowl set over a pan of gently simmering water. Stir together until melted. Set aside.

2 Put the sugar in a bowl and sift over the flour and ginger. Stir into the butter mixture, then beat well until combined. Cover with clear film (plastic wrap) and chill for about 25 minutes, until firm.

3 Preheat the oven to 180°C/350°F/Gas 4 and lightly grease two or three baking sheets.

4 Roll teaspoonfuls of the cookie mixture into balls between your hands and place them, spaced well apart to allow room for spreading, on the prepared baking sheets.

5 Place a second piece of baking parchment on top and roll the cookies as thinly as possible. Peel off the top sheet, then stamp each cookie with a 7.5 or 9cm/3 or 3½in cookie cutter.

6 Bake for 5–6 minutes, or until golden. Leave for a few seconds on the baking sheets to firm up slightly, then either leave flat or curl over in half. Leave to cool completely.

> **Cook's Tip**
> Use unlipped baking sheets so you can roll the cookies thinly.

Iced Ginger Cookies

If your children enjoy cooking with you, mixing and rolling the dough, or cutting out different shapes, this is the ideal recipe to let them practise on.

Makes about 16
115g/4oz/¹/₂ cup soft brown sugar
115g/4oz/¹/₂ cup butter
pinch of salt

few drops vanilla extract
175g/6oz/1¹/₃ cups wholemeal (whole-wheat) flour, plus extra for dusting
15g/¹/₂oz/1 tbsp unsweetened cocoa powder, sifted
10ml/2 tsp ground ginger
a little milk
glacé icing and glacé (candied) cherries, to decorate

1 Preheat the oven to 190°C/375°F/Gas 5. Lightly grease two baking sheets.

2 In a large bowl, beat together the sugar, butter, salt and vanilla extract until soft and fluffy. Work in the flour, cocoa powder and ginger, adding a little milk, if necessary, to bind the mixture. Knead lightly on a floured surface until smooth.

3 Roll out the dough on a lightly floured surface to about 5mm/¹/₄in thick. Stamp out shapes using cookie cutters and place on the prepared baking sheets.

4 Bake the cookies for 10–15 minutes, leave to cool on the baking sheets until firm, then transfer to a wire rack to cool completely. Decorate with glacé icing and glacé cherries.

Chocolate Gingerbread

Chocolate and ginger form a classic partnership in these fabulous cookies.

Makes 12
175g/6oz/1¹/₂ cup plain (all-purpose) flour, plus extra for dusting
10ml/2 tsp mixed (apple pie) spice

pinch of salt
2.5ml/¹/₂ tsp bicarbonate of soda (baking soda)
25g/1oz/¹/₄ cup unsweetened cocoa powder
75g/3oz/6 tbsp unsalted butter, diced
75g/3oz/1/3 cup light muscovado (brown) sugar
1 egg

1 Sift together the flour, spice, salt, bicarbonate of soda and cocoa powder. Blend in a food processor, with the butter, until the mixture resembles fine breadcrumbs.

2 Add the sugar and egg and mix to a firm dough. Knead lightly. Wrap in clear film (plastic wrap) and chill for 30 minutes.

3 Preheat the oven to 180°C/350°F/Gas 4. Lightly grease two large baking sheets.

4 Roll out the dough to 10mm/¹/₂in thickness. Stamp out shapes and transfer to the prepared baking sheets.

5 Bake for 12 minutes until the cookies are just beginning to colour around the edges. Transfer to a wire rack to cool.

Ginger Glass Cookies Energy 55kcal/231kJ; Protein 0.3g; Carbohydrate 8.9g, of which sugars 6.2g; Fat 2.3g, of which saturates 1.5g; Cholesterol 6mg; Calcium 6mg; Fibre 0.1g; Sodium 21mg.
Iced Ginger Cookies Energy 119kcal/497kJ; Protein 1.6g; Carbohydrate 14.7g, of which sugars 7.8g; Fat 6.4g, of which saturates 3.9g; Cholesterol 15mg; Calcium 11mg; Fibre 1.1g; Sodium 53mg.
Chocolate Gingerbread Energy 133kcal/560kJ; Protein 2.3g; Carbohydrate 18.1g, of which sugars 6.8g; Fat 6.5g, of which saturates 3.7g; Cholesterol 29mg; Calcium 29mg; Fibre 0.7g; Sodium 64mg.

Shaker-style Spiced Cookies

These delicious spicy cookies can be packed up in pretty boxes to make elegant gifts for all ages. They are great to give to children or to make with children, as a gift for older relatives.

Makes about 25

50g/2oz/4tbsp butter
100g/4oz/scant ¹/₂ cup soft light brown sugar
45ml/3 tbsp clear honey

30ml/2 tbsp orange juice or milk
225g/8oz/2 cups plain (all-purpose) flour, plus extra for dusting
2.5ml/¹/₂ tsp bicarbonate of soda (baking soda)
5ml/1 tsp ground ginger
1.25ml/¹/₄ tsp ground allspice
1.25ml/¹/₄ tsp ground cinnamon

To decorate

45ml/3 tbsp orange juice or water
100g/4oz/1 cup icing (confectioners') sugar

1 Brush two baking sheets with a little oil.

2 Put the butter, sugar and honey into a pan and heat gently, stirring occasionally, until the butter has melted.

3 Add the orange juice or milk to the pan. Sift the flour, bicarbonate of soda and spices into the pan and mix with a wooden spoon, until you have a smooth dough. Leave the mixture to cool for 15 minutes.

4 Preheat the oven to 160°C/325°F/Gas 3. Turn out the ginger dough on to a floured surface, knead lightly and then roll out. Use cookie cutters to stamp out heart and hand shapes.

5 Transfer to the baking sheets. Cook for 8–10 minutes, until browned. Leave to cool on the baking sheet, then transfer to a wire rack to cool completely.

6 To make the icing, gradually mix the orange juice or water with the icing sugar to make a thick paste. Pipe borders of lines and dots, to decorate.

7 Leave to dry overnight before packing into boxes or tins. Keep for up to 10 days at room temperature.

Golden Gingerbread

Maple syrup is the secret ingredient that gives this spicy gingerbread its extra special flavour and lovely rich colour.

Makes 20

175g/6oz/1¹/₂ cups plain (all-purpose) flour, plus extra for dusting
1.5ml/¹/₄ tsp bicarbonate of soda (baking soda)

pinch of salt
5ml/1 tsp ground ginger
5ml/1 tsp ground cinnamon
65g/2¹/₂oz/5 tbsp unsalted butter, diced
75g/3oz/scant ¹/₂ cup caster (superfine) sugar
30ml/2 tbsp maple or golden (light corn) syrup
1 egg yolk, beaten

1 In a large bowl, sift together the flour, bicarbonate of soda, salt and spices.

2 Rub the butter into the flour until the mixture resembles fine breadcrumbs. Alternatively, blend in a food processor.

3 Add the sugar, syrup and egg yolk and mix or process to a firm dough. Knead lightly. Wrap in clear film (plastic wrap) and chill in the refrigerator for 30 minutes.

4 Preheat the oven to 180°C/350°F/Gas 4. Lightly grease two large baking sheets.

5 Roll out the dough on a lightly floured surface to 10mm/¹/₂in thick. Stamp out shapes using your choice of cookie cutter and transfer to the prepared baking sheets.

6 Bake for 12 minutes, until the cookies are just beginning to colour around the edges. Transfer to a wire rack and leave to cool completely.

> **Cook's Tip**
> If you want to make the darker cocoa gingerbread, replace 15g/¹/₂oz flour with unsweetened cocoa powder.

Shaker-style Spiced Cookies Energy 67kcal/285kJ; Protein 0.9g; Carbohydrate 12.7g, of which sugars 5.8g; Fat 1.8g, of which saturates 1.1g; Cholesterol 4mg; Calcium 16mg; Fibre 0.3g; Sodium 13mg.
Golden Gingerbread Energy 78kcal/327kJ; Protein 1g; Carbohydrate 12.1g, of which sugars 5.3g; Fat 3.1g, of which saturates 1.8g; Cholesterol 17mg; Calcium 17mg; Fibre 0.3g; Sodium 24.8mg.

Ginger-topped Shortbread Fingers

Topping a ginger shortbread base with a sticky ginger mixture may be gilding the lily, but it tastes delicious!

Makes about 40
225g/8oz/2 cups plain
  (all-purpose) flour
5ml/1 tsp ground ginger
75g/3oz/6 tbsp caster
  (superfine) sugar

3 pieces preserved stem ginger,
  finely chopped
175g/6oz/³⁄₄ cup butter

For the topping
15ml/1 tbsp golden (light
  corn) syrup
50g/2oz/¹⁄₄ cup butter
60ml/4 tbsp icing (confectioners')
  sugar, sifted
5ml/1 tsp ground ginger

1 Preheat the oven to 180°C/350°F/Gas 4. Lightly grease a shallow rectangular 28 x 18cm/11 x 7in baking tin (pan).

2 Sift the flour and ground ginger into a bowl and stir in the sugar and preserved stem ginger.

3 Rub in the butter until the mixture begins to bind together. Press the mixture into the prepared tin and smooth over the top with a metal spatula.

4 Bake for 40 minutes, until the ginger shortbread base is very lightly browned.

5 To make the topping, put the syrup and butter in a small pan. Heat gently until both have melted. Stir in the sifted icing sugar and ginger.

6 Remove the shortbread from the oven and pour the topping over the base while both are still hot. Leave to cool slightly, then cut into fingers. Remove to wire racks to cool completely.

> **Cook's Tip**
> Use the syrup from the jar of preserved stem ginger instead of golden syrup in the topping, if you prefer.

Lebkuchen

These luxurious and elegant cookies would make a delightful and special gift.

Makes 40
115g/4oz/¹⁄₂ cup unsalted butter
115g/4oz/¹⁄₂ cup light muscovado
  (brown) sugar
1 egg, eaten
155g/4oz/¹⁄₃ cup black treacle
  (molasses)
400g/14oz/3¹⁄₂ cups self-raising
  (self-rising) flour, plus extra
  for dusting
5ml/1 tsp ground ginger

2.5ml/¹⁄₂ tsp ground cloves
1.5ml/¹⁄₄ tsp chilli powder

For the decoration
115g/4oz plain (semisweet)
  chocolate
115g/4oz milk chocolate
115g/4oz white chocolate
chocolate sprinkles
unsweetened cocoa powder or
  icing (confectioners') sugar,
  for dusting

1 Beat together the butter and sugar until pale and fluffy. Beat in the egg and black treacle. Sift the flour, ginger, cloves and chilli powder into the bowl. Using a wooden spoon, gradually mix the ingredients together to make a stiff paste.

2 Turn out on to a lightly floured work surface and knead lightly until smooth. Wrap and chill for 30 minutes.

3 Preheat the oven to 180°C/350°F/Gas 4. Lightly grease two large baking sheets.

4 Roll out the dough to 8mm/³⁄₄in thickness and stamp out your choice of shapes using cookie cutters. Roll dough balls with the trimmings and flatten them. Place on the prepared baking sheets and bake for 8–10 minutes, until just beginning to colour around the edges. Transfer to a wire rack to cool.

5 For the decoration, melt the chocolate in separate bowls over a pan of gently simmering water. Spoon a little of each into three piping (pastry) bags. Cover a third of the cookies with plain chocolate, a third with milk chocolate, and a third with white chocolate. Pipe decorations on some cookies. Sprinkle icing sugar, cocoa or chocolate sprinkles over the rest.

Ginger-topped Shortbread Fingers Energy 62kcal/257kJ; Protein 0.5g; Carbohydrate 6.7g, of which sugars 3.2g; Fat 3.8g, of which saturates 2.4g; Cholesterol 10mg; Calcium 9mg; Fibre 0.1g; Sodium 29mg.
Lebkuchen Energy 105kcal/444kJ; Protein 2.4g; Carbohydrate 16.3g, of which sugars 11.7g; Fat 3.9g, of which saturates 0.4g; Cholesterol 19mg; Calcium 33mg; Fibre 0.7g; Sodium 16mg.

Sake and Ginger Cookies

Light and crisp, these cookies have a unique taste created by a combination of maple syrup and sake, complemented by a hint of ginger. They are delicious served with green tea.

Makes 20–30
250g/12oz/3 cups plain
  (all-purpose) flour, plus extra
  for dusting
45ml/3 tbsp sesame oil
25g/1oz fresh root ginger, peeled
  and grated

90ml/6 tbsp sake or rice wine
90ml/6 tbsp maple syrup or
  golden (light corn) syrup
2.5ml/½ tsp white pepper
30ml/2 tbsp pine nuts
vegetable oil, for deep-frying
salt

For the syrup
250ml/8fl oz/1 cup water
200g/7oz/1 cup sugar
30ml/2 tbsp clear honey
5ml/1 tsp ground cinnamon
pinch of salt

1 Sift the flour into a large bowl. Add the sesame oil. Mix in the grated ginger, sake, syrup, pepper and a splash of water. Knead into an elastic dough.

2 Roll out on a floured surface to about 1cm/½in thick. Use a cookie cutter to stamp out the dough into rounds.

3 To make the syrup, place the water, sugar and honey in a pan, and add a pinch of salt. Bring to the boil without stirring, then add the cinnamon and stir until the syrup thickens and becomes sticky. Pour into a bowl and set aside.

4 Grind the pine nuts to a fine powder in a mortar and pestle or using a food processor fitted with a metal blade.

5 Pour a generous amount of vegetable oil into a pan, and heat over medium heat until a small piece of day-old bread browns in about 20 seconds. Add the cookies, in batches if necessary, and deep-fry until golden brown.

6 Drain well to remove any excess oil and dip the cookies into the syrup to coat. Arrange on a serving plate and dust with ground pine nuts.

Three-colour Ribbon Cookies

These crisp twists of wafer-thin dough have a hint of gingery spiciness.

Makes 12–15
vegetable oil, for deep-frying
30ml/2 tbsp pine nuts,
  finely ground

For the green cookies
115g/4oz/1 cup plain
  (all-purpose) flour
2.5ml/½ tsp salt
10g/¼oz grated fresh root ginger
30ml/2 tbsp seaweed,
  finely ground

For the yellow cookies
115g/4oz/1 cup plain
  (all-purpose) flour

2.5ml/½ tsp salt
10g/¼oz grated fresh root ginger
50g/2oz sweet pumpkin, finely
  minced (ground)

For the pink cookies
115g/4oz/1 cup plain
  (all-purpose) flour
2.5ml/½ tsp salt
10g/¼oz grated fresh root ginger
50g/2oz apricot flesh, finely
  minced (ground)

For the syrup
250ml/8fl oz/1 cup water
200g/7oz/1 cup sugar
30ml/2 tbsp clear honey
2.5ml/½ tsp ground cinnamon
pinch of salt

1 To make the green cookies, sift the flour and salt into a large bowl and mix in the grated ginger, ground seaweed and a splash of water. Knead gently into a smooth, elastic dough. Place on a lightly floured surface and roll out the dough to about 3mm/⅛in thick. Cut into strips approximately 2 x 5cm/¾ x 2in. Make the yellow and pink cookies in the same way.

2 Score three cuts lengthways into each cookie, and bring one end of the strip back through the centre slit to form a knot.

3 Put the water, sugar and honey in a pan, and add a pinch of salt. Bring to the boil. Add the cinnamon and continue to boil, stirring until the syrup becomes sticky. Pour into a bowl.

4 Pour a generous amount of vegetable oil into a heavy pan, and heat over medium heat. Add the cookies and deep-fry until golden brown. Drain on kitchen paper, then dip into the cinnamon syrup. Dust with the ground pine nuts.

Sake and Ginger Cookies Energy 95kcal/403kJ; Protein 0.9g; Carbohydrate 16g, of which sugars 10.2g; Fat 3.3g, of which saturates 0.4g; Cholesterol 0mg; Calcium 14mg; Fibre 0.25g; Sodium 8.8mg.
Three-colour Ribbon Cookies Energy 178kcal/753kJ; Protein 2.6g; Carbohydrate 16.8g, of which sugars 16.1g; Fat 69.2g, of which saturates 0.5g; Cholesterol 0mg; Calcium 41mg; Fibre 0.8g; Sodium 132mg.

Viennese Whirls

These crisp, melt-in-the-mouth piped cookies are filled with a creamy coffee buttercream.

Makes 20
175g/6oz/12 tbsp butter
50g/2oz/¹⁄₂ cup icing
   (confectioners') sugar
2.5ml/¹⁄₂ tsp vanilla extract
115g/4oz/1 cup plain
   (all-purpose) flour
50g/2oz/¹⁄₂ cup cornflour
   (cornstarch)

icing (confectioners') sugar and
   unsweetened cocoa powder,
   for dusting

For the filling
15ml/1 tbsp ground coffee
60ml/4 tbsp single (light) cream
75g/3oz/6 tbsp butter, softened
115g/4oz/1 cup icing
   (confectioners') sugar, sifted

1 Preheat the oven to 180°C/350°F/Gas 4. Lightly grease a baking sheet.

2 Beat together the butter, icing sugar and vanilla extract until light and fluffy.

3 Sift in the flour and cornflour and beat until smooth. Spoon into a piping (pastry) bag fitted with a 1cm/¹⁄₂in fluted nozzle. Pipe small rosettes well apart on greased baking sheets. Bake for 12–15 minutes, until golden. Transfer to a wire rack to cool.

4 To make the filling, put the coffee in a bowl. Heat the cream to near-boiling and pour it over. Infuse for 4 minutes, then strain through a fine sieve (strainer).

5 Beat the butter, icing sugar and coffee-flavoured cream until light. Use to sandwich the cookies in pairs. Dust with icing sugar and unsweetened cocoa powder.

Variation
For mocha Viennese whirls, substitute 25g/1oz/¹⁄₄ cup unsweetened cocoa powder for 25g/1oz/¹⁄₄ cup of the flour.

Spicy Pepper Cookies

Hot and spicy, these little nuggets are perfect for a cold winter's day.

Makes 48
200g/7oz/ cups plain
   (all-purpose) flour
55g/2oz cornflour (cornstarch)
2.5ml/¹⁄₂ tsp ground cardamom
2.5ml/¹⁄₂ tsp ground cinnamon
2.5ml/¹⁄₂ tsp grated nutmeg
2.5ml/¹⁄₂ tsp ground ginger
2.5ml/¹⁄₂ tsp ground allspice

pinch of salt
2.5ml/¹⁄₂ tsp freshly ground
   black pepper
225g/8oz/1 cup butter, softened
100g/3¹⁄₂oz light brown sugar
2.5ml/¹⁄₂ tsp vanilla extract
5ml/1tsp finely grated lemon rind
65ml/2fl oz whipping cream
85g/3oz finely ground almonds
30ml/2 tbsp icing (confectioners')
   sugar, for dusting

1 Preheat the oven to 180°C/350°F/Gas 4.

2 Sift the flour, cornflour, spices, salt and pepper into a bowl. Set aside.

3 Beat the butter and sugar together until light and fluffy. Beat in the vanilla extract and lemon rind.

4 Add the flour and spice mixture in batches, alternating it with the cream, and beating well after each addition. Begin and end with the flour.

5 Stir in the ground almonds until all the ingredients are thoroughly combined.

6 Shape the dough into 2cm/³⁄₄in balls in the palms of your hands. Place them on ungreased baking trays set about 2.5cm/1in apart to allow room for spreading during baking. Bake in the oven for 15–20 minutes until the cookies are golden brown.

7 Leave the cookies to firm up on the baking sheets for 1–2 minutes then, using a metal spatula, carefully transfer them to a wire rack to cool completely. Sift icing sugar over the surface before serving.

Viennese Whirls Energy 210kcal/877kJ; Protein 2.2g; Carbohydrate 21.3g, of which sugars 11.2g; Fat 13.5g, of which saturates 7.6g; Cholesterol 22mg; Calcium 28mg; Fibre 0.8g; Sodium 64mg.
Spicy Pepper Cookies Energy 75kcal/314kJ; Protein 0.8g; Carbohydrate 6.8g, of which sugars 2.6g; Fat 5.2g, of which saturates 2.8g; Cholesterol 11mg; Calcium 12mg; Fibre 0.2g; Sodium 30mg.

Coffee Ice Cream Sandwiches

The perfect treat for a summer's afternoon or an unusual way to end an *al fresco* dinner party, these cookies are guaranteed to hit the spot.

Makes 8
115g/4oz/½ cup butter, at room
   temperature
50g/2oz/¼ cup caster
   (superfine) sugar
115g/4oz/1 cup plain
   (all-purpose) flour
2 tbsp instant coffee powder
icing (confectioners') sugar,
   for dusting
450ml/16fl oz/2 cups coffee
   ice cream
2 tbsp unsweetened cocoa
   powder, for dusting

1 In a large bowl, cream the butter until soft. Beat in the sugar. Add the flour and coffee and mix by hand to form an evenly blended dough. Wrap in a plastic bag and chill for 1 hour.

2 Lightly sprinkle the work surface with icing sugar. Knead the dough on the sugared surface for a few minutes to soften it. Lightly grease two or three baking trays.

3 Using a rolling pin dusted with icing sugar, roll out the dough to ⅛in/3mm thick. With a 2½in/6cm cookie cutter, stamp out 16 rounds. Transfer the rounds to the baking trays. Chill for at least 30 minutes.

4 Preheat the oven to 300°F/150°C/Gas 2. Bake the cookies for about 30 minutes, until they are lightly golden. Let them firm up for a couple of minutes before removing them to a wire rack to cool completely.

5 Remove the ice cream from the freezer and let soften for 10 minutes at room temperature. With a metal spatula, spread the ice cream evenly on the flat side of eight of the cookies. Top with the remaining cookies, flat side down.

6 Arrange the ice cream sandwiches on a baking tray. Cover and freeze for at least 1 hour, longer if a firmer sandwich is desired. Sift the cocoa powder over the tops before serving.

Cappuccino Swirls

A melt-in-the-mouth, mocha-flavoured cookie drizzled with white and dark chocolate is just the thing to have with that mid-morning caffè latte.

Makes 18
10ml/2 tsp instant coffee powder
10ml/2 tsp boiling water
225g/8oz/1 cup unsalted
   butter, at room temperature,
   diced
50g/2oz/¼ cup golden caster
   (superfine) sugar
150g/5oz/1¼ cups plain
   (all-purpose) flour
115g/4oz/½ cup cornflour
   (cornstarch)
15ml/1 tbsp unsweetened
   cocoa powder

For the decoration
50g/2oz white chocolate
25g/1oz dark (bittersweet)
   chocolate

1 Preheat the oven to 190°C/375°F/Gas 5. Line two baking sheets with baking parchment.

2 Put the coffee powder in a cup, add the boiling water and stir until dissolved. Set aside to cool.

3 In a bowl, beat the butter and sugar until pale and creamy. Stir in the coffee. Sift in the flour, cornflour and cocoa powder. Mix well.

4 Spoon into a piping (pastry) bag fitted with a plain nozzle. Pipe 18 spirals, slightly apart, on to the prepared baking sheets.

5 Bake for 10–15 minutes, until firm but not browned. Leave on the baking sheets for 1 minute, then transfer to a wire rack to cool. Place the cooled cookies on kitchen paper.

6 Melt the white and dark chocolate separately in heatproof bowls set over a pan of hot water.

7 Using a teaspoon, take some white chocolate and moving your hand speedily from left to right create small lines of chocolate drizzle over the cookies. Repeat the process with the dark chocolate, flicking it over the cookies. Leave until the chocolate has set and then remove the cookies from the paper.

Coffee Ice Cream Sandwiches Energy 281kcal/1176kJ; Protein 3.4g; Carbohydrate 31.7g, of which sugars 20.2g; Fat 16.5g, of which saturates 10.4g; Cholesterol 45mg; Calcium 88mg; Fibre 0.5g; Sodium 122mg. **Cappuccino Swirls** Energy 179kcal/746kJ; Protein 1.3g; Carbohydrate 18.1g, of which sugars 5.7g; Fat 11.8g, of which saturates 7.3g; Cholesterol 27mg; Calcium 19mg; Fibre 0.5g; Sodium 88mg.

Dark Chocolate Fingers

With their understated elegance and distinctly grown-up flavour, these deliciously decadent chocolate fingers are ideal for serving with after-dinner coffee and liqueurs.

Makes about 26
115g/4oz/1 cup plain
    (all-purpose) flour
2.5ml/½ tsp baking powder
30ml/2 tbsp unsweetened
    cocoa powder
50g/2oz/¼ cup unsalted
    butter, softened
50g/2oz/¼ cup caster
    (superfine) sugar
20ml/4 tsp golden (light
    corn) syrup
150g/5oz dark (bittersweet)
    chocolate
chocolate-flavour mini flakes,
    for sprinkling

1 Preheat the oven to 160°C/325°F/Gas 3. Line two baking sheets with baking parchment.

2 Put the flour, baking powder, cocoa powder, butter, caster sugar and golden syrup in a large mixing bowl. Work the ingredients together with your fingertips to combine and form into a dough.

3 Roll the dough out between sheets of baking parchment to an 18 × 24cm/7 × 9½in rectangle. Remove the top sheet. Cut in half lengthways, then into bars 2cm/¾in wide. Place on the baking sheets.

4 Bake for about 15 minutes, taking care not to allow the bars to brown or they will taste bitter. Transfer to a wire rack to cool.

5 Melt the chocolate in a heatproof bowl set over a pan of gently simmering water. Half-dip the cookies, place on baking parchment, sprinkle with chocolate flakes, then leave to set.

Variation
If you're making these cookies for children, dip them in melted plain (semisweet) or milk chocolate.

Chunky Chocolate Drops

Do not allow these cookies to cool completely on the baking sheet or they will become crisp and may break when you try to lift them on to a wire rack.

Makes 18
175g/6oz plain (semisweet)
    chocolate, chopped
115g/4oz/½ cup unsalted
    butter, diced
2 eggs
90g/3½oz/½ cup sugar
50g/2oz/¼ cup soft light
    brown sugar
40g/1½oz/⅓ cup plain
    (all-purpose) flour
25g/1oz/¼ cup unsweetened
    cocoa powder
5ml/1 tsp baking powder
10ml/2 tsp vanilla extract
pinch of salt
115g/4oz/1 cup pecan nuts,
    toasted and coarsely chopped
175g/6oz/1 cup plain (semisweet)
    chocolate chips
115g/4oz good-quality white
    chocolate, chopped into
    5mm/¼in pieces
115g/4oz good-quality milk
    chocolate, chopped into
    5mm/¼in pieces

1 Preheat the oven to 160°C/325°F/Gas 3. Lightly grease two large baking sheets.

2 Melt the plain chocolate and butter in a pan over a low heat, stirring constantly. Remove from the heat and set aside to cool.

3 In a large mixing bowl, whisk the eggs and sugars until pale and creamy. Gradually pour in the melted chocolate mixture, beating until blended.

4 Beat in the flour, cocoa powder, baking powder, vanilla extract and salt until just blended. Stir in the nuts, chocolate chips and white and milk chocolate pieces.

5 Drop mounded tablespoonfuls of the mixture on to the baking sheets, 10cm/4in apart. Flatten each to 7.5cm/3in rounds. Bake for 8–10 minutes, until the edges look crisp.

6 Leave to cool for 2 minutes, then transfer to a wire rack to cool completely.

Dark Chocolate Fingers Energy 72kcal/303kJ; Protein 0.9g; Carbohydrate 9.9g, of which sugars 6.3g; Fat 3.5g, of which saturates 2.1g; Cholesterol 4mg; Calcium 11mg; Fibre 0.4g; Sodium 25mg.
Chunky Chocolate Drops Energy 264kcal/1101kJ; Protein 3.4g; Carbohydrate 21.1g, of which sugars 20.7g; Fat 19.1g, of which saturates 9.1g; Cholesterol 37mg; Calcium 48mg; Fibre 0.9g; Sodium 73mg.

Chewy Chocolate Cookies

The texture of these dark and delicious cookies is sublime – soft on the inside with a crisper, crunchier outside – matched only by their subtle mocha flavour.

Makes 18
4 egg whites
300g/11oz/2½ cups icing
   (confectioners') sugar
115g/4oz/1 cup unsweetened
   cocoa powder
30ml/2 tbsp plain
   (all-purpose) flour
5ml/1 tsp instant coffee powder
15ml/1 tbsp water
115g/4oz/1 cup walnuts, finely
   chopped

1 Preheat the oven to 180°C/350°F/Gas 4. Line two or three baking sheets with baking parchment and grease the paper well.

2 Whisk the egg whites in a grease-free bowl until frothy, using an electric whisk. Sift the sugar, cocoa powder, flour and coffee into the egg whites.

3 Add the water and continue beating on low speed to blend, then on high speed for a few minutes until the mixture thickens. Gently fold in the walnuts with a flexible spatula or metal spoon.

4 Place spoonfuls of the mixture 2.5cm/1in apart on the baking sheets. Bake in batches for 12–15 minutes until firm and cracked on top but soft inside. Using a metal spatula, transfer the cookies to a wire rack to cool.

Cook's Tip
• *These cookies are best eaten the day they are cooked, but can be stored for 24 hours in an airtight container.*
• *Always buy fresh nuts in small quantities, as they quickly become rancid, and chop them only when you need to use them to prevent them from tasting stale.*
• *You could substitute pecans for the walnuts, if you like.*

Chocolate Crackle-tops

Older children will enjoy making these distinctive-looking cookies. The dough needs to be chilled for an hour but then is easy to handle and roll.

Makes 38
200g/7oz plain (semisweet)
   chocolate, chopped
90g/3½oz/scant ½ cup unsalted
   (sweet) butter
115g/4oz/generous ½ cup caster
   (superfine) sugar
3 eggs
5ml/1 tsp vanilla extract
215g/7½oz/scant 2 cups plain
   (all-purpose) flour
25g/1oz/¼ cup unsweetened
   cocoa powder
2.5ml/½ tsp baking powder
pinch of salt
175g/6oz/1½ cups icing
   (confectioners') sugar,
   for dusting

1 In a pan set over a low heat, melt the chocolate and butter until smooth, stirring frequently. Remove from the heat.

2 Stir in the sugar and continue stirring for 2–3 minutes, until it dissolves. Add the eggs, one at a time, beating well after each addition. Stir in the vanilla extract.

3 Sift the flour, cocoa powder, baking powder and salt into the chocolate mixture, in batches, until blended. Cover and chill for 1 hour, until the dough is cold and is able to hold its shape.

4 Preheat the oven to 160°C/325°F/Gas 3. Lightly grease two or three large baking sheets.

5 Sift the icing sugar into a bowl. Using a teaspoon, scoop out the cold dough and roll into 4cm/1½in balls. Drop each ball into the icing sugar and roll until heavily coated. Shake to remove any excess icing sugar.

6 Place on the baking sheets about 4cm/1½in apart. Bake for 10–15 minutes, until the tops feel slightly firm when touched.

7 Remove to a wire rack for 2–3 minutes, then transfer the cookies to the wire rack to cool completely.

Chewy Chocolate Cookies Energy 138kcal/580kJ; Protein 3g; Carbohydrate 19.7g, of which sugars 17.6g; Fat 5.8g, of which saturates 1.2g; Cholesterol 0mg; Calcium 26mg; Fibre 1.1g; Sodium 76mg.
Chocolate Crackle-tops Energy 102kcal/428kJ; Protein 1.5g; Carbohydrate 15.8g, of which sugars 11.4g; Fat 4.1g, of which saturates 2.3g; Cholesterol 20mg; Calcium 17mg; Fibre 0.4g; Sodium 27mg.

Mini Chocolate Marylands

These delicious little cookies are perfect for any age group and for any time of day. They're quick and easy to make, too, and because they're small they bake superfast.

Makes 40–45
125g/4¼oz/generous ½ cup unsalted butter, at room temperature, diced

90g/3½oz/ ½ cup caster (superfine) sugar
1 egg
1 egg yolk
5ml/1 tsp vanilla extract
175g/6oz/1½ cups self-raising (self-rising) flour
90g/3½oz/scant ½ cup milk
90g/3½oz/generous ½ cup chocolate chips

1 Preheat the oven to 180°C/350°F/Gas 4. Lightly grease two or three baking sheets.

2 In a large bowl, beat together the butter and sugar until pale and creamy. Add the egg, egg yolk, vanilla extract, flour, milk and half the chocolate chips and stir well with a wooden spoon until thoroughly combined.

3 Using two teaspoons, place small mounds of the mixture on the baking sheets, spacing them slightly apart to allow room for spreading.

4 Press the remaining chocolate chips on to the mounds of cookie dough and press down gently.

5 Bake for 10–15 minutes, until pale golden brown. Leave the cookies on the baking sheets for 2 minutes to firm up slightly, then, using a metal spatula, carefully transfer them to wire racks to cool completely.

Cook's Tip
This recipe makes quite a large quantity. If you like, you can freeze half of the cookies for another time. Simply thaw, then return to the oven for a few minutes to re-crisp before serving.

Chocolate Chip and Walnut Cookies

Rich-tasting and crunchy, these wonderful cookies are just perfect at any time of day.

Makes 24
115g/4oz/½ cup butter, at room temperature
50g/2oz/¼ cup caster (superfine) sugar
90g/3½oz/scant ½ cup soft dark brown sugar

1 egg
2.5ml/½ tsp vanilla extract
175g/6oz/1½ cups plain (all-purpose) flour
2.5ml/½ tsp bicarbonate of soda (baking soda)
pinch of salt
175g/6oz/1 cup chocolate chips
50g/2oz/½ cup walnuts, chopped

1 Preheat the oven to 180°C/350°F/Gas 4. Lightly grease two large baking sheets.

2 In a large bowl, beat the butter and two sugars together until light and fluffy.

3 In a small bowl, mix the egg and vanilla, then gradually beat the liquid into the butter mixture. Sift over the flour, bicarbonate of soda and salt and beat to combine. Add the chocolate chips and walnuts and mix well.

4 Place heaped teaspoonfuls of the dough 5cm/2in apart on the prepared sheets. Bake for 10–15 minutes until lightly coloured. Transfer to a wire rack to cool.

Chocolate Chip Cookies

The lovely light texture of these cookies gives an old favourite a new twist.

Makes 16
75g/3oz/6 tbsp butter
50g/2oz/¼ cup light soft brown sugar
50g/2oz/¼ cup caster (superfine) sugar

1 egg
5ml/1 tsp vanilla extract
75g/3oz/¾ cup cornmeal
75g/3oz/¾ cup rice flour
5ml/1 tsp baking powder
pinch of salt
115g/4oz/⅔ cup plain (semisweet) chocolate chips, or a mixture of milk and white chocolate chips

1 Preheat the oven to 190°C/375°F/Gas 5. Lightly grease two baking sheets.

2 Place the butter and sugars in a bowl and beat together until light and fluffy.

3 Beat in the egg and vanilla extract. Fold in the cornmeal, rice flour, baking powder and salt, then fold in the chocolate chips with a flexible spatula.

4 Place spoonfuls of the mixture on the prepared baking sheets, leaving space for spreading between each one. Bake for 10–15 minutes, until the cookies are lightly browned.

5 Remove the cookies from the oven and leave to cool for a few minutes, then transfer to a wire rack and leave to cool.

Mini Chocolate Marylands Energy 54kcal/227kJ; Protein 0.7g; Carbohydrate 6.4g, of which sugars 3.5g; Fat 3g, of which saturates 1.8g; Cholesterol 10mg; Calcium 19mg; Fibre 0.2g; Sodium 33mg. **Chocolate Chip and Walnut Cookies** Energy 138kcal/578kJ; Protein 1.7g; Carbohydrate 16.5g, of which sugars 10.9g; Fat 7.7g, of which saturates 3.9g; Cholesterol 19mg; Calcium 20mg; Fibre 0.5g; Sodium 33mg. **Chocolate Chip Cookies** Energy 139kcal/581kJ; Protein 1.7g; Carbohydrate 16.7g, of which sugars 11.1g; Fat 7.7g, of which saturates 3.9g; Cholesterol 19mg; Calcium 20mg; Fibre 0.5g; Sodium 33mg.

Giant Triple Chocolate Cookies

Here is the ultimate cookie, packed full of chocolate and macadamia nuts. You will have to be patient when they come out of the oven, as they are too soft to move until completely cold.

Makes 12 large cookies
90g/3½oz milk chocolate
90g/3½oz white chocolate
300g/11oz dark (bittersweet) chocolate (minimum 70 per cent cocoa solids)
90g/3½oz/7 tbsp unsalted butter, at room temperature, diced
5ml/1 tsp vanilla extract
150g/5oz/¾ cup light muscovado (brown) sugar
150g/5oz/1¼ cups self-raising (self-rising) flour
100g/3½oz/scant 1 cup macadamia nut halves

1 Preheat the oven to 180°C/350°F/Gas 4. Line two baking sheets with baking parchment.

2 Coarsely chop the milk and white chocolate and put them in a bowl. Chop 200g/7oz of the dark chocolate into very large chunks, at least 2cm/¾in in size. Put them into another bowl and set aside.

3 Break the remaining dark chocolate into pieces and place them in a heatproof bowl set over a pan of barely simmering water. Heat, stirring frequently, until the chocolate has melted and is smooth. Remove the bowl from the heat and stir in the butter. Add the vanilla extract and muscovado sugar and stir well until fully incorporated.

4 Add the flour and mix gently. Add half the dark chocolate chunks, all the milk and white chocolate and the nuts and fold together.

5 Spoon 12 mounds on to the prepared baking sheets, spacing them well apart. Press the remaining dark chocolate chunks into the top of each cookie. Bake for abut 12 minutes, until just beginning to colour. Remove from the oven and leave the cookies on the baking sheets to cool completely.

Chunky Double Chocolate Cookies

Twice the flavour and twice the fun, these crunchy cookies are packed with chunks of plain and white chocolate for the maximum taste impact.

Makes 18–20
115g/4oz/½ cup unsalted (sweet) butter, softened
115g/4oz/½ cup light muscovado (brown) sugar
1 egg
5ml/1 tsp vanilla extract
150g/5oz/1¼ cups self-raising (self-rising) flour
75g/3oz/¾ cup rolled oats
115g/4oz plain (semisweet) chocolate, coarsely chopped
115g/4oz white chocolate, coarsely chopped

1 Preheat the oven to 190°C/375°F/Gas 5. Lightly grease two baking sheets.

2 Beat the butter with the sugar in a bowl until pale and fluffy. Add the egg and vanilla extract and beat well.

3 Sift the flour over the mixture and fold in lightly with a metal spoon, then add the oats and chopped plain and white chocolate and stir until evenly mixed.

4 Place small spoonfuls of the mixture in 18–20 rocky heaps on the baking sheets, leaving space for spreading.

5 Bake for 12–15 minutes, or until the cookies are beginning to turn pale golden. Cool for 2–3 minutes on the baking sheets, then, using a metal spatula, lift on to wire racks to cool completely. The cookies will be soft when freshly baked but will harden on cooling.

> **Variation**
> Instead of the rolled oats, use 75g/3oz/¾ cup ground almonds. Omit the chopped chocolate and use 175g/6oz/1 cup chocolate chips instead. Top each heap of cookie mixture with half a glacé (candied) cherry before baking.

Giant Triple Chocolate Cookies Energy 416kcal/1738kJ; Protein 4.3g; Carbohydrate 47.6g, of which sugars 37.8g; Fat 24.4g, of which saturates 11.8g; Cholesterol 21mg; Calcium 71mg; Fibre 1.6g; Sodium 84mg. **Chunky Double Chocolate Cookies** Energy 169kcal/710kJ; Protein 2.3g; Carbohydrate 21.6g, of which sugars 13.1g; Fat 8.8g, of which saturates 5.1g; Cholesterol 22mg; Calcium 36mg; Fibre 0.6g; Sodium 47mg.

Chocolate Chip Nut Cookies

You can bake a batch of these nutty delights in no time at all – and they'll be eaten just as fast.

Makes 36
115g/4oz/1 cup plain (all-purpose) flour
5ml/1 tsp baking powder
5ml/1 tsp salt
75g/3oz/6 tbsp butter
115g/4oz/generous ½ cup caster (superfine) sugar
50g/2oz/¼ cup soft light brown sugar
1 egg
5ml/1 tsp vanilla extract
115g/4oz/⅔ cup plain (semisweet) chocolate chips
50g/2oz/½ cup hazelnuts, chopped

1 Preheat the oven to 180°C/350°F/Gas 4. Lightly grease two or three baking sheets.

2 Sift the flour, baking powder and salt into a small bowl. Set the bowl aside.

3 In a large bowl, beat the butter and sugars together until light and fluffy. Beat in the egg and vanilla extract. Sift the dry ingredients into the mixture and beat well.

4 Stir in the chocolate chips and half of the hazelnuts. Drop teaspoonfuls of the mixture on to the prepared baking sheets, to form 2cm/¾in mounds. Space the cookies about 5cm/2in apart to allow room for spreading.

5 Flatten each cookie lightly with a wet fork. Sprinkle the remaining hazelnuts on top of the cookies and press lightly into the surface.

6 Bake for 10–12 minutes, until golden brown. Transfer the cookies to a wire rack and leave to cool.

Variation
If you like, you could substitute almonds or macadamia nuts for the hazelnuts – both go well with chocolate.

Chocolate Delights

These crispy cookies are simply packed with flavour and are irresistible for a mid-morning coffee break.

Makes 50
25g/1oz plain (semisweet) chocolate
25g/1oz dark (bittersweet) cooking chocolate
225g/8oz/1 cup unsalted butter, at room temperature
225g/8oz/generous 1 cup caster (superfine) sugar
2 eggs
5ml/1 tsp vanilla extract
225g/8oz/2 cups plain (all-purpose) flour
pinch of salt
115g/4oz/1 cup finely chopped walnuts

1 Melt the chocolates in a heatproof bowl set over a pan of gently simmering water. Set aside.

2 In a large bowl, beat the butter and sugar together until the mixture is light and fluffy.

3 Mix the eggs with the vanilla, then gradually stir into the butter mixture. Stir in the melted chocolate. Sift the flour and salt into the mixture and stir to combine. Stir in the nuts.

4 Divide the mixture into four and roll each into 5cm/2in diameter logs. Wrap tightly in foil and chill until firm.

5 Preheat the oven to 190°C/375°F/Gas 5. Lightly grease two baking sheets. Cut the logs into 5mm/¼in slices. Place the rounds on the baking sheets and bake for about 10 minutes until lightly coloured. Transfer to a rack to cool.

Variation
For two-tone cookies, melt half the chocolate. Combine all the ingredients as above except the chocolate. Divide the mixture in half. Add the chocolate to one half. Roll out the plain mixture on to a flat sheet. Roll out the chocolate mixture, place on top of the plain one and roll up. Slice and bake as above.

Chocolate Chip Nut Cookies Energy 64kcal/271kJ; Protein 0.8g; Carbohydrate 9.9g, of which sugars 5g; Fat 2.7g, of which saturates 1.2g; Cholesterol 4mg; Calcium 14mg; Fibre 0.3g; Sodium 68mg.
Chocolate Delights Energy 90kcal/377kJ; Protein 1.1g; Carbohydrate 8.9g, of which sugars 5.5g; Fat 5.8g, of which saturates 2.7g; Cholesterol 17mg; Calcium 13mg; Fibre 0.2g; Sodium 31mg.

Chocolate Chip Oat Cookies

The lovely texture of these cookies is matched by the delicious chocolate and vanilla flavour – a perfect thank you gift.

Makes 60
115g/4oz/1 cup plain (all-purpose) flour
2.5ml/½ tsp bicarbonate of soda (baking soda)
1.5ml/¼ tsp baking powder
pinch of salt
115g/4oz/½ cup butter
115g/4oz/generous ½ cup caster (superfine) sugar
90g/3½oz/scant ½ cup light brown sugar
1 egg
2.5ml/½ tsp vanilla extract
75g/3oz/¾ cup rolled oats
175g/6oz/1 cup chocolate chips

1 Preheat the oven to 180°C/350°F/Gas 4. Grease three or four baking sheets.

2 Sift the flour, bicarbonate of soda, baking powder and salt into a mixing bowl.

3 Beat together the butter and the two sugars. Add the egg and vanilla extract and beat until light and fluffy. Beat in the flour mixture until blended.

4 Stir in the oats and chocolate chips. The dough should be crumbly. Drop teaspoonfuls of the dough on to the baking sheets, spacing the cookies well apart so that they can spread during baking.

5 Bake for 15 minutes, until firm around the edge but soft to the touch in the centre. Transfer the cookies to a wire rack and leave to cool completely.

> **Variations**
> • Use either milk chocolate or plain (semisweet) chocolate chips, as both go well with the nutty texture.
> • If you like, decorate the cookies by drizzling them with zig-zag lines of melted chocolate once they have cooled.

Chocolate Amaretti

As an alternative decoration lightly press a few coffee sugar crystals on top of each cookie before baking.

Makes 24
140g/5oz/1¼ cup blanched whole almonds
100g/3½oz/½ cup caster (superfine) sugar
15ml/1 tbsp unsweetened cocoa powder
30ml/2 tbsp icing (confectioners') sugar
2 egg whites
pinch of cream of tartar
5ml/1 tsp almond extract
flaked (sliced) almonds, to decorate

1 Preheat the oven to 180°C/350°F/Gas 4. Line a large non-stick baking sheet with baking parchment. Place the almonds on the baking sheet and bake until golden, 12 minutes. Leave to cool. Reduce the oven temperature to 160°C/325°F/Gas 3.

2 In a processor or blender fitted with a metal blade, process the almonds with half of the sugar until finely ground. Transfer to a medium bowl and sift the cocoa and icing sugar on top. Stir to blend. Set aside.

3 In a medium mixing bowl, using an electric mixer, beat the egg whites and cream of tartar until stiff peaks form. Sprinkle in the remaining sugar, a tablespoon at a time, beating well after each addition, and continue beating until the mixture is glossy and stiff. Beat in the almond extract.

4 Sprinkle the almond-sugar mixture over the beaten egg whites and fold in gently until just blended. Spoon the mixture into a large piping (pastry) bag fitted with a plain 1cm/½ in nozzle. Pipe 4cm/1½ in rounds about 2.5cm/1 in apart on the prepared baking sheets. Press a flaked almond into the centre of each.

5 Bake the cookies for 12–15 minutes, or until they appear crisp. Remove to a wire rack to cool completely. When cool, store in an airtight container.

Chocolate Chip Oat Cookies Energy 207kcal/864kJ; Protein 3.2g; Carbohydrate 22.1g, of which sugars 12g; Fat 12.4g, of which saturates 5g; Cholesterol 32mg; Calcium 30mg; Fibre 1.1g; Sodium 46mg.
Chocolate Amaretti Energy 65kcal/270kJ; Protein 1.8g; Carbohydrate 5.8g, of which sugars 5.5g; Fat 4g, of which saturates 0.4g; Cholesterol 0mg; Calcium 20mg; Fibre 0.6g; Sodium 12mg.

Chocolate Caramel Nuggets

Inside each of these buttery cookies lies a soft-centred chocolate-coated caramel. They're at their most delicious served an hour or so after baking, so you might want to shape them in advance, then put the baking sheet of uncooked nuggets in the refrigerator until you are ready to bake them.

Makes 14

150g/5oz/1¹⁄₄ cups self-raising (self-rising) flour, plus extra for dusting
90g/3¹⁄₂oz/7 tbsp unsalted (sweet) butter, chilled and diced
50g/2oz/¹⁄₄ cup golden caster (superfine) sugar
1 egg yolk
5ml/1 tsp vanilla extract
14 soft-centred chocolate caramels
icing (confectioners') sugar and unsweetened cocoa powder, for dusting

1 Put the flour and butter in a food processor and process until the mixture resembles fairly fine breadcrumbs.

2 Add the sugar, egg yolk and vanilla extract to the food processor and process to a smooth dough. Wrap the dough in clear film (plastic wrap) and chill for 30 minutes.

3 Preheat the oven to 200°C/400°F/Gas 6. Lightly grease two large baking sheets.

4 Roll out the dough thinly on a lightly floured surface and cut out 28 rounds using a 5cm/2in cutter.

5 Place one chocolate caramel on a cookie round, then place a second round on top. Pinch the edges of the dough together so that the chocolate caramel is completely enclosed, then place on the prepared baking sheet. Make the remaining cookies in the same way. Bake for about 10 minutes, until pale golden.

6 Using a metal spatula transfer the cookies to a wire rack and leave to cool. Serve lightly dusted with sifted icing sugar and unsweetened cocoa powder.

Chunky Pecan Chocolate Drops

Toasted pecan nuts, chocolate chips and a mixture of white and milk chocolate chunks make these larger cookies extra special.

Makes 18

175g/6oz plain (semisweet) chocolate, chopped
115g/4oz/¹⁄₂ cup unsalted butter, chopped
2 eggs
90g/3¹⁄₂oz/¹⁄₂ cup caster (superfine) sugar
50g/2oz/¹⁄₄ cup light brown sugar
40g/1¹⁄₂oz/¹⁄₃ cup plain (all-purpose) flour
25g/1oz/¹⁄₄ cup unsweetened cocoa powder
5ml/1 tsp baking powder
10ml/2 tsp vanilla extract
pinch of salt
115g/4oz/1 cup pecan nuts, toasted and coarsely chopped
175g/6oz/1 cup chocolate chips
115g/4oz fine quality white chocolate, chopped into 5mm/¹⁄₄in pieces
115g/4 oz fine quality milk chocolate, chopped into 5mm/¹⁄₄in pieces

1 Preheat the oven to 160°C/325°F/Gas 3. Lightly grease two baking sheets.

2 In a heatproof bowl set over a pan of gently simmering water, melt together the plain chocolate and butter. Remove from the heat and set aside to cool.

3 In a large bowl and using an electric mixer, beat the eggs and sugars for about 2 minutes, until creamy.

4 Pour in the melted chocolate mixture, beating until well blended. Sift in the flour, cocoa powder, baking powder, vanilla extract and salt in batches into the egg mixture and beat well after each addition. Stir in the nuts and remaining chocolate.

5 Drop tablespoonfuls of mixture on to the baking sheets. Bake for 8–10 minutes, until crisp.

6 Remove the baking sheets to a wire rack to cool for 2 minutes, then transfer the cookies to the wire rack.

Chunky Pecan Chocolate Drops Energy 259kcal/1080kJ; Protein 3.3g; Carbohydrate 24g, of which sugars 21.9g; Fat 17.3g, of which saturates 8g; Cholesterol 37mg; Calcium 52mg; Fibre 0.8g; Sodium 73mg. **Chocolate Caramel Nuggets** Energy 149kcal/625kJ; Protein 1.8g; Carbohydrate 18.7g, of which sugars 9.5g; Fat 8g, of which saturates 4.6g; Cholesterol 30mg; Calcium 34mg; Fibre 0.3g; Sodium 58mg.

Chocolate Cinnamon Tuiles

These crisp French cookies are classically plain – this special version is flavoured with cocoa and cinnamon.

Makes 12
1 egg white
50g/2oz/¼ cup caster
　(superfine) sugar
30ml/2 tbsp plain
　(all-purpose) flour
40g/1½oz/3 tbsp butter, melted
15ml/1 tbsp unsweetened
　cocoa powder
2.5ml/½ tsp ground cinnamon

1 Preheat the oven to 200°C/400°F/Gas 6. Lightly grease two baking sheets.

2 Whisk the egg white in a grease-free bowl until it forms soft peaks. Gradually whisk in the sugar.

3 Sift the flour over the mixture and fold in evenly. Stir in the melted butter. Transfer about 45ml/3 tbsp of the mixture to a small bowl and set aside.

4 Sift together the cocoa and ground cinnamon over the flour and butter mixture, in batches, stirring well after each addition.

5 Leaving room for spreading, drop spoonfuls of the chocolate-flavoured mixture on to the prepared baking sheets, then spread each gently with a metal spatula to make a neat round.

6 Using a small spoon, carefully drizzle the reserved unflavoured mixture over the rounds to create a softly marbled effect.

7 Bake for 4–6 minutes, until just set. Using a metal spatula, lift each cookie carefully and quickly drape it over a rolling pin to give a curved shape as it hardens.

8 Leave the tuiles to cool until set, then remove them gently and place on a wire rack to cool completely. Serve on the same day.

Fruity Chocolate Cookie Cakes

The combination of spongy cookie, fruity preserve and dark chocolate makes irresistible eating. As cookies go, these are a little fiddly to make.

Makes 18
90g/3½oz/½ cup caster
　(superfine) sugar
2 eggs
50g/2oz/½ cup plain
　(all-purpose) flour
75g/3oz/6 tbsp orange
　marmalade or apricot jam
125g/4¼oz plain (semisweet)
　chocolate

1 Preheat the oven to 190°C/375°F/Gas 5. Lightly grease 18 patty tins (muffin pans), preferably non-stick.

2 Stand a mixing bowl in very hot water for a couple of minutes to heat through, keeping the inside of the bowl dry. Put the sugar and eggs in the bowl and whisk with a hand-held electric mixer until light and frothy and the beaters leave a ribbon trail when lifted. Sift the flour over the mixture and stir in gently using a large metal spoon.

3 Divide the sponge mixture among the patty tins. Bake for 10 minutes, until just firm and pale golden around the edges. Using a metal spatula, carefully lift from the sponges from the tins and transfer to a wire rack to cool.

4 Press the marmalade or jam through a sieve (strainer) to remove any rind or fruit pieces. Spoon a little of the smooth jam on to the centre of each sponge.

5 Break the chocolate into pieces and place in a heatproof bowl set over a pan of gently simmering water. Heat, stirring frequently, until melted and smooth.

6 Spoon a little chocolate on to the top of each cookie and spread to the edges, covering the jam completely. Once the chocolate has just started to set, very gently press it with the back of a fork to give a textured surface. Leave to set for at least 1 hour.

Chocolate Cinnamon Tuiles Energy 55kcal/229kJ; Protein 0.8g; Carbohydrate 6.5g, of which sugars 4.4g; Fat 3g, of which saturates 1.9g; Cholesterol 7mg; Calcium 8mg; Fibre 0.2g; Sodium 38mg.
Fruity Chocolate Cookie Cakes Energy 84kcal/353kJ; Protein 1.3g; Carbohydrate 14.7g, of which sugars 12.5g; Fat 2.6g, of which saturates 1.3g; Cholesterol 22mg; Calcium 12mg; Fibre 0.3g; Sodium 11mg.

Chocolate Pretzels

These scrumptious snacks look so charming twisted into little knots. Sweet pretzels are a speciality of Germany and Austria.

Makes 28
115g/4oz/1 cup plain
  (all-purpose) flour
pinch of salt

45ml/3 tbsp unsweetened
  cocoa powder
115g/4oz/½ cup butter
150g/5oz/¾ cup caster
  (superfine) sugar
1 egg
1 egg white, lightly beaten,
  for glazing
sugar crystals, for sprinkling

1 Sift together the flour, salt and cocoa powder. Set aside. Lightly grease two baking sheets.

2 In a large bowl, beat the butter until pale and soft. Add the sugar and continue beating until light and fluffy. Beat in the egg.

3 Add the dry ingredients and stir to blend. Gather the dough into a ball, wrap in greaseproof (waxed) paper and chill for 1 hour or freeze for 30 minutes.

4 Preheat the oven to 190°C/375°F/Gas 5.

5 Roll the dough into 28 small balls. Roll each ball into a rope about 25cm/10in long. With each rope, form a loop with the two ends facing you. Twist the ends and fold back on to the circle, pressing in, to make a pretzel shape.

6 Place on the prepared baking sheets. Brush with the egg white and sprinkle sugar crystals over the tops to decorate.

7 Bake for 10–12 minutes, until firm. Transfer to a wire rack to cool.

Cook's Tip
To make mocha-flavoured pretzels, replace 10ml/2 tsp of the unsweetened cocoa powder with instant coffee powder.

Chocolate-filled Cookies

Concealed chunks of plain chocolate are baked inside these delectable cookies to make a wonderful, melt-in-the-mouth surprise when you bite into them.

Makes about 16
150g/5oz/⅔ cup butter, softened
150g/5oz/¾ cup caster
  (superfine) sugar
1 egg yolk
15ml/1 tbsp ground almonds

225g/8oz/2 cups self-raising
  (self-rising) flour, plus extra
  for dusting
25g/1oz/¼ cup unsweetened
  cocoa powder
150g/5oz plain (semisweet)
  chocolate
icing (confectioners') sugar,
  for dusting

1 Preheat the oven to 190°C/375°F/Gas 5. Lightly grease two baking sheets.

2 Beat together the butter and sugar until pale and fluffy. Beat in the egg yolk and ground almonds.

3 Sift the flour and unsweetened cocoa powder over the mixture and gently fold in with a flexible spatula to make a firm dough. Knead lightly for a few seconds, then wrap in clear film (plastic wrap) and chill in the refrigerator for about 30 minutes.

4 Cut off slightly more than one-third of the dough. Cover the remaining dough with clear film until required. Roll out the smaller piece of dough on a lightly floured surface to a thickness of about 3mm/⅛in. Stamp out 16 rounds using a 4cm/1½in cookie cutter. Break the chocolate into 16 squares and put one square into the centre of each dough round.

5 Roll out the remaining dough and cut into 16 larger rounds using a 5cm/2in cutter. Place these over the chocolate-covered cookie rounds and press the edges together. Bake for 10 minutes, until firm.

6 Dust the cookies with icing sugar and, using a metal spatula carefully transfer to a wire rack. Serve warm while the filling is still soft and melted.

Variations
• For a fruity flavour and a different texture, substitute 30ml/2 tbsp dried sour cherries or dried cranberries for the ground almonds.
• For a moister mix, use desiccated (dry unsweetened shredded) coconut instead of the ground almonds.
• For an unusual and more sophisticated filling, use dark (bittersweet) chocolate and add candied chillies. Put 25g/1oz/2 tbsp caster (superfine) sugar into a small pan and add 30ml/2 tbsp water. Heat gently, stirring until the sugar has dissolved, then add 2 seeded and very finely chopped red chillies. Bring to the boil and boil for 2 minutes, without stirring. Remove from the heat, strain the chillies and leave to cool. Discard the syrup. Divide the chillies among the cookie rounds with the squares of chocolate.

Triple Chocolate Sandwiches

Chocolate shortbread is a great base for sandwiching or coating in lashings of melted chocolate.

Makes 15
125g/4¼oz/generous ½ cup unsalted butter, chilled and diced
150g/5oz/1¼ cups plain (all-purpose) flour
30ml/2 tbsp unsweetened cocoa powder
50g/2oz/¼ cup caster (superfine) sugar

For the filling
75g/3oz white chocolate
25g/1oz/2 tbsp unsalted butter
115g/4oz milk chocolate

1 Put the butter, flour and cocoa in a food processor. Process until the mixture resembles breadcrumbs. Add the sugar and process again until the mixture forms a dough.

2 Transfer the dough to a clean surface and knead lightly. Wrap in clear film (plastic wrap) and chill for 30 minutes.

3 Preheat the oven to 200°C/400°F/Gas 6. Lightly grease a large baking sheet.

4 Roll out the chilled dough on a floured surface to a 33 × 16cm/13 × 6¼in rectangle. Place on the baking sheet. Cut the dough in half lengthways, then cut across at 2cm/¾in intervals to make 30 small bars. Prick each bar with a fork.

5 Bake for 12–15 minutes, until just beginning to darken. Leave for 2 minutes, then transfer to a wire rack to cool.

6 To make the filling, break the white chocolate into a heatproof bowl. Add half the butter and set the bowl over a pan of gently simmering water. Stir frequently until melted.

7 Spread a little of the filling on to half of the bars. Place another bar on top and push together to sandwich the cookies.

8 Melt the milk chocolate with the remaining butter. Using a teaspoon, drizzle over the cookies, then leave to set.

Chocolate Thumbprint Cookies

Chunky, chocolatey and gooey all at the same time, these gorgeous cookies are filled with a spoonful of chocolate spread after baking to really add to their indulgent quality.

Makes 16
115g/4oz/½ cup unsalted butter, at room temperature, diced
115g/4oz/½ cup light muscovado (brown) sugar
1 egg
75g/3oz/⅔ cup plain (all-purpose) flour
25g/1oz/¼ cup unsweetened cocoa powder
2.5ml/½ tsp bicarbonate of soda (baking soda)
115g/4oz/generous 1 cup rolled oats
75–90ml/5–6 tbsp chocolate spread

1 Preheat the oven to 180°C/350°F/Gas 4. Lightly grease two large baking sheets.

2 In a bowl, beat together the butter and sugar until creamy.

3 Add the egg and beat well. Sift over the flour, cocoa powder and bicarbonate of soda and stir to combine. Add the rolled oats to the bowl and mix well.

4 Using your hands, roll spoonfuls of the mixture into balls. Place the balls on the baking sheet, spacing them well apart to allow room for spreading. Flatten slightly.

5 Dip a thumb in flour and press into the centre of each cookie to make an indent. Bake the cookies for 10 minutes. Leave for 2 minutes, then transfer to a wire rack to cool.

6 Spoon a little chocolate spread into the centre of each indented cookie.

Cook's Tip
Use chocolate and hazelnut spread instead of the plain one.

Chocolate Thumbprint Cookies Energy 163kcal/682kJ; Protein 2.3g; Carbohydrate 19.3g, of which sugars 10.3g; Fat 9g, of which saturates 4.1g; Cholesterol 27mg; Calcium 19mg; Fibre 0.8g; Sodium 66mg. **Triple Chocolate Sandwiches** Energy 189kcal/790kJ; Protein 2.4g; Carbohydrate 18.8g, of which sugars 11g; Fat 12.1g, of which saturates 7.5g; Cholesterol 22mg; Calcium 50mg; Fibre 0.6g; Sodium 88mg.

Chocolate and Prune Cookies

When freshly baked, these cookies have a deliciously gooey centre. As they cool down the mixture hardens slightly to form a firmer, fudge-like consistency.

Makes 18

150g/5oz/²⁄₃ cup butter, at room temperature, diced
150g/5oz/³⁄₄ cup caster (superfine) sugar
1 egg yolk

250g/9oz/2¹⁄₄ cups self-raising (self-rising) flour
25g/1oz/¹⁄₄ cup unsweetened cocoa powder
about 90g/3¹⁄₂oz plain (semisweet) chocolate, coarsely chopped

For the topping
50g/2oz plain (semisweet) chocolate
9 ready-to-eat prunes, halved

1 Preheat the oven to 190°C/375°F/Gas 5. Line two baking sheets with baking parchment.

2 Beat the butter and sugar together until light and creamy. Beat in the egg yolk. Sift over the flour and cocoa powder and stir in to make a firm yet soft dough.

3 Roll out a third of the dough on baking parchment. Using a 5cm/2in cookie cutter, stamp out 18 rounds and place them on the baking sheets. Sprinke the chopped chocolate in the centre of each cookie.

4 Roll out the remaining dough in the same way and, using a 7.5cm/3in round cookie cutter, stamp out 18 "lids". Place the lids over the cookie bases and press the edges together to seal.

5 Bake for about 10 minutes, until the cookies have spread a little and are just firm to the touch. Leave them on the baking sheets for a few minutes to firm up, then, using a metal spatula, transfer to a wire rack to cool completely.

6 For the topping, melt the chocolate in a heatproof bowl set over a pan of gently simmering water. Dip the cut side of the prunes in the chocolate, then place one on top of each cookie. Spoon any remaining chocolate over the prunes.

Chocolate Marzipan Cookies

These crisp little cookies are deliciously sweet and have a delightful almond surprise inside. Piped with zig-zag lines of white chocolate, they make a perfect party treat.

Makes 36

200g/7oz/scant 1 cup unsalted butter at room temperature, diced

200g/7oz/scant 1 cup light muscovado (brown) sugar
1 egg
300g/11oz/2³⁄₄ cups plain (all-purpose) flour, plus extra for dusting
60ml/4 tbsp unsweetened cocoa powder
200g/7oz white almond paste
115g/4oz white chocolate, chopped

1 Preheat the oven to 190°C/375°F/Gas 5. Lightly grease two large baking sheets.

2 In a bowl, beat the butter with the sugar until pale and fluffy. Add the egg and beat well.

3 Sift the flour and cocoa powder over the mixture. Stir in, first with a wooden spoon, then with clean hands, pressing the mixture together to make a fairly soft dough. If the dough seems sticky, wrap it in clear film (plastic wrap) and chill for about 30 minutes.

4 Roll out half the dough on a lightly floured surface to a thickness of about 5mm/¹⁄₄in. Using a 5cm/2in cutter, stamp out rounds until you have about 36 rounds.

5 Cut the almond paste into 36 equal pieces. Roll into balls, flatten slightly and place one on each dough round. Roll out the remaining dough, stamp out more rounds, then place on top of the almond paste. Press the dough edges to seal. Bake the cookies for 10–12 minutes, until well risen.

6 Transfer the cookies to a wire rack, using a spatula, and leave to cool completely. Melt the white chocolate, spoon into a paper piping (pastry) bag and pipe zig-zag lines on to the cookies. Leave to set before serving.

Chocolate and Prune Cookies Energy 197kcal/825kJ; Protein 2.3g; Carbohydrate 26.4g, of which sugars 15.5g; Fat 9.8g, of which saturates 5.9g; Cholesterol 29mg; Calcium 33mg; Fibre 1.1g; Sodium 66mg. **Chocolate Marzipan Cookies** Energy 137kcal/576kJ; Protein 1.9g; Carbohydrate 18.1g, of which sugars 11.6g; Fat 6.9g, of which saturates 3.8g; Cholesterol 17mg; Calcium 31mg; Fibre 0.6g; Sodium 57mg.

Chocolate Treacle Snaps

These elegantly thin, treacle-flavoured snap cookies have a delicate hint of spice and a decorative lick of chocolate on top. They are particularly good with a steaming cup of hot coffee.

Makes about 35

90g/3¹/₂oz/7 tbsp unsalted butter, diced
175ml/6fl oz/³/₄ cup golden (light corn) syrup
50ml/2fl oz/¹/₄ cup black treacle (molasses)
250g/9oz/2¹/₄ cups plain (all-purpose) flour
150g/5oz/³/₄ cup golden caster (superfine) sugar
5ml/1 tsp bicarbonate of soda (baking soda)
1.5ml/¹/₄ tsp mixed (apple pie) spice)
100g/3¹/₂oz milk chocolate
100g/3¹/₂oz white chocolate

1 Preheat the oven to 180°C/350°F/Gas 4. Line two or three baking sheets with baking parchment.

2 Put the butter, syrup and treacle in a small pan. Heat gently, stirring constantly, until the butter has melted. Remove from the heat and set aside until required.

3 Sift the flour into a large mixing bowl. Add the sugar, bicarbonate of soda and mixed spice and mix well using a wooden spoon. Slowly pour in the butter and treacle mixture and stir to combine well.

4 Place large teaspoonfuls of the mixture well apart on the prepared baking sheets. Bake the cookies for 10–12 minutes, until just beginning to brown around the edges. Leave them to cool for a few minutes on the baking sheets. When firm enough to handle, using a metal spatula, transfer the cookies to a wire rack to cool completely.

5 Melt the milk chocolate and white chocolate separately in heatproof bowls set over pans of gently simmering water. Stir frequently. Swirl a little of each into the centre of each cookie and leave to set.

Mocha Viennese Swirls

Sophisticated cookies that look elegant and taste superb, these swirls can be served with morning coffee to impress your guests or just please your friends.

Makes 20

250g/9oz plain (semisweet) chocolate, chopped
200g/7oz/scant 1 cup unsalted butter at room temperature, diced
50g/2oz/¹/₂ cup icing (confectioners') sugar
30ml/2 tbsp strong black coffee
200g/7oz/1³/₄ cups plain (all-purpose) flour
50g/2oz/¹/₂ cup cornflour (cornstarch)
about 20 blanched almonds

1 Preheat the oven to 190°C/375°F/Gas 5. Lightly grease two large baking sheets.

2 Melt 115g/4oz of the chocolate in a heatproof bowl set over a pan of gently simmering water, then remove from the heat and leave to cool slightly.

3 Beat the butter with the icing sugar in a bowl until smooth and pale. Beat in the melted chocolate, then the black coffee.

4 Sift the flour and cornflour over the mixture. Fold in lightly and evenly to make a soft mixture. Spoon the mixture into a piping (pastry) bag fitted with a large star nozzle and pipe 20 swirls on the baking sheets, allowing room for spreading.

5 Press an almond into the centre of each swirl. Bake for about 15 minutes, until the cookies are firm and just beginning to brown. Leave to cool for about 10 minutes on the baking sheets, then, using a metal spatula, transfer to a wire rack to cool completely.

6 Melt the remaining chocolate in a heatproof bowl over a pan of gently simmering water. Dip the base of each swirl into the chocolate to coat. Place on a sheet of baking parchment and leave to set.

Chocolate Treacle Snaps Energy 109kcal/459kJ; Protein 1.2g; Carbohydrate 18.2g, of which sugars 12.8g; Fat 4g, of which saturates 2.4g; Cholesterol 6mg; Calcium 35mg; Fibre 0.2g; Sodium 38mg.
Mocha Viennese Swirls Energy 231kcal/965kJ; Protein 2.4g; Carbohydrate 23.5g, of which sugars 12.4g; Fat 14.8g, of which saturates 8.3g; Cholesterol 24mg; Calcium 31mg; Fibre 0.9g; Sodium 70mg.

Chocolate Truffle Cookies

Deeply decadent, chocolatey truffle cookies are given a wicked twist by the addition of cherry brandy – the perfect way to end dinner.

Makes 18

50g/2oz/½ cup plain
  (all-purpose) flour
25g/1oz/¼ cup unsweetened
  cocoa powder

2.5ml/½ tsp baking powder
90g/3½oz/½ cup caster
  (superfine) sugar
25g/1oz/2 tbsp butter, diced
1 egg, beaten
5ml/1 tsp cherry brandy
50g/2oz/½ cup icing
  (confectioners') sugar

1 Preheat the oven to 200°C/400°F/Gas 6. Line two baking sheets with baking parchment.

2 Sift together the flour, unsweetened cocoa powder and baking powder into a large bowl and stir in the caster sugar. Add the butter and rub in lightly with your fingertips until the mixture resembles breadcrumbs.

3 Mix together the beaten egg and cherry brandy and stir into the flour mixture. Cover with clear film (plastic wrap) and chill for 30 minutes.

4 Put the icing sugar into a bowl. Shape walnut-size pieces of dough roughly into a ball between the palms of your hands and drop into the icing sugar. Toss until thickly coated, then place on the baking sheets.

5 Bake for about 10 minutes, or until just set. Transfer to a wire rack, and leave to cool completely.

Variations
• Other liqueurs with an affinity with chocolate, such as amaretto and Cointreau, could also be used.
• If you're making these cookies for children, use orange juice instead of the cherry brandy.

Carob Chip Shorties

Perfect for anyone on a gluten-free or dairy-free diet, these lovely cookies are best eaten freshly made, preferably while still slightly warm.

75g/3oz/6 tbsp vegetable
  margarine
50g/2oz/⅓ cup carob chips
15–25ml/1–1½ tbsp clear honey,
  warmed
demerara (raw) or caster
  (superfine) sugar, for sprinkling

Makes 12

175g/6oz/1½ cups gluten-free
  flour
25g/1oz/2 tbsp soft light
  brown sugar

1 Preheat the oven to 160°C/325°F/Gas 3. Line one large baking sheet with baking parchment.

2 Put the flour and brown sugar in a mixing bowl and rub in the margarine.

3 Add the carob chips, then stir in just enough honey to bring the mixture together but not make it sticky.

4 Roll out the dough between two sheets of baking parchment to about 8mm/⅜in thick. Stamp out 12 rounds using a plain 5cm/2in round cookie cutter. Place the rounds on the prepared baking sheet, spaced apart to allow room for spreading. Prick each cookie once with a fork and sprinkle lightly with demerara or caster sugar.

5 Bake for about 15–20 minutes, until firm and golden brown. Using a metal spatula, carefully transfer the cookies to a wire rack to cool completely.

Cook's Tips
• Gluten-free flour can be bought at most health-food stores.
• Some margarines contain animal products, such as whey. The health-conscious and vegetarians should check the label.

Chocolate Truffle Cookies Energy 59kcal/249kJ; Protein 0.9g; Carbohydrate 10.5g, of which sugars 8.2g; Fat 1.8g, of which saturates 1g; Cholesterol 14mg; Calcium 12mg; Fibre 0.3g; Sodium 26mg.
Carob Chip Shorties Energy 133kcal/553kJ; Protein 1.2g; Carbohydrate 17.5g, of which sugars 5.8g; Fat 6.4g, of which saturates 2.9g; Cholesterol 1mg; Calcium 6mg; Fibre 0.4g; Sodium 51mg.

Iced Carob Cookies

If you are unable to eat chocolate but still crave it, these heavenly cookies, with their creamy topping, may provide the answer.

Makes 12–16
115g/4oz/½ cup butter
10ml/2 tsp carob powder
115g/4oz/1 cup wholemeal
(whole-wheat) flour
5ml/1 tsp baking powder

75g/3oz/⅓ cup dark muscovado
(molasses) sugar
50g/2oz/generous ½ cup
rolled oats

For the topping
50g/2oz carob bar,
coarsely chopped
45ml/3 tbsp double
(heavy) cream
15ml/1 tbsp chopped ready-to-eat
dried apricots

1 Preheat the oven to 190°C/375°F/Gas 5. Line the base and sides of an 18cm/7in square shallow cake tin (pan) with baking parchment.

2 Put the butter in a large pan and add the carob powder. Stir over a low heat until the butter has melted and the mixture is smooth and thoroughly combined. Remove the pan from the heat, stir in the flour, baking powder, sugar and rolled oats and mix well.

3 Press the mixture into the prepared tin and bake for about 20–25 minutes, until just set. Mark into squares or bars while still hot. Leave to cool in the tin.

4 To make the topping, stir the carob bar and cream in a small pan over a low heat until combined. Remove the pan from the heat and spread the mixture over the cookies. Sprinkle the apricots on top and leave to cool completely and set.

Cook's Tip
Carob is derived from the carob bean, which has a nutritious, flavoursome pulp. Its taste is similar to chocolate and it has a high sugar content, but unlike chocolate, it does not contain any caffeine.

Carob and Cherry Cookies

Simplicity itself to make, these little cookies are given a chocolate-like flavour by the addition of carob powder and are deliciously crisp and crunchy.

Makes about 20
90g/3½oz/7 tbsp unsalted
butter, at room
temperature, diced
75g/3oz/scant ½ cup caster
(superfine) sugar

75g/3oz/⅓ cup light muscovado
(brown) sugar
1 egg
150g/5oz/1¼ cups self-raising
(self-rising) flour
25g/1oz/2 tbsp carob powder
50g/2oz/¼ cup glacé (candied)
cherries, quartered
50g/2oz carob bar, chopped

1 Preheat the oven to 180°C/350°F/Gas 4. Line two large baking sheets with baking parchment.

2 Put the butter, both sugars and the egg in a large mixing bowl and beat well until the mixture is smooth and creamy.

3 Add the flour, carob powder, cherries and chopped carob bar to the mixture and mix well.

4 Shape the mixture into walnut-size balls and place, spaced slightly apart to allow room for spreading, on the prepared baking sheets.

5 Bake for about 15 minutes, until golden brown and just firm. Leave on the baking sheets for 5 minutes to cool slightly, then, using a metal spatula, carefully transfer the cookies to a wire rack to cool completely.

Variations
• If you aren't on a diet, use unsweetened cocoa powder and a bar of chocolate instead of the carob.
• Use raisins, dried cranberries or dried sour cherries instead of cherries, if you like.

Iced Carob Cookies Energy 140kcal/585kJ; Protein 1.7g; Carbohydrate 14.3g, of which sugars 7.4g; Fat 8.9g, of which saturates 5.3g; Cholesterol 19mg; Calcium 12mg; Fibre 1.1g; Sodium 52mg.
Carob and Cherry Cookies Energy 114kcal/481kJ; Protein 1.4g; Carbohydrate 16.9g, of which sugars 11.2g; Fat 5g, of which saturates 3g; Cholesterol 19mg; Calcium 36mg; Fibre 0.5g; Sodium 71mg.

Chocolate Florentines

These big, flat, crunchy cookies are just like traditional Florentines but use tiny seeds instead of nuts. Rolling the edges of the cookies in milk or white chocolate turns them into a real treat.

Makes 12
50g/2oz/ ¼ cup unsalted butter
50g/2oz/¼ cup caster (superfine) sugar
15ml/1 tbsp milk

25g/1oz/scant ¼ cup pumpkin seeds
40g/1½oz/generous ¼ cup sunflower seeds
50g/2oz/scant ½ cup raisins
25g/1oz/2 tbsp multi-coloured glacé (candied) cherries, chopped
30ml/2 tbsp plain (all-purpose) flour
125g/4¼oz milk or white chocolate

1 Preheat the oven to 180°C/350°F/Gas 4. Lightly grease two baking sheets.

2 Put the butter and sugar into a pan and set over a low heat, stirring constantly, until the butter has melted and the sugar has dissolved, then cook until bubbling. Remove the pan from the heat and stir in the milk, pumpkin and sunflower seeds, raisins, glacé cherries and flour. Mix well with a wooden spoon until thoroughly incorporated.

3 Spoon 6 teaspoonfuls of the mixture on to each baking sheet, spacing them well apart.

4 Bake for 8–10 minutes, until the cookies are turning dark golden. Using a metal spatula, push back the edges of the cookies to neaten them. Leave on the baking sheets for about 5 minutes to firm up, then carefully transfer to a wire rack to cool completely.

5 Break up the chocolate and put in a heatproof bowl set over a pan of gently simmering water. Heat, stirring frequently, until melted. Roll the edges of the cookies in the chocolate and leave to set on a clean sheet of baking parchment for about 1 hour.

Mini Florentines with Grand Marnier

Orange liqueur adds a note of glorious luxury to these ever-popular nut and dried fruit cookies. These mini versions would be delicious with dessert or after-dinner coffee and liqueurs.

Makes about 24
50g/2oz/¼ cup soft light brown sugar
15ml/1 tbsp clear honey

15ml/1 tbsp Grand Marnier
50g/2oz/¼ cup butter
40g/1½oz/⅓ cup plain (all-purpose) flour
25g/1oz/¼ cup hazelnuts, coarsely chopped
50g/2oz/½ cup flaked (sliced) almonds, chopped
50g/2oz/¼ cup glacé (candied) cherries, chopped
115g/4oz dark (bittersweet) chocolate, melted, for coating

1 Preheat the oven to 180°C/350°F/Gas 4. Line two or three baking sheets with baking parchment.

2 Combine the sugar, honey, Grand Marnier and butter in a small pan and melt over a low heat.

3 Remove the pan from the heat and tip in the flour, hazelnuts, almonds and cherries. Stir well.

4 Spoon small heaps of the mixture on to the baking sheets. Bake for about 10 minutes, until golden brown. Leave the cookies on the baking sheets until the edges begin to harden a little, then remove and cool on a wire rack.

5 Spread the melted chocolate over the underside of each Florentine with a round-bladed knife. When the chocolate is just beginning to set, drag a fork through to make wavy lines. Leave to set completely.

> **Variation**
> For an extra decoration, pour melted milk, plain (semisweet) or white chocolate into a paper piping (pastry) bag, snip off the end and pipe zig-zag lines over the plain side of each Florentine.

Chocolate Florentines Energy 157kcal/656kJ; Protein 2.2g; Carbohydrate 17.5g, of which sugars 14.8g; Fat 9.1g, of which saturates 4.3g; Cholesterol 11mg; Calcium 40mg; Fibre 0.6g; Sodium 38mg.
Mini Florentines with Grand Marnier Energy 82kcal/342kJ; Protein 1g; Carbohydrate 8.6g, of which sugars 7.2g; Fat 4.9g, of which saturates 2g; Cholesterol 5mg; Calcium 13mg; Fibre 0.4g; Sodium 14mg.

Florentine Bites

Very sweet and rich, these little mouthfuls are great with after-dinner coffee and liqueurs, and would also make an ideal and special gift to offer to a dinner party host.

Makes 36
200g/7oz good-quality dark (bittersweet) chocolate (minimum 70 per cent cocoa solids)

50g/2oz/2 1/2 cups cornflakes
50g/2oz/scant 1/2 cup sultanas (golden raisins)
115g/4oz/1 cup toasted flaked (sliced) almonds
115g/4oz/1/2 cup glacé (candied) cherries, halved
50g/2oz/1/3 cup cut mixed (candied) peel
200ml/7fl oz/scant 1 cup sweetened condensed milk

1 Line the base of a shallow 20cm/8in cake tin (pan) with baking parchment. Lightly grease the sides.

2 Break the chocolate into pieces and put them into a small heatproof bowl set over a pan of gently simmering water. When the chocolate has melted, remove from the heat and spread it evenly over the base of the prepared tin. Chill in the refrigerator until set.

3 Preheat the oven to 180°C/350°F/Gas 4.

4 Put the cornflakes, sultanas, almonds, cherries and mixed peel in a large bowl. Pour over the condensed milk and toss the mixture gently, using a fork.

5 Spread the mixture evenly over the chocolate base and bake for 12–15 minutes, until golden brown. Cool in the tin, then chill for 20 minutes. Cut into squares.

> **Cook's Tip**
> Condensed milk is creamy and rich and may be sweetened or unsweetened. Do not confuse it with evaporated milk, which is not sweetened and has a slightly "boiled" flavour.

Black-and-White Ginger Florentines

These Florentines can be kept in the refrigerator in an airtight container for one week.

Makes 30
120ml/4fl oz/1/2 cup double (heavy) cream
50g/2oz/1/4 cup unsalted butter
90g/3 1/2oz/1/2 cup sugar
30ml/2 tbsp clear honey
150g/5oz/1 1/4 cups flaked (sliced) almonds

40g/1 1/2oz/1/3 cup plain (all-purpose) flour
2.5ml/1/2 tsp ground ginger
50g/2oz/1/3 cup diced candied orange peel
65g/2 1/2oz/1/2 cup diced preserved stem ginger
200g/7oz plain (semisweet) chocolate, chopped
150g/5oz fine quality white chocolate, chopped

1 Preheat the oven to 180°C/350°F/Gas 4. Lightly grease two large baking sheets.

2 In a medium pan over a medium heat, stir the cream, butter, sugar and honey until the sugar dissolves. Bring the mixture to the boil, stirring constantly.

3 Remove from the heat and stir in the almonds, flour and ground ginger. Stir in the orange peel, preserved stem ginger and 50g/2oz/1/3 cup chopped plain chocolate.

4 Drop teaspoons of the mixture on to the baking sheets, spaced 7.5cm/3in apart. Spread thinly.

5 Bake for 8–10 minutes until the edges are golden brown. Leave to firm up for 10 minutes. Transfer to a wire rack to cool.

6 In separate heatproof bowls set over pans of gently simmering water, melt the remaining plain chocolate and the white chocolate. Cool slightly.

7 Spread plain chocolate on the flat side of half the Florentines. Spread the remaining Florentines with the white chocolate. Chill for 10–15 minutes to set.

Florentine Bites Energy 87kcal/364kJ; Protein 1.6g; Carbohydrate 12g, of which sugars 10.7g; Fat 3.9g, of which saturates 1.4g; Cholesterol 2mg; Calcium 30mg; Fibre 0.5g; Sodium 27mg.
Black-and-White Ginger Florentines Energy 71kcal/298kJ; Protein 0.9g; Carbohydrate 8.6g, of which sugars 7.8g; Fat 3.9g, of which saturates 1.3g; Cholesterol 2mg; Calcium 16mg; Fibre 0.3g; Sodium 11mg.

Late Night Cookies

Crisp yet crumbly and packed with chocolate chips, these are a must with tall glasses of ice-cold milk or stacked with a large amount of ice cream.

Makes about 12 large or 20 small cookies
75g/3oz/6 tbsp butter, softened
75g/3oz/scant ¹/₂ cup golden caster (superfine) sugar
75g/3oz/¹/₃ cup soft light brown sugar, sifted
1 large (US extra large) egg, beaten
2.5ml/¹/₂ tsp vanilla extract
150g/5oz/1¹/₄ cups self-raising (self-rising) flour
25g/1oz/¹/₄ cup unsweetened cocoa powder
pinch of salt
100g/4oz chopped chocolate or plain (semisweet) chocolate chips
ice cream, to serve

1 Preheat the oven to 180°C/350°F/Gas 4. Lightly grease two non-stick baking sheets.

2 Beat the butter and sugars together until pale and fluffy. Beat in the egg and vanilla extract.

3 Sift the flour with the cocoa and salt. Gently fold into the egg mixture with the chopped chocolate or chocolate chips, using a flexible spatula.

4 Place four heaped tablespoonfuls of the mixture, spaced well apart, on each baking sheet. Press down and spread out with the back of a wet spoon.

5 Bake the cookies for about 12 minutes, until a rich golden brown. Leave on the baking sheets for 1 minute to firm up slightly, then using a metal spatula, carefully transfer to a wire rack to cool completely.

6 When the baking sheets have cooled, lightly grease them again. Place teaspoons of the remaining mixture on them as before and bake. Continue in this way until all the cookies have been baked. When cold, serve sandwiched together with ice cream or on their own.

Chocolate and Pistachio Wedges

These cookies are rich and grainy textured, with a bitter chocolate flavour. They go extremely well with vanilla ice cream and are especially delicious with bananas and custard.

Makes 16
200g/7oz/scant 1 cup unsalted butter, at room temperature, diced
90g/3¹/₂oz/¹/₂ cup golden caster (superfine) sugar
250g/9oz/2¹/₄ cups plain (all-purpose) flour
50g/2oz/¹/₂ cup unsweetened cocoa powder
25g/1oz/¹/₄ cup shelled pistachio nuts, finely chopped
unsweetened cocoa powder, for dusting

1 Preheat the oven to 180°C/350°F/Gas 4. Line a shallow 23cm/9in round sandwich tin (layer cake pan) with baking parchment.

2 In a large bowl, beat the butter and sugar together until light and creamy.

3 Sift the flour and cocoa powder over the butter mixture and mix in first with a wooden spoon, then work in with your hands until the mixture is smooth. Knead until soft and pliable.

4 Spread the mixture evenly in the tin. Sprinkle the pistachio nuts over the top and press in gently. Prick with a fork, then mark into 16 segments using a knife.

5 Bake for about 15–20 minutes. Do not allow to brown or the cookies will taste bitter.

6 Remove from the oven and dust the cookies with cocoa powder. Cut through the marked sections with a round-bladed knife and leave to cool before removing from the tin.

> **Cook's Tip**
> *Always sift cocoa powder before dusting cookies.*

Late Night Cookies Energy 170kcal/711kJ; Protein 2.8g; Carbohydrate 21g, of which sugars 11.5g; Fat 8.9g, of which saturates 5.2g; Cholesterol 34mg; Calcium 72mg; Fibre 0.7g; Sodium 117mg.
Chocolate and Pistachio Wedges Energy 188kcal/783kJ; Protein 2.4g; Carbohydrate 18.6g, of which sugars 6.3g; Fat 12g, of which saturates 7.1g; Cholesterol 27mg; Calcium 33mg; Fibre 1g; Sodium 115mg.

Ice Cream Sandwich Cookies

These are great when you get those midnight munchies – keep them in an airtight container and sandwich together each time with ice cream of your choice or make the sandwiches complete with ice cream and coating and freeze until required.

Makes 12
115g/4oz/½ cup unsalted butter, at room temperature, diced
115g/4oz/generous ½ cup caster (superfine) sugar
1 egg, beaten
200g/7oz/1¾ cups plain (all-purpose) flour
25g/1oz/¼ cup unsweetened cocoa powder, sifted
ice cream, to fill
toasted nuts, cookie crumbs, chocolate flakes or demerara (raw) sugar, to coat

1 Preheat the oven to 180°C/350°F/Gas 4. Lightly grease two baking sheets.

2 In a bowl, beat the butter and sugar together until light and fluffy, then beat in the egg. Stir in the flour and cocoa powder to make a firm dough.

3 Roll the dough out to a thickness of 5mm/¼in on baking parchment. Using a 7.5cm/3in plain round cookie cutter, stamp out 24 rounds and place on the baking sheets. Bake the cookies for about 15 minutes. Set aside on the baking sheets to cool.

4 To serve, spread 2 spoonfuls of softened ice cream on a cookie and press a second cookie on top.

5 Put your chosen coating on a plate and roll the cookies in it.

> **Cook's Tip**
> For super deluxe cookies, half-dip the ice cream cookies in melted chocolate. When the chocolate has set, either eat or wrap in foil and freeze for up to 2 weeks.

Chocolate and Coconut Slices

Rich, sweet and delicious, these slices will keep hunger at bay.

Makes 24
175g/6oz digestive biscuits (graham crackers)
115g/4oz/½ cup butter
115g/4oz/1 cup walnuts
55g/2oz/½ cup caster (superfine) sugar
pinch of salt
85g/3oz/1 cup desiccated (dry unsweetened shredded) coconut
260g/9oz/1½ cups plain (semisweet) chocolate chips
250ml/8fl oz/1 cup sweetened condensed milk

1 Preheat the oven to 180°C/350°F/Gas 4.

2 Put half the digestive biscuits in a clear plastic bag and use a rolling pin to crush them into small pieces, slightly larger than crumbs. Decant the contents of the bag into a bowl and repeat with the remaining cookies.

3 In a small pan set over a low heat, gently melt the butter, stirring occasionally.

4 In a blender or processor fitted with a metal blade, grind the walnuts, or chop them finely using a sharp knife.

5 Add the sugar and salt to the bowl with the crushed cookies and pour on the melted butter. Mix well to combine.

6 Press the mixture evenly over the bottom of an ungreased 33 x 23cm/13 x 9in baking dish using the back of a spoon.

7 Sprinkle the coconut over the biscuit base, then sprinkle over the chocolate chips. Pour the condensed milk over the chocolate. Top the condensed milk with the chopped walnuts.

8 Bake in the oven for 30 minutes until just beginning to turn golden brown. Leave to firm up slightly, then unmould on to a wire rack and leave to cool, preferably overnight. Use a sharp knife to cut into slices.

Chocolate and Coconut Slices Energy 217kcal/907kJ; Protein 2.8g; Carbohydrate 20g, of which sugars 15.8g; Fat 14.6g, of which saturates 7.5g; Cholesterol 18mg; Calcium 48mg; Fibre 1g; Sodium 89mg.
Ice Cream Sandwich Cookies Energy 184kcal/771kJ; Protein 3.3g; Carbohydrate 20.1g, of which sugars 13.5g; Fat 10.7g, of which saturates 4.7g; Cholesterol 18mg; Calcium 36mg; Fibre 0.8g; Sodium 73mg.

Nutty Marshmallow and Chocolate Squares

Unashamedly sweet, with chocolate, marshmallows, cherries, nuts and coconut, this recipe is a favourite with sweet-tooths.

Makes 9

200g/7oz digestive biscuits (graham crackers)
90g/3½oz plain (semisweet) chocolate
200g/7oz coloured mini marshmallows
150g/5oz/1¼ cups chopped walnuts
90g/3½oz/scant ½ cup glacé (candied) cherries, halved
50g/2oz/⅔ cup desiccated (dry unsweetened shredded) coconut
350g/12oz milk chocolate

1 Put the digestive biscuits in a plastic bag and, using a rolling pin, crush them until they are fairly small. Transfer the crumbs to a bowl.

2 Melt the plain chocolate in a heatproof bowl set over a pan of gently simmering water. Pour the melted plain chocolate over the broken biscuits and stir well.

3 Spread the mixture in the base of a 20cm/8in square shallow cake tin (pan).

4 Put the marshmallows, walnuts, cherries and coconut in a large bowl.

5 Melt the milk chocolate in a heatproof bowl set over a pan of gently simmering water. Pour the melted milk chocolate over the marshmallow and nut mixture and toss gently together until almost everything is coated. Spread the mixture over the chocolate base. Chill until set, then cut into squares.

> **Variation**
> Other nuts can be used instead of the walnuts – the choice is yours.

Almond-scented Chocolate Cherry Wedges

These cookies are a chocoholic's dream, and use the very best quality chocolate. Erratically shaped, they are packed with crunchy cookies, juicy raisins and munchy nuts.

Makes about 15

50g/2oz ratafia biscuits (almond macaroons) or small amaretti
90g/3½oz shortcake biscuits (cookies)
150g/5oz/1 cup jumbo raisins
50g/2oz/¼ cup natural glacé (candied) cherries, quartered
450g/1lb dark (bittersweet) chocolate (minimum 70 per cent cocoa solids)
90g/3½oz/scant ½ cup unsalted butter, diced
30ml/2 tbsp amaretto liqueur (optional)
25g/1oz/¼ cup toasted flaked (sliced) almonds

1 Line a baking sheet with baking parchment.

2 Put the ratafia biscuits in a large bowl. Break half of them into coarse pieces. Break the shortcakes into three or four pieces and add to the bowl. Add the raisins and glacé cherries and mix well.

3 Melt the chocolate and butter with the liqueur, if using, in a heatproof bowl set over a pan of gently simmering water, stirring until smooth and combined. Remove from the heat and set aside to cool slightly.

4 Pour the chocolate over the cookie mixture and toss lightly together until everything is coated in chocolate. Spread out over the prepared baking sheet.

5 Sprinkle over the almonds and push them in at angles so they stick well to the chocolate-coated cookies. Leave in a cool place until set.

6 When the mixture is completely cold and set, cut into long thin triangles.

Nutty Marshmallow and Chocolate Squares Energy 603kcal/2523kJ; Protein 8.6g; Carbohydrate 69.7g, of which sugars 53.2g; Fat 34.1g, of which saturates 14.7g; Cholesterol 19mg; Calcium 133mg; Fibre 2.5g; Sodium 179mg. **Almond-scented Chocolate Cherry Wedges** Energy 288kcal/1206kJ; Protein 2.7g; Carbohydrate 34.6g, of which sugars 29.7g; Fat 16.4g, of which saturates 9.5g; Cholesterol 20mg; Calcium 31mg; Fibre 1.3g; Sodium 75mg.

Rich Chocolate Cookie Slice

These rich, dark chocolate refrigerator cookies are perfect served with strong coffee, either as a mid-morning treat or even in place of dessert. They are always very popular.

Makes about 10
275g/10oz fruit and nut plain (semisweet) chocolate
130g/4½oz/½ cup unsalted butter, diced
90g/3½oz digestive biscuits (graham crackers)
90g/3½oz white chocolate

1 Lightly grease and line the base and sides of a 450g/1lb loaf tin (pan) with baking parchment.

2 Break the fruit and nut chocolate into even-size pieces and place in a heatproof bowl together with the butter.

3 Set the bowl over a pan of barely simmering water and stir gently until melted and smooth. Remove the bowl from the heat and set aside to cool for 20 minutes.

4 Break the digestive biscuits into small pieces. Finely chop the white chocolate.

5 Stir the broken biscuits and white chocolate into the cooled, melted fruit and nut chocolate until combined. Turn the mixture into the prepared tin and pack down gently. Chill for 2 hours, or until set.

6 To serve, turn out the mixture and remove the lining paper. Cut into slices with a sharp knife.

Variations
You can use this simple basic recipe for all kinds of variations.
• Try different kinds of chocolate, such as ginger, hazelnut, honey and almond, peanut or mocha.
• Substitute different cookies for the digestive biscuits (graham crackers) – shortbread, Petit-Beurre, Marie, ginger nuts (gingersnaps) or peanut butter cookies.

Rocky Road Wedges

Free from gluten and wheat, these crumbly chocolate wedges contain home-made popcorn in place of broken cookies, which are the classic ingredient in many no-bake cookies. This recipe uses an orange-flavoured chocolate bar, but any flavour can be used.

Makes 8
15ml/1 tbsp vegetable oil
25g/1oz/2½ tbsp popping corn
150g/5oz orange-flavoured plain (semisweet) chocolate
25g/1oz/2 tbsp unsalted butter, diced
75g/3oz soft vanilla fudge, diced
icing (confectioners') sugar, for dusting

1 Heat the oil in a heavy pan. Add the popping corn, cover with a lid and heat, shaking the pan once or twice, until the popping noises die down. (It is important not to lift the lid until the popping stops.)

2 Remove the pan from the heat and leave for about 30 seconds before removing the lid. Be careful, as there may be quite a lot of steam trapped inside. Transfer the popcorn to a bowl and leave to cool for about 5 minutes.

3 Meanwhile, line the base of an 18cm/7in sandwich tin (layer cake pan) with baking parchment.

4 Once cooled, tip the corn into a plastic bag and tap with a rolling pin to break up into small pieces.

5 Break the chocolate into a heatproof bowl. Add the butter and set the bowl over a pan of gently simmering water. Stir frequently until melted. Remove the bowl from the heat and leave to cool for 2 minutes.

6 Stir the popcorn and fudge into the cooled melted chocolate mixture until well coated, then turn the mixture into the prepared tin and press down firmly in an even layer. Leave to set for about 30 minutes.

7 Turn the cookie out on to a board and cut into eight wedges. Serve lightly dusted with icing sugar.

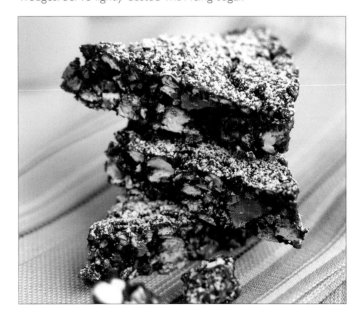

Rich Chocolate Cookie Slice Energy 326kcal/1361kJ; Protein 2.7g; Carbohydrate 29g, of which sugars 23.8g; Fat 23g, of which saturates 13.9g; Cholesterol 33mg; Calcium 44mg; Fibre 0.9g; Sodium 144mg. **Rocky Road Wedges** Energy 191kcal/798kJ; Protein 1.5g; Carbohydrate 21g, of which sugars 19.3g; Fat 11.8g, of which saturates 5.9g; Cholesterol 11mg; Calcium 19mg; Fibre 0.5g; Sodium 33mg.

Ice Mountain

To create an alternative shape to rounds and squares, this refrigerator cookie is set in the corner of a cake tin, giving it a "pyramid" shape for slicing into triangles.

Makes 12
75g/3oz malted milk cookies
90g/3½oz milk chocolate
75g/3oz white chocolate mint sticks
250g/9oz white chocolate
60ml/4 tbsp double (heavy) cream
several clear mints (hard mint candies), to decorate

1 Cut one 23cm/9in square of baking parchment. Grease one side, and 5cm/2in of the base of an 18cm/7in square cake tin (pan). Line one side and the base of the tin.

2 Break the cookies into small pieces, chop the milk chocolate into small dice and break the chocolate mint sticks into short lengths. Keep these ingredients separate.

3 Reserve 50g/2oz of the white chocolate. Put the remainder in a small heatproof bowl with the cream and set the bowl over a pan of gently simmering water. Melt, stirring frequently. Remove from the heat.

4 Stir the cookies into the white chocolate mixture followed by the chocolate mint sticks. Add the milk chocolate, stir quickly to combine, then turn the mixture into the lined section of the tin. Hold the tin at an angle, then smooth the surface of the chocolate. Chill the mixture in the refrigerator, propping the tin up to maintain the angle to form the pyramid shape. Leave to set. Remove from the tin, place on a flat plate and peel off the paper.

5 In their wrappers, crush the mints with a rolling pin. Melt the reserved white chocolate in a heatproof bowl set over a pan of hot water.

6 Spread the white chocolate over the top sloping side of the pyramid, sprinkle with the crushed mints and press in lightly.

Chocolate Salami

This after-dinner sweetmeat resembles a salami, hence its name. It is very rich and will serve a lot of people. Slice it very thinly and serve with espresso coffee and amaretto liqueur.

Serves 8–12
24 Petit Beurre cookies, broken into pieces

350g/12oz plain (semisweet) chocolate, broken into squares
225g/8oz/1 cup unsalted butter, softened
60ml/4 tbsp amaretto liqueur
2 egg yolks
50g/2oz/½ cup flaked (sliced) almonds, lightly toasted and thinly shredded lengthways
25g/1oz/¼ cup ground almonds

1 Place the cookies in a food processor and process until crushed into coarse crumbs.

2 Put the chocolate, a small knob (pat) of the butter and the liqueur in a heatproof bowl, set over a pan of barely simmering water. Heat until the chocolate melts, stirring occasionally.

3 Remove the bowl from the heat, leave to cool for a minute or two, stir in the egg yolks, then the remaining butter, a little at a time. Tip in most of the crushed cookies, leaving behind a good handful, and stir well. Stir in the flaked almonds. Leave the mixture in a cold place for 1 hour.

4 Process the remaining crushed cookies in the food processor until they are very finely ground. Mix with the ground almonds. Cover and set aside.

5 Turn the chocolate and cookie mixture on to a sheet of lightly oiled baking parchment, then shape into a 35cm/14in long sausage using a metal spatula. Wrap securely in the paper and freeze the roll for at least 4 hours, until solid.

6 To serve, spread the finely ground cookies and almonds out on a clean sheet of baking parchment and roll the salami in them until evenly coated. Transfer to a board and leave to stand for about 1 hour before cutting into slices with a sharp knife to serve.

Ice Mountain Energy 234kcal/977kJ; Protein 3.2g; Carbohydrate 24.8g, of which sugars 21.5g; Fat 14.2g, of which saturates 8.4g; Cholesterol 11mg; Calcium 100mg; Fibre 0.2g; Sodium 63mg.
Chocolate Salami Energy 453kcal/1885kJ; Protein 4.5g; Carbohydrate 36.6g, of which sugars 26.9g; Fat 32.3g, of which saturates 16.8g; Cholesterol 96mg; Calcium 47mg; Fibre 1.4g; Sodium 173mg.

Midnight Cookies

These cookies are so-called because you can make them up before you go to bed and leave them to bake slowly in the switched-off oven. How presto, there they are in the morning, lightly crunchy on the outside and deliciously soft in the middle.

Makes 9
1 egg white
90g/3½oz/½ cup caster
   (superfine) sugar
50g/2oz/½ cup ground almonds
90g/3½oz/generous ½ cup milk
   chocolate chips
90g/3½oz/scant ½ cup glacé
   (candied) cherries, chopped
50g/2oz/⅔ cup dessicated
   (dry unsweetened
   shredded) coconut

1 Preheat the oven to 220°C/425°F/Gas 7. Line a baking sheet with baking parchment.

2 Put the egg white in a large, clean, grease-free bowl and whisk until stiff peaks form.

3 Add the sugar to the egg white, a spoonful at a time, whisking well between each addition until the sugar is fully incorporated. The mixture should be completely smooth and glossy in appearance.

4 Fold in the ground almonds, chocolate chips, glacé cherries and shredded coconut with a flexible spatula. Place 9 spoonfuls of the mixture on the baking sheet, spaced apart. Place the baking sheet in the oven, close the door and turn the oven off. Leave overnight (or for at least 6 hours) and don't open the oven door. Serve for breakfast or store in airtight container.

> **Cook's Tip**
> *Given that time is always short in the morning, these cookies make a great breakfast treat – even children will find time to eat them. For a nourishing start to the day, serve them with fresh fruit. Alternatively, quickly whiz up a fresh fruit smoothie in the blender.*

Chocolate Macaroons

The Italians claim to have invented these little cookies during the Renaissance and this classic combination of almonds and chocolate certainly suggests that this is true.

Makes 20
50g/2oz plain (semisweet)
   chocolate, chopped into
   small pieces
2 egg whites
200g/7oz/1 cup caster
   (superfine) sugar
2.5ml/½ tsp vanilla extract
1.5ml/¼ tsp almond extract
115g/4oz/1 cup ground almonds
icing (confectioners') sugar,
   for dusting

1 Preheat the oven to 150°C/300°F/Gas 2. Line two baking sheets with baking parchment.

2 Melt the chocolate in a heatproof bowl placed over a pan of barely simmering water, stirring occasionally. Leave to cool.

3 In a grease-free bowl, whisk the egg whites until they form soft peaks. Gently fold in the sugar, vanilla and almond extracts, ground almonds and melted chocolate. The mixture should just hold its shape. If it is too soft, chill it for 15 minutes.

4 Place mounded teaspoonfuls of the mixture, spaced well apart, on the prepared baking sheets and flatten slightly. Brush each with a little water and sift over a thin layer of icing sugar.

5 Bake the macaroons for 20–25 minutes until just firm. Transfer to a wire rack to cool.

> **Cook's Tip**
> *To make Chocolate Pine Nut Macaroons, spread 75g/3oz/ ¾ cup pine nuts in a shallow dish. Press the balls of chocolate macaroon dough into the nuts to cover one side of each ball and place them, nut side up, on lined baking sheets, then bake as above.*

Midnight Cookies Energy 185kcal/777kJ; Protein 2.7g; Carbohydrate 23.5g, of which sugars 23.4g; Fat 9.6g, of which saturates 5g; Cholesterol 2mg; Calcium 48mg; Fibre 1.3g; Sodium 21mg.
Chocolate Macaroons Energy 94kcal/393kJ; Protein 2.1g; Carbohydrate 11.6g, of which sugars 11.4g; Fat 4.7g, of which saturates 0.7g; Cholesterol 0mg; Calcium 23mg; Fibre 0.6g; Sodium 9mg.

Sweet Hearts

These cookies are for Valentine's Day or an anniversary, but you could use different-shaped cutters in the same way to make cookies for other occasions.

Makes 12–14

50g/2oz/¼ cup unsalted butter, softened

75g/3oz/scant ½ cup caster (superfine) sugar
I egg yolk
150g/5oz/1¼ cups plain (all-purpose) flour
25g/1oz dark (bittersweet) chocolate, melted and cooled
25–50g/1–2oz dark (bittersweet) chocolate, to decorate

1 Preheat the oven to 180°C/350°F/Gas 4. Line two baking sheets with baking parchment.

2 Put the butter, sugar and egg yolk in a mixing bowl and beat well. Stir in the flour and then knead until smooth.

3 Divide the dough in half, then knead the melted chocolate into one half until it is evenly coloured.

4 Roll out each piece of dough between sheets of baking parchment, to 3mm/⅛in thick.

5 Stamp out shapes from both doughs using a 7.5cm/3in cookie cutter. Place the cookies on the prepared baking sheets.

6 Using a smaller cookie cutter, stamp out the centres from all the cookies. Place a light-coloured cookie in the centre of a larger chocolate cookie and vice versa.

7 Bake the cookies for 10 minutes, or until just beginning to turn brown. Remove from the oven and leave to cool.

8 To decorate, melt the chocolate in a heatproof bowl set over a pan of hot water. Leave to cool slightly. Put into a piping (pastry) bag. Pipe dots on to the outer part of the large chocolate hearts. Pipe zig-zags on the pale part of the large plain hearts. Leave in a cool place until they are set.

Chinese Fortune Cookies

Whether you're a rabbit or a dragon, a snake or a tiger, these charming cookies are sure to delight and are a wonderful way to celebrate the Chinese New Year with family and friends.

Makes about 35

2 egg whites
50g/2oz/½ cup icing (confectioners') sugar, sifted, plus extra for dusting
5ml/1 tsp almond or vanilla extract

25g/1oz/2 tbsp unsalted butter, melted
50g/2oz/½ cup plain (all-purpose) flour
25g/1oz/⅓ cup desiccated (dry unsweetened shredded) coconut, lightly toasted
tiny strips of paper with "good luck", "health, wealth and happiness" and other appropriate messages typed or written on them, to decorate

1 Preheat the oven to 190°C/375°F/Gas 5. Line two or three baking sheets with baking parchment.

2 Put the egg whites into a grease-free bowl and whisk until foamy and white. Whisk in the icing sugar, a little at a time, beating well after each addition. Beat in the almond or vanilla extract and the melted butter. Fold in the flour with a flexible spatula and mix gently until smooth.

3 Place three seperate teaspoonfuls of mixture on to each prepared baking sheet and spread out evenly with the back of a spoon. Sprinkle with a little coconut. Bake one sheet at a time (as you will only have enough time to shape one sheetful of cookies before they set) for about 5 minutes, or until very lightly brown on the edges.

4 Remove the cookies from the oven, immediately loosely fold in half and place on the rim of a glass. Leave until firm, then transfer to a wire rack. Continue baking one sheet of cookies at a time.

5 Tuck the messages into the side of each cookie. Dust very lightly with icing sugar before serving.

Sweet Hearts Energy 107kcal/449kJ; Protein 1.4g; Carbohydrate 16.2g, of which sugars 8g; Fat 4.5g, of which saturates 2.6g; Cholesterol 22mg; Calcium 21mg; Fibre 0.4g; Sodium 23mg.
Chinese Fortune Cookies Energy 21kcal/87kJ; Protein 0.4g; Carbohydrate 2.7g, of which sugars 1.6g; Fat 1g, of which saturates 0.8g; Cholesterol 2mg; Calcium 3mg; Fibre 0.1g; Sodium 8mg.

Oznei Haman

These little cookies, shaped like three-cornered hats, are eaten at the Jewish summer feast of Purim.

Makes about 20
115g/4oz/½ cup unsalted butter, at room temperature, diced
115g/4oz/generous ½ cup caster (superfine) sugar
2.5ml/½ tsp vanilla extract
3 egg yolks
250g/9oz/2¼ cups plain (all-purpose) flour, plus extra for dusting
beaten egg, to seal and glaze

For the filling
40g/1½oz/3 tbsp poppy seeds
15ml/1 tbsp clear honey
25g/1oz/2 tbsp caster (superfine) sugar
finely grated rind of 1 lemon
15ml/1 tbsp lemon juice
40g/1½oz/⅓ cup ground almonds
1 small (US medium) egg, beaten
25g/1oz/scant ¼ cup raisins

1 Beat the butter with the sugar until light and creamy. Beat in the vanilla and egg yolks. Sift over the flour, stir in, then work into a dough with your hands. Knead until smooth. Wrap in clear film (plastic wrap) and chill.

2 For the filling, put the poppy seeds, honey, sugar, lemon rind and juice into a pan with 60ml/4 tbsp water and bring to the boil, stirring. Remove from the heat and beat in the almonds, egg and raisins. Leave to cool.

3 Preheat the oven to 180°C/350°F/Gas 4. Line two large baking sheets with baking parchment.

4 Roll out the dough on a lightly floured surface to 3mm/⅛in thick. Using a 7.5cm/3in cookie cutter, stamp out rounds. Place a heaped teaspoon of filling on each round. Brush the edges with beaten egg, then bring the sides to the centre to form a tricorne shape. Seal and place on the prepared baking sheets, spaced slightly apart.

5 Brush with beaten egg and bake for 20–30 minutes, or until golden brown. Transfer to a wire rack and leave to cool.

Ma'amoul

Jews eat these date and nut cookies at Purim, Christians enjoy them at Easter and Muslims serve them at Iftar, the after-sunset meal that breaks the Ramadan fast. They are made in special wooden moulds, which seal the rose-scented pastry around the filling.

Makes 35–40
450g/1lb/4 cups plain (all-purpose) flour
225g/8oz/1 cup unsalted butter, diced
45ml/3 tbsp rose water
60–75ml/4–5 tbsp milk
icing (confectioners') sugar, for dusting

For the filling
225g/8oz/1⅓ cups dried dates, stoned (pitted) and chopped
175g/6oz/1½ cup walnuts, finely chopped
115g/4oz/1 cup blanched almonds, chopped
50g/2oz/½ cup pistachio nuts, chopped
120ml/4fl oz/½ cup water
115g/4oz/½ cup sugar
10ml/2 tsp ground cinnamon

1 Preheat the oven to 160°C/325°F/Gas 3. Lightly grease one or two large baking sheets.

2 To make the filling, place the dates, walnuts, almonds, pistachio nuts, water, sugar and cinnamon in a small pan and cook over a low heat, until the dates are soft and the water has been absorbed. Set aside.

3 Place the flour in a bowl and add the butter, working it into the flour with your fingertips. Add the rose water and milk and knead until soft. Take walnut-size pieces of dough. Roll each into a ball and hollow with your thumb. Pinch the sides.

4 Place a spoonful of date mixture in the hollow, then press the dough back over the filling to enclose it, pressing the edges together to seal.

5 Arrange the cookies on the prepared baking sheets, spaced well apart. Press gently to flatten them slightly. Bake for 20 minutes. Do not allow them to brown or they will become hard. Leave to cool slightly and sprinkle with icing sugar.

Oznei Haman Energy 156kcal/653kJ; Protein 2.8g; Carbohydrate 18.7g, of which sugars 9.1g; Fat 8.3g, of which saturates 3.6g; Cholesterol 52mg; Calcium 46mg; Fibre 0.7g; Sodium 42mg.
Ma'amoul Energy 163kcal/680kJ; Protein 2.8g; Carbohydrate 16.1g, of which sugars 7.4g; Fat 10.1g, of which saturates 3.4g; Cholesterol 12mg; Calcium 35mg; Fibre 1g; Sodium 43mg.

Simnel Cookies

Enjoy these mini variations on the sweet, marzipan-covered simnel cake that is traditionally eaten at Easter and, originally, Mothering Sunday in Britain.

Makes about 18
175g/6oz/³⁄₄ cup unsalted butter, at room temperature, diced
115g/4oz/generous ¹⁄₂ cup caster (superfine) sugar
finely grated rind of 1 lemon

2 egg yolks
225g/8oz/2 cups plain (all-purpose) flour
50g/2oz/¹⁄₄ cup currants

For the topping
400g/14oz marzipan
200g/7oz/1³⁄₄ cups icing (confectioners') sugar, sifted
2–3 shades of food colouring
mini sugar-coated chocolate Easter eggs

1 Preheat the oven to 180°C/350°F/Gas 4.

2 Put the butter, sugar and lemon rind in a bowl and beat until light and fluffy. Beat in the egg yolks, then stir in the flour and currants and mix to a firm dough. If it is a little soft, chill in the refrigerator until firm.

3 Roll out the dough on baking parchment to 5mm/¹⁄₄in thick. Using a 9cm/3¹⁄₂in cookie cutter, stamp out rounds and place, spaced slightly apart, on non-stick baking sheets.

4 To make the topping, roll out the marzipan to 5mm/¹⁄₄in thick and use a 6cm/2¹⁄₂in cookie cutter to stamp out the same number of rounds as there are cookies. Place a marzipan round on top of each cookie and press down gently.

5 Bake the cookies for about 12 minutes, or until just golden. Remove from the oven and leave to cool on the baking sheets.

6 Put the icing sugar in a bowl and add water to mix to a smooth consistency. Colour the icing as desired. Three different colours have been used here.

7 Ice the cooled cookies. While the icing is still wet, press a few sugar-coated eggs on top of each cookie and leave to set.

Easter Cookies

These traditional English cookies are sweet, lightly spiced and flecked with currants. They have a soft and crunchy texture and are a filling treat.

Makes 16–18
115g/4oz/¹⁄₂ cup soft butter
75g/3oz/scant ¹⁄₂ cup caster (superfine) sugar, plus extra for sprinkling

1 egg
200g/7oz/1³⁄₄ cups plain (all-purpose) flour, plus extra for dusting
2.5ml/¹⁄₂ tsp mixed (apple pie) spice
2.5ml/¹⁄₂ tsp ground cinnamon
50g/2oz/¹⁄₄ cup currants
15ml/1 tbsp chopped mixed (candied) peel
15–30ml/1–2 tbsp milk

1 Preheat the oven to 200°C/400°F/Gas 6. Lightly grease two baking sheets.

2 Beat together the butter and sugar until light and fluffy.

3 Separate the egg, reserving the white, and beat the yolk into the butter mixture.

4 Sift the flour and spices over the mixture, then fold in the currants and peel, adding sufficient milk to make a fairly soft dough.

5 Knead the dough lightly on a floured surface, then roll out to 5mm/¹⁄₄in thick. Stamp out rounds using a 5cm/2in fluted cookie cutter. Arrange on the baking sheets, spaced well apart, and bake for 10 minutes.

6 Beat the egg white and brush gently over the cookies. Sprinkle with caster sugar and return to the oven for 10 minutes, until golden. Using a metal spatula, transfer to a wire rack to cool.

Variation
Substitute freshly grated nutmeg for the cinnamon.

Simnel Cookies Energy 285kcal/1197kJ; Protein 2.9g; Carbohydrate 45g, of which sugars 35.4g; Fat 11.6g, of which saturates 5.5g; Cholesterol 43mg; Calcium 48mg; Fibre 0.9g; Sodium 66mg.
Easter Cookies Energy 116kcal/485kJ; Protein 1.5g; Carbohydrate 15.4g, of which sugars 7g; Fat 5.7g, of which saturates 3.4g; Cholesterol 24mg; Calcium 25mg; Fibre 0.4g; Sodium 46mg.

Fourth of July Blueberry Softbakes

These are simply wonderful when eaten still warm from the oven. However, they are also good if allowed to cool and then packed for a traditional Independence Day picnic.

Makes 10
150g/5oz/1¼ cups plain (all-purpose) flour
7.5ml/1½ tsp baking powder
5ml/1 tsp ground cinnamon
50g/2oz/¼ cup unsalted butter, at room temperature, diced
50g/2oz/¼ cup demerara (raw) sugar, plus extra for sprinkling
120ml/4fl oz/½ cup sour cream
90g/3½oz/scant 1 cup fresh blueberries
50g/2oz/½ cup semi-dried cranberries

1 Preheat the oven to 190°C/375°F/Gas 5. Line two baking sheets with baking parchment.

2 Sift together the flour, baking powder and cinnamon into a large mixing bowl. Add the diced butter and rub in with your fingers until the mixture resembles fine breadcrumbs. Stir in the demerara sugar.

3 Add the sour cream, blueberries and cranberries and stir until just combined.

4 Spoon ten mounds of the mixture, spaced well apart, on to the prepared baking sheets. Sprinkle with the extra demerara sugar and bake for about 20 minutes, or until golden and firm in the centre. Serve warm.

Variations
• For Thanksgiving, substitute fresh cranberries for the blueberries and chopped preserved stem ginger for the semi-dried cranberries.
• For Halloween, substitute chocolate chips and chopped almonds for the fruit.
• For Christmas, substitute raisins soaked in rum for 20 minutes for the blueberries.

Neuris

These melt-in-the-mouth sweet and spicy samosas are traditionally eaten during the Hindu festival of Diwali and are also given as little gifts to friends and family.

Makes 12
75g/3oz/1 cup desiccated (dry unsweetened shredded) coconut
50g/2oz/¼ cup light muscovado (brown) sugar
25g/1oz/¼ cup cashew nuts, chopped
50g/2oz/⅓ cup seedless raisins
250ml/8fl oz/1 cup evaporated milk
large pinch grated nutmeg
2.5ml/½ tsp ground cinnamon
12 sheets filo pastry, about 28 x 18cm/11 x 7in each
sunflower oil, for brushing

For the topping
15ml/1 tbsp evaporated milk
15ml/1 tbsp caster (superfine) sugar
desiccated (dry unsweetened shredded) coconut

1 For the filling, put the coconut, sugar, cashews, raisins and evaporated milk into a pan. Bring to the boil, stirring occasionally. Reduce the heat and cook for 10 minutes, stirring, until the milk is absorbed. Add the nutmeg and cinnamon. Cool.

2 Preheat the oven to 180°C/350°F/Gas 4. Line two baking sheets with baking parchment.

3 Brush one sheet of filo pastry with sunflower oil. Fold the sheet in half lengthways, then brush with more oil and fold widthways. Brush the edges of the folded pastry with water.

4 Put a spoonful of filling on one half of the pastry sheet. Fold the other half over the filling, and press the edges together. Place on the baking sheet. Repeat with the remaining mixture.

5 To make the topping, put the evaporated milk and sugar into a pan and heat gently, stirring until the sugar has dissolved. Brush over the cookies and sprinkle them with the coconut.

6 Bake for about 20 minutes, until golden brown. Transfer to a wire rack and leave to cool.

Fourth of July Blueberry Softbakes Energy 185kcal/775kJ; Protein 3.3g; Carbohydrate 25.2g, of which sugars 9.8g; Fat 8.4g, of which saturates 4.6g; Cholesterol 78mg; Calcium 48mg; Fibre 0.8g; Sodium 42mg. **Neuris** Energy 164kcal/689kJ; Protein 4.2g; Carbohydrate 24.6g, of which sugars 11.6g; Fat 6.1g, of which saturates 4.1g; Cholesterol 4mg; Calcium 88mg; Fibre 1.5g; Sodium 37mg.

85 FESTIVAL AND CELEBRATION COOKIES

Panellets

The Catalan name for these nutty festival cakes means "little bread", but they are, in fact, much closer to marzipan, with a slightly soft centre that is produced by their secret ingredient – sweet potato. Patisseries make hundreds of these little cakes for All Saints' Day, on 1st November, when families take flowers to the graveyards of their relatives.

Makes about 24

115g/4oz sweet potato
butter, for greasing
1 large (US extra large) egg, separated
225g/8oz/2 cups ground almonds
200g/7oz/1 cup caster (superfine) sugar, plus extra for sprinkling
finely grated rind of 1 small lemon
7.5ml/1½ tsp vanilla extract
60ml/4 tbsp pine nuts
60ml/4 tbsp pistachio nuts, chopped

1 Peel and dice the sweet potato and cook it in a pan of boiling water for about 15 minutes, until soft but not falling apart. Drain well and leave to cool.

2 Preheat the oven to 200°C/400°F/Gas 6. Line one or two baking sheets with foil and grease well with butter.

3 Put the cooled sweet potato into a food processor and process to a smooth purée. Gradually work in the egg yolk, ground almonds, caster sugar, lemon rind and vanilla extract, processing to make a soft dough. Transfer the dough to a bowl, cover with clear film (plastic wrap) and chill in the refrigerator for 30 minutes.

4 Spoon walnut-size balls of dough on to the prepared baking sheets, spacing them about 2.5cm/1in apart, then flatten them out slightly.

5 Lightly beat the egg white and brush over the cookies. Sprinkle half with pine nuts, slightly less than 5ml/1 tsp each, and half with pistachio nuts. Sprinkle lightly with sugar. Bake for 10 minutes, or until lightly browned.

6 Leave to cool on the foil, then lift off with a metal spatula.

Speculaas

These Dutch cookies are made from a spicy dough wrapped around a wonderfully rich marzipan filling. They are eaten in Holland around the Feast of St Nicholas on 6 December.

Makes about 35

175g/6oz/1½ cups ground hazelnuts
175g/6oz/1½ cups ground almonds
175g/6oz/scant 1 cup caster (superfine) sugar
175g/6oz/1½ cups icing (confectioners') sugar

1 egg, beaten
10–15ml/2–3 tsp lemon juice

For the pastry

250g/9oz/2¼ cups self-raising (self-rising) flour, plus extra for dusting
5ml/1 tsp mixed (apple pie) spice
75g/3oz/⅓ cup brown sugar
115g/4oz/½ cup unsalted butter, diced
2 eggs
15ml/1 tbsp milk
15ml/1 tbsp caster (superfine) sugar
about 35 blanched almond halves

1 For the filling, mix the hazelnuts, almonds, sugars, egg and 10ml/2 tsp lemon juice to a firm paste, adding more lemon juice if needed. Halve the paste and roll into sausages 25cm/10in long. Wrap and chill.

2 For the pastry, sift the flour and spice into a bowl, then stir in the brown sugar. Add the butter and rub in well. Add one egg and mix to form dough. Knead, wrap and chill for 15 minutes.

3 Preheat the oven to 180°C/350°F/Gas 4. Line a large baking sheet with baking parchment.

4 Roll out the pastry on a lightly floured surface to a 30cm/12in square and cut in half to make two equal rectangles. Beat the remaining egg and brush some over the pastry.

5 Place a roll of filling on each piece of pastry and roll the pastry around it. Place, join side down, on the baking sheet. Beat the remains of the egg with the milk and sugar and brush over the rolls. Press almond halves along the top. Bake for 35 minutes, until golden brown.

Panellets Energy 130kcal/541kJ; Protein 3.1g; Carbohydrate 10.7g, of which sugars 9.6g; Fat 8.6g, of which saturates 0.8g; Cholesterol 8mg; Calcium 32mg; Fibre 1g; Sodium 20mg.
Speculaas Energy 168kcal/703kJ; Protein 3.1g; Carbohydrate 19.4g, of which sugars 13.7g; Fat 9.2g, of which saturates 2.3g; Cholesterol 23mg; Calcium 39mg; Fibre 0.9g; Sodium 28mg.

Christmas Honey Cookies

Gloriously sticky, these spicy cookies are an irresistible festive treat.

Makes 20

2.5ml/½ tsp bicarbonate of soda (baking soda)
grated rind and juice of 1 large orange
150ml/¼ pint/⅔ cup extra virgin olive oil
75g/3oz/scant ½ cup caster (superfine) sugar
60ml/4 tbsp brandy
7.5ml/1½ tsp ground cinnamon
400g/14oz/3½ cups self-raising (self-rising) flour sifted with a pinch of salt
115g/4oz/1 cup shelled walnuts, chopped

For the syrup

225g/8oz/1 cup clear honey
115g/4oz/generous ½ cup caster (superfine) sugar

1 Mix together the bicarbonate of soda and orange juice.

2 Beat the oil and sugar with an electric mixer until blended. Beat in the brandy and 2.5ml/½ tsp of the cinnamon, then the orange juice and soda. Using your hands, gradually work the flour and salt into the mixture. Add the orange rind and knead for 10 minutes, or until the dough is soft and pliable.

3 Preheat the oven to 180°C/350°F/Gas 4.

4 Flour your hands and pinch off small pieces of the dough. Shape them into 6cm/2½in long ovals and place on ungreased baking sheets. Using a fork dipped in water, flatten each cookie. Bake for 25 minutes, until golden. Cool slightly, then transfer to a wire rack to harden.

5 To make the syrup, put the honey, sugar and 150ml/¼ pint/⅔ cup water in a small pan. Bring gently to the boil, skim, then lower the heat and simmer for 5 minutes.

6 Immerse the cold cookies, about six at a time, into the hot syrup and leave them for 1–2 minutes.

7 Lift them with a slotted spoon and place on a platter in a single layer. Sprinkle with the walnuts and remaining cinnamon.

Christmas Tree Cookies

These cookies make an appealing gift. They look wonderful hung on a Christmas tree.

Makes 12

175g/6oz/1½ cups plain (all-purpose) flour, plus extra for dusting
75g/3oz/⅓ cup butter, chopped
40g/1½oz/3 tbsp caster (superfine) sugar
1 egg white
30ml/2 tbsp orange juice
225g/8oz coloured fruit sweets (candies)
coloured ribbons, to decorate

1 Preheat the oven to 180°C/350°F/Gas 4. Line two baking sheets with baking parchment.

2 Sift the flour into a mixing bowl. Add the butter and rub into the flour with your fingertips until the mixture resembles fine breadcrumbs. Stir in the sugar, egg white and enough orange juice to form a soft dough. Turn out on to a lightly floured surface and knead lightly until smooth.

3 Roll out thinly and stamp out as many shapes as possible using a floured Christmas tree cookie cutter. Transfer the shapes to the prepared baking sheets, spacing them well apart. Knead the trimmings together.

4 Using a 1cm/½in round cutter or the end of a large plain piping nozzle, stamp out and remove six rounds from each tree shape. Cut each sweet into three and place a piece in each hole. Make a small hole at the top of each tree to thread through the ribbon. Repeat until you have used up the remaining cookie dough and sweets.

5 Bake for 15–20 minutes, until the cookies are slightly gold in colour and the sweets have melted and filled the holes. If the holes for threading the ribbons have closed up during baking, pierce them again while the cookies are still hot. Leave to cool on the baking sheets.

6 Thread short lengths of ribbon through the holes so that the trees can be hung up.

Christmas Honey Cookies Energy 173kcal/724kJ; Protein 2.7g; Carbohydrate 19.5g, of which sugars 4.6g; Fat 9.2g, of which saturates 1.1g; Cholesterol 0mg; Calcium 78mg; Fibre 0.8g; Sodium 73mg.
Christmas Tree Cookies Energy 147kcal/622kJ; Protein 1.9g; Carbohydrate 28.7g, of which sugars 16g; Fat 3.6g, of which saturates 2.1g; Cholesterol 15mg; Calcium 31mg; Fibre 0.5g; Sodium 45mg.

Stained Glass Windows

Baking coloured sweets inside a cookie frame creates a stained glass effect, particularly if you hang the cookies in the light.

Makes 12–14
175g/6oz/1½ cups plain
  (all-purpose) flour, plus extra
  for dusting
2.5ml/½ tsp bicarbonate of soda
  (baking soda)
2.5ml/½ tsp ground cinnamon
75g/3oz/6 tbsp unsalted butter,
  chilled and diced
75g/3oz/scant ½ cup caster
  (superfine) sugar
30ml/2 tbsp golden (light
  corn) syrup
1 egg yolk
150g/5oz brightly coloured, clear
  boiled sweets (hard candies)
fine ribbon

1 Put the flour, bicarbonate of soda, cinnamon and butter into a bowl and rub the fat into the flour until the mixture resembles breadcrumbs. Add the sugar, syrup and egg yolk and mix until the mixture starts to cling together in a dough. Turn the dough out on to a lightly floured surface and knead until smooth. Wrap in clear film (plastic wrap) and chill for at least 30 minutes.

2 Preheat the oven to 180°C/350°F/Gas 4. Line two large baking sheets with baking parchment.

3 Roll out the dough thinly on a lightly floured surface. Stamp out 12 diamonds using a cookie cutter. Cut a smaller diamond from the centre of each and remove to leave a 1cm/½in frame. Make a hole at one end for hanging. Bake for 5 minutes.

4 Lightly crush the sweets with a rolling pin. Remove the cookies from the oven and fill the centre of each with two crushed sweets of the same colour.

5 Return the cookies to the oven for another 5 minutes until the sweets have melted. Spread the melted sweets to fill the space with the tip of a skewer. Leave to cool.

6 Thread ribbon through the holes in the cookies, then hang up the cookies as decorations.

Christmas Tree Angels

Why not make these charming edible decorations to brighten your Yuletide?

Makes 20–30
90g/3½oz/scant ½ cup
  demerara (raw) sugar
200g/7oz/scant1 cup golden
  (light corn) syrup
5ml/1 tsp ground ginger
5ml/1 tsp ground cinnamon
1.5ml/¼ tsp ground cloves
115g/4oz/½ cup unsalted
  butter, diced
10ml/2 tsp bicarbonate of soda
  (baking soda)
1 egg, beaten
500g/1¼lb/5 cups plain
  (all-purpose) flour, sifted

For the decoration
1 egg white
175–225g/6–8oz/1½–2 cups
  icing (confectioners')
  sugar, sifted
silver and gold balls
fine ribbon

1 Preheat the oven to 160°C/325°F/Gas 3. Line two or three large baking sheets with baking parchment.

2 Put the sugar, syrup, ginger, cinnamon and cloves into a heavy pan and bring to the boil over a low heat, stirring constantly. Once the mixture has boiled, remove the pan from the heat.

3 Put the butter in a heatproof bowl and pour over the hot sugar and syrup mixture. Add the bicarbonate of soda and stir until the butter has melted. Beat in the egg, then stir in the flour. Mix thoroughly and then knead to form a smooth dough.

4 Divide the dough into four. Roll each out between sheets of baking parchment, to a 3mm/⅛in thickness. Stamp out angels using a cookie cutter.

5 Using a skewer, make a hole in the cookies through which ribbon can be threaded. Place on the baking sheets. Bake for 10–15 minutes, until golden. Transfer to a wire rack to cool.

6 For the decoration, beat the egg white. Whisk in icing sugar until a soft-peak consistency forms. Put the icing in a piping (icing) bag fitted with a plain nozzle and decorate the cookies. Add silver and gold balls. Thread ribbon through the holes.

Stained Glass Windows Energy 145kcal/612kJ; Protein 1.2g; Carbohydrate 26.4g, of which sugars 16.8g; Fat 4.6g, of which saturates 2.8g; Cholesterol 11mg; Calcium 22mg; Fibre 0.4g; Sodium 42mg.
Christmas Tree Angels Energy 147kcal/622kJ; Protein 1.9g; Carbohydrate 28.7g, of which sugars 16g; Fat 3.6g, of which saturates 2.1g; Cholesterol 15mg; Calcium 31mg; Fibre 0.5g; Sodium 45mg.

Christmas Cookies with Walnuts

At Christmas time, these are individually wrapped in small squares of brightly coloured tissue paper and arranged in large bowls. Transform them into gifts by wrapping five or six into packages and tying them with pretty coloured ribbons.

Makes 24
115g/4oz/½ cup lard, softened and diced
75g/3oz/¾ cup icing (confectioners') sugar
5ml/1 tsp vanilla extract
150g/5oz/1¼ cups unbleached plain (all-purpose) flour
75g/3oz/¾ cup broken walnuts, finely chopped

For the topping
50g/2oz/½ cup icing (confectioners') sugar
10ml/2 tsp ground cinnamon

1 Preheat the oven to 190°C/375°F/Gas 5. Lightly grease two baking sheets.

2 Place the lard in a large bowl and beat with an electric whisk until light and aerated. Gradually beat in 75g/3oz/¾ cup icing sugar, then add the vanilla extract and beat well.

3 Add the flour by hand, working it gently into the mixture. Do not be tempted to use a spoon or the mixture will be too sticky. Add the walnuts and mix in.

4 Divide the dough evenly into 24 small pieces, roll each into a ball and space well apart on baking sheets. Bake for 10–15 minutes, until golden. Leave to cool on wire racks.

5 Put the remaining icing sugar in a bowl and stir in the cinnamon. Add a few cookies at a time, shaking them in the icing sugar until they are heavily coated. Shake off the excess sugar. Serve wrapped in coloured paper.

> **Variation**
> *Pecan nuts or toasted almonds can be used instead of the walnuts, if you like.*

Festive Cookies

These cookies are great fun to make as gifts. For a change, omit the lemon rind and add 25g/1oz/¼ cup ground almonds and a few drops of almond extract.

Makes about 12
75g/3oz/6 tbsp butter
50g/2oz/½ cup icing (confectioners') sugar
grated rind of 1 lemon
1 egg yolk
175g/6oz/1½ cups plain (all-purpose) flour, plus extra for dusting
pinch of salt

To decorate
2 egg yolks
red and green food colourings

1 In a large bowl, beat together the butter, sugar and lemon rind until fluffy. Beat in the egg yolk and then sift in the flour and the salt. Knead to form a dough. Wrap in clear film (plastic wrap) and chill for 30 minutes.

2 Preheat the oven to 190°C/375°F/Gas 5. Lightly grease two large baking sheets.

3 On a lightly floured surface, roll out the dough thinly. Using a cookie cutter, stamp out the cookies. Transfer the cookies to the baking sheets.

4 Mark the tops with a holly leaf cutter and use a plain piping nozzle for the berries. Chill for about 10 minutes, until firm. Put each egg yolk into a cup. Mix red food colour into one and green into the other. Paint the leaves and berries.

5 Bake for 10–12 minutes, or until they begin to colour around the edges. Leave to cool slightly on the baking sheets, and then transfer them to a wire rack to cool completely.

> **Cook's Tip**
> *You can freeze the cookies, raw or baked. Baked cookies that have been frozen will benefit from being refreshed in the oven after they have thawed.*

Christmas Cookies with Walnuts Energy 141kcal/591kJ; Protein 1.7g; Carbohydrate 15.4g, of which sugars 9g; Fat 8.5g, of which saturates 2g; Cholesterol 4mg; Calcium 22mg; Fibre 0.5g; Sodium 1mg.
Festive Cookies Energy 118kcal/494kJ; Protein 1.7g; Carbohydrate 15.7g, of which sugars 4.6g; Fat 5.8g, of which saturates 3.4g; Cholesterol 30mg; Calcium 26mg; Fibre 0.5g; Sodium 39mg.

Festive Gingerbreads

These brightly decorated gingerbread cookies are fun to make and may be used as tasty edible Christmas tree decorations.

Makes 20

30ml/2 tbsp golden (light corn) syrup
15ml/1 tbsp black treacle (molasses)
50g/2oz/¼ cup light soft brown sugar
25g/1oz/2 tbsp butter
175g/6oz/1½ cups plain (all-purpose) flour, plus extra for dusting
¾ tsp bicarbonate of soda (baking soda)
½ tsp ground mixed (apple pie) spice
1½ tsp ground ginger
1 egg yolk

To decorate

small quantity royal icing
red, yellow and green food colourings
brightly coloured ribbons

1 Preheat the oven to 190°C/375°F/Gas 5. Line several baking sheets with baking parchment.

2 Put the syrup, treacle, sugar and butter into a pan. Heat gently, stirring occasionally, until the butter has melted.

3 Sift the flour, bicarbonate of soda and mixed spice and ginger into a bowl. Stir in the treacle mixture and the egg yolk. Mix to a soft dough. Knead on a lightly floured surface until smooth.

4 Roll out the dough thinly. Using cookie cutters, stamp out as many shapes as possible. Arrange well spaced on the baking sheets. Make a hole in the top of each.

5 Bake in the oven for 15–20 minutes, or until risen and golden. Leave to cool slightly before transferring to a wire rack.

6 Divide the royal icing into four and colour one part red, one part yellow and one part green using food colouring. Fill a piping (icing) bag fitted with a writing nozzle with each.

7 Pipe lines, dots, and zig-zags on the cookies. Leave to dry. Thread ribbons through the holes in the cookies.

Christmas Cookies

These cookies taste rich and buttery. If you want Christmas cookies for adults you could add your choice of Christmas spices to the recipe.

Makes 30

175g/6oz/¾ cup unsalted butter, at room temperature
275g/10oz/scant 1½ cups caster (superfine) sugar
1 egg
1 egg yolk
5ml/1 tsp vanilla extract
grated rind of 1 lemon
pinch of salt
275g/10oz/2½ cups plain (all-purpose) flour, plus extra for dusting

For the decoration

coloured icing
small decorations

1 Preheat the oven to 350°F/180°C/Gas 4.

2 In a large bowl, beat the butter until soft. Add the sugar and continue beating until light and fluffy.

3 Using a wooden spoon, gradually mix in the whole egg and the egg yolk. Add the vanilla extract, lemon rind and salt. Stir until thoroughly combined.

4 Add the flour and stir until blended. Gather the mixture into a ball with your fingertips, wrap in cling film (plastic wrap), and chill in the refrigerator for at least 30 minutes.

5 On a lightly floured surface, roll out the mixture to 3mm/⅛in thick.

6 Stamp out Christmas shapes or rounds with cookie cutters and place on a non-stick baking sheet. Gather up the trimmings and continue rolling and stamping out cookies until the mixture has been used up.

7 Bake the cookies in the oven for about 8 minutes until lightly coloured. Leave to stand for a few minutes before transferring to a wire rack with a metal spatula to cool completely. Ice and decorate, as you like.

Festive Gingerbreads Energy 2kcal/217kJ; Protein 0.6g; Carbohydrate 6.3g, of which sugars 2.4g; Fat 2.9g, of which saturates 1.8g; Cholesterol 9.4mg; Calcium 9.6mg; Fibre 0.1g; Sodium 20mg.
Christmas Cookies Energy 118kcal/495kJ; Protein 1.3g; Carbohydrate 17.3g, of which sugars 10.1g; Fat 5.3g, of which saturates 3.2g; Cholesterol 26mg; Calcium 21mg; Fibre 0.3g; Sodium 39mg.

New Mexico Christmas Biscochitos

The aniseed flavour in these cookies is very pronounced, and the addition of brandy makes them a distinctly adult cookie.

Makes 24
175g/6oz/1½ cups plain
    (all-purpose) flour, plus extra
    for dusting
5ml/1 tsp baking powder

pinch of salt
50g/2oz/¼ cup unsalted
    butter, softened
90g/3½oz/scant ½ cup sugar
1 egg
5ml/1 tsp whole aniseed
15ml/1 tbsp brandy
50g/2oz/¼ cup sugar mixed with
    2.5ml/½ tsp ground cinnamon,
    for sprinkling

1 Sift together the flour, baking powder and salt into a large bowl. Set aside.

2 In another bowl, beat the butter with the sugar until soft and fluffy. Add the egg, aniseed and brandy and beat until incorporated. Fold in the dry ingredients until just blended to a dough. Shape into a ball, wrap in clear film (plastic wrap) and chill in the refrigerator for at least 30 minutes.

3 Preheat the oven to 180°C/350°F/Gas 4. Lightly grease two baking sheets.

4 On a lightly floured surface, roll out the chilled cookie dough to about 3mm/⅛in thick.

5 Using cookie cutters, stamp out shapes from the dough.

6 Place the cookies on the prepared baking sheets and sprinkle lightly with the cinnamon sugar.

7 Bake for about 10 minutes, until just barely golden. Leave to cool on the baking sheets for 5 minutes, then, using a metal spatula, carefully transfer the cookies to a wire rack to cool completely.

8 The cookies can be stored in an airtight container for up to 1 week.

Cinnamon and Orange Tuiles

The tempting aroma of cinnamon and orange evokes a feeling of Christmas and, served with coffee, these chocolate dipped tuiles are perfect for festive occasions.

Serves 15
2 egg whites
90g/3½oz/½ cup caster
    (superfine) sugar
7.5ml/1½ tsp ground cinnamon

finely grated rind of 1 orange
50g/2oz/½ cup plain
    (all-purpose) flour
75g/3oz/6 tbsp butter, melted

For the dipping chocolate
75g/3oz plain (semisweet)
    chocolate
45ml/3 tbsp milk
75–90ml5–6 tbsp double (heavy)
    or whipping cream

1 Preheat the oven to 200°C/400°F/Gas 6. Lightly grease two or three large baking sheets.

2 In a grease-free glass bowl, whisk the egg whites until softly peaking, then whisk in the sugar until smooth and glossy.

3 Add the cinnamon and orange rind, sift over the flour and fold in with the melted butter. When well blended, add 15ml/ 1 tbsp of recently boiled water to thin the mixture.

4 Place 4–5 teaspoons of the mixture on each tray, well apart. Flatten out and bake, one sheet at a time, for 7 minutes, until just golden. Cool for a few seconds, then remove from the sheet with a metal spatula and immediately roll around the handle of a wooden spoon. Place on a rack to cool.

5 Melt the chocolate in the milk, then stir in the cream. Dip one or both ends of the cookies in the chocolate and leave to cool and set.

Variation
You could substitute 5ml/1 tsp ground ginger or a few drops of peppermint extract for the cinnamon, if you like.

New Mexico Christmas Biscochitos Energy 68kcal/286kJ; Protein 1g; Carbohydrate 11.8g, of which sugars 6.2g; Fat 2g, of which saturates 1.2g; Cholesterol 12mg; Calcium 15mg; Fibre 0.2g; Sodium 16mg. Cinnamon and Orange Tuiles Energy 125kcal/523kJ; Protein 1.2g; Carbohydrate 12.3g, of which sugars 9.7g; Fat 8.3g, of which saturates 5.2g; Cholesterol 18mg; Calcium 17mg; Fibre 0.2g; Sodium 42mg.

Festive Orange and Almond Cookies

Lightly spiced and delicately flavoured with orange flower water and almonds, these crisp little crescents are perfect for parties and festive occasions such as christenings and weddings.

Makes about 20
115g/4oz/1/2 cup unsalted
   butter, softened
pinch of ground nutmeg

10ml/2 tsp orange flower water
50g/2oz/1/2 cup icing
   (confectioners') sugar, plus
   extra for dusting
90g/31/2oz/3/4 cup plain
   (all-purpose) flour
115g/4oz/1 cup ground almonds
25g/1oz/1/4 cup whole almonds,
   toasted and chopped

1 Preheat the oven to 160°C/325°F/Gas 3. Line two large baking sheets with baking parchment.

2 In a large bowl, beat the butter until soft and creamy. Add the nutmeg and orange flower water and beat to combine. Add the icing sugar and beat the mixture until fluffy.

3 Add the flour, ground and chopped almonds and mix well, then use your hands to bring the mixture together to form a dough, being careful not to overwork it.

4 Shape pieces of dough into sausages about 7.5cm/3in long. Curve each one into a crescent and place, spaced well apart, on the prepared baking sheets.

5 Bake for about 15 minutes, or until firm but still pale in colour. Leave to stand for about 5 minutes, then dust with a little icing sugar and, using a metal spatula, transfer the cookies to a wire rack to cool completely.

Cook's Tip
Made from the blossoms of the bitter orange, orange flower water has a wonderful fragrance that lends an exotic touch to these cookies. It is widely available from supermarkets.

Jewelled Shortbread Fingers

These shortbread fingers are made using a classic, buttery shortbread base, drizzled with icing and decorated with sparkling, crushed sweets and glistening gold or silver balls.

Makes 14
90g/31/2oz/7 tbsp unsalted
   butter, diced
175g/6oz/11/2 cups plain
   (all-purpose) flour

50g/2oz/1/4 cup caster
   (superfine) sugar

To decorate
150g/5oz/11/4 cups icing
   (confectioners') sugar
10–15ml/2–3 tsp lemon juice
coloured boiled sweets
   (hard candies)
gold or silver balls

1 Preheat the oven to 160°C/325°F/Gas 3. Lightly grease an 18cm/7in square shallow baking tin (pan).

2 Put the butter and flour in a food processor and process until the mixture resembles breadcrumbs. Add the sugar and process until the ingredients form a dough.

3 Put the dough in the baking tin and press down in an even layer. Bake for 35 minutes, or until just beginning to colour. Leave to cool in the tin.

4 To make the topping, put the icing sugar in a bowl, add lemon juice to make a thick paste that just holds its shape.

5 Tap the boiled sweets (in their wrappers) with a rolling pin to break them up. Unwrap the sweets and put in a bowl.

6 Turn out the shortbread base on to a board. Cut in half, then across into fingers. Drizzle with the icing, then sprinkle with the sweets and gold or silver balls. Leave to set.

Cook's Tip
Use a serrated knife and a sawing action to cut the shortbread.

Festive Orange and Almond Cookies Energy 131kcal/546kJ; Protein 2.3g; Carbohydrate 9.5g, of which sugars 3.5g; Fat 9.6g, of which saturates 2.9g; Cholesterol 16mg; Calcium 28mg; Fibre 0.7g; Sodium 5mg. **Jewelled Shortbread Fingers** Energy 147kcal/618kJ; Protein 1.3g; Carbohydrate 24.7g, of which sugars 15.2g; Fat 5.5g, of which saturates 3.4g; Cholesterol 14mg; Calcium 26mg; Fibre 0.4g; Sodium 40mg.

Mexican Wedding Cookies

Almost hidden beneath their veil of icing sugar, these little shortbread cookies are traditionally served at weddings, and are absolutely delicious. Serve them after dinner with coffee.

Makes 30
225g/8oz/1 cup butter, softened
175g/6oz/1½ cups icing (confectioners') sugar
5ml/1 tsp vanilla extract
300g/11oz/2¾ cups plain (all-purpose) flour
pinch of salt
150g/5oz/1¼ cups pecan nuts, finely chopped

1 Preheat the oven to 190°C/375°F/Gas 5. Lightly grease two baking sheets.

2 In a large mixing bowl, beat the butter until it is light and fluffy, then beat in 115g/4oz/1 cup of the icing sugar, with the vanilla extract.

3 Gradually add the flour and salt to the creamed mixture, using a wooden spoon at first until it starts to form a dough. Add the finely chopped pecans with the remaining flour. Pull the dough together with your hands and then knead the dough lightly.

4 Divide the dough into 30 equal pieces and roll them into balls. Space about 5mm/¼in apart on baking sheets. Press each ball lightly with your thumb, to flatten it slightly.

5 Bake the cookies for 10–15 minutes, until they start to brown. Leave to stand on the baking sheets for 10 minutes, then, using a metal spatula, carefully transfer the cookies to wire racks to cool completely.

6 Put the remaining icing sugar in a bowl. Add a few cookies at a time, shaking them in the icing sugar until they are heavily coated.

7 Store them, interleaved with baking parchment in an airtight container for up to 3 days.

Cinnamon-spiced Wedding Cookies

These melt-in-the-mouth cinnamon and vanilla cookies are also served at Mexican weddings. They are perfect for serving with coffee.

Makes about 40
225g/8oz/1 cup butter, softened
50g/2oz/¼ cup caster (superfine) sugar

5ml/1 tsp vanilla extract
225g/8oz/2 cups plain (all-purpose) flour
115g/4oz/1 cup cornflour (cornstarch)

For the topping
50g/2oz/½ cup icing (confectioners') sugar
5ml/1 tsp ground cinnamon

1 Preheat the oven to 160°C/325°F/Gas 3. Lightly grease two or three baking sheets.

2 In a bowl, beat the butter with the caster sugar until light and fluffy. Add the vanilla extract. Sift the flour and cornflour together over the mixture and gradually work into the creamed butter and sugar mixture in batches.

3 Roll heaped teaspoons of the mixture into balls and place on the baking sheets. Bake for 30 minutes, or until pale golden. Loosen on the baking tray and leave to cool slightly.

4 Sift the icing sugar and ground cinnamon into a bowl. While the cookies are still warm, toss them in the icing sugar mixture. Leave on a wire rack to cool.

5 Store in an airtight container for up to 2 weeks.

> **Variation**
> *For a special surprise, shape the dough balls around squares of chocolate or pieces of crystallized (candied) fruit.*

> **Cook's Tip**
> *The cookie mixture can be prepared in a food processor.*

Mexican Wedding Cookies Energy 147kcal/615kJ; Protein 1.5g; Carbohydrate 14.2g, of which sugars 6.5g; Fat 9.8g, of which saturates 4.2g; Cholesterol 16mg; Calcium 22mg; Fibre 0.5g; Sodium 46mg.
Cinnamon-spiced Wedding Cookies Energy 81kcal/339kJ; Protein 0.6g; Carbohydrate 9.7g, of which sugars 2.7g; Fat 4.7g, of which saturates 2.9g; Cholesterol 12mg; Calcium 11mg; Fibre 0.2g; Sodium 36mg.

Persian Celebration Cookies

These prettily decorated cookies are traditionally served on special occasions with black tea. However, they taste as good with coffee or even a glass of chilled dry white wine.

Makes about 22
75g/3oz/³⁄₄ cup icing
  (confectioners') sugar, sifted
225g/8oz/1 cup unsalted
  butter, softened
300g/10oz/2¹⁄₂ cups rice flour
75g/3oz/³⁄₄ cup self-raising
  (self-rising) flour
1 egg yolk
15ml/1 tbsp rose water

For the topping
150g/5oz/1¹⁄₄ cups icing
  (confectioners') sugar, sifted
rose water
pink food colouring
crystallized rose petals or violets
  or pink sugar balls or
  sugar sprinkles

1 In a large bowl, beat together the sugar and butter until light and fluffy. Add the flours, egg yolk and rose water and mix first with a wooden spoon and then with your hands until a dough forms. Gather into a ball. Wrap with cling film (plastic wrap) and chill for 30 minutes.

2 Preheat the oven to 160°C/325°F/Gas 3. Line two baking sheets with baking parchment.

3 Shape small pieces of the dough into balls. Place well apart on the prepared baking sheets and flatten each one slightly.

4 Bake for 15–20 minutes, until firm but still quite pale in colour. Leave to cool completely on the baking sheets.

5 To make the topping, put the icing sugar into a bowl and add just enough rose water to mix to a thick, flowing consistency. Add just a light touch of pink food colouring to make a very pale shade.

6 Drizzle the icing in random squiggles and circles over all the cookies. Place a few crystallized rose petals or violets or pink sugar balls on top, or sprinkle with a little sugar sprinkles. Leave to set completely.

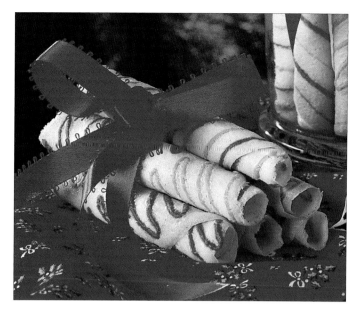

Striped Party Cookies

These cookies can be made in different flavours and colours and look wonderful tied in bundles or packed into decorative jars or boxes. Eat them with ice cream or light desserts.

Makes 25
2 egg whites
90g/3¹⁄₂oz/¹⁄₂ cup caster
  (superfine) sugar
50g/2oz/¹⁄₂ cup plain
  (all-purpose) flour
50g/2oz/¹⁄₄ cup unsalted
  butter, melted
25g/1oz white chocolate, melted
red and green food colouring

1 Preheat the oven to 190°C/375°F/Gas 5. Line two baking sheets with baking parchment. Lightly grease several wooden spoon handles.

2 Place the egg whites in a bowl and whisk until stiff. Add the sugar gradually, whisking well after each addition.

3 Add the flour and melted butter and whisk until smooth. Drop four separate teaspoonfuls of the mixture on to the prepared baking sheets and spread into thin rounds.

4 Divide the melted chocolate in half and add a little food colouring to each half. Fill piping (icing) bags with coloured chocolate. Pipe lines or zig-zags of green and red chocolate over each round of cookie mixture.

5 Bake one sheet at a time for about 3 minutes, until pale golden. Loosen the rounds with a metal spatula and return to the oven for a few seconds to soften.

6 Taking one cookie at a time, turn it over and roll it around a spoon handle. Leave for a few seconds to set. Repeat to shape the remaining cookies.

7 When the cookies are set, slip them off the spoon handles on to a wire rack. If the cookies are too hard to shape, simply return them to the oven for a few seconds to soften. Store in an airtight container for 2–3 days.

Persian Celebration Cookies Energy 180kcal/753kJ; Protein 1.4g; Carbohydrate 24.3g, of which sugars 10.8g; Fat 8.8g, of which saturates 5.4g; Cholesterol 31mg; Calcium 24mg; Fibre 0.4g; Sodium 76mg. **Striped Party Cookies** Energy 42kcal/177kJ; Protein 0.5g; Carbohydrate 5.9g, of which sugars 4.4g; Fat 2g, of which saturates 1.2g; Cholesterol 4mg; Calcium 8mg; Fibre 0.1g; Sodium 18mg.

Black Russian Party Cookies

The ingredients of the famous cocktail – coffee and vodka – flavour these fabulous and unusual adult party cookies.

Makes 16

30ml/2 tbsp ground espresso or other strong-flavoured coffee
60ml/4 tbsp near-boiling milk
115g/4oz/½ cup butter
115g/4oz/½ cup soft light brown sugar
1 egg
225g/8oz/2 cups plain (all-purpose) flour
5ml/1 tsp baking powder
pinch of salt

For the icing

115g/4oz/1 cup icing (confectioners') sugar
about 25ml/1½ tbsp vodka

1 Preheat the oven to 180°C/350°F/Gas 4. Lightly grease two baking sheets.

2 Put the coffee in a small bowl and pour the hot milk over. Leave to infuse (steep) for 4 minutes, then strain through a fine sieve (strainer) and leave to cool.

3 Beat the butter and sugar together until light and fluffy. Gradually beat in the egg. Sift the flour, baking powder and salt together and fold in with the coffee-flavoured milk to make a fairly stiff mixture.

4 Place dessertspoonfuls of the mixture on the baking sheets, spacing them slightly apart to allow room for a little spreading. Bake the cookies for about 15 minutes, until lightly browned. Using a metal spatula, carefully transfer the cookies to a wire rack to cool.

5 To make the icing, mix the icing sugar and enough vodka together to make a thick icing. Spoon into a small baking parchment piping (icing) bag.

6 Snip off the end of the piping bag and lightly drizzle the icing over the top of each cookie. Leave the icing to set before serving.

Celebration Hearts and Stars

These soft, sweet cookies have a wonderfully chewy texture and a deliciously warm, fragrant flavour. Serve with coffee at the end of a festive meal, or make them as a gift on a special occasion.

50g/2oz/1½ tbsp golden (light corn) syrup
50g/2oz/1½ tbsp black treacle (molasses)
100g/11 1oz/3½ cups self-rising (self-rising) flour, plus extra for dusting
10ml/2 tsp ground ginger

Makes about 25

115g/4oz/½ cup unsalted butter, softened
115g/4oz/½ cup light muscovado (brown) sugar
1 egg

For the toppings

200g/7oz plain (semisweet) or milk chocolate
150g/5oz/1¼ cups icing (confectioners') sugar, sifted

1 In a large bowl, beat together the butter and sugar until light and creamy.

2 Beat in the egg, syrup and treacle, stirring carefully after each addition. Sift in the flour and ginger and mix to form a firm dough. Chill for 20 minutes.

3 Preheat the oven to 180°C/350°F/Gas 4. Lightly grease two large baking sheets.

4 Roll out the dough on a lightly floured surface to just under 1cm/½in thick and use cookie cutters to stamp out heart and star shapes. Place, spaced slightly apart to allow for spreading during baking, on the prepared baking sheets and bake in the oven for about 10 minutes, or until risen. Leave to cool on a wire rack.

5 To make the toppings, melt the chocolate in a heatproof bowl set over a pan of barely simmering water. Use the melted chocolate to coat the heart-shaped cookies.

6 Put the icing sugar into a bowl and mix with warm water to make a coating consistency, then use this to glaze the stars.

Black Russian Party Cookies Energy 168kcal/706kJ; Protein 2g; Carbohydrate 26.2g, of which sugars 15.5g; Fat 6.5g, of which saturates 3.9g; Cholesterol 27mg; Calcium 35mg; Fibre 0.4g; Sodium 51mg.
Celebration Hearts and Stars Energy 185kcal/781kJ; Protein 2.3g; Carbohydrate 31.5g, of which sugars 19.3g; Fat 6.5g, of which saturates 3.8g; Cholesterol 18mg; Calcium 44mg; Fibre 0.7g; Sodium 41mg.

Italian Glazed Lemon Party Rings

These delicately flavoured, pretty cookies look almost too good to eat. The icing is flavoured with Italian liqueur, so they are strictly for adults.

Makes about 16
200g/7oz/1¾ cups self-raising (self-rising) flour
50g/2oz/¼ cup unsalted butter, at room temperature, diced
25ml/1½ tbsp milk
50g/2oz/¼ cup caster (superfine) sugar
finely grated rind of ½ lemon
1 egg, beaten

For the topping
150g/5oz/1¼ cups icing (confectioners') sugar, sifted
30ml/2 tbsp Limoncello liqueur
15ml/1 tbsp chopped candied angelica

1 Preheat the oven to 180°C/350°F/Gas 4. Lightly grease two large baking sheets.

2 Put the flour into a bowl and rub in the butter with your fingertips until the mixture resembles breadcrumbs.

3 Put the milk, sugar and lemon rind in a small pan and stir over a low heat until the sugar has dissolved. Add to the flour mixture, together with the egg, and mix well. Knead lightly until smooth.

4 Roll walnut-size pieces of dough into strands 15cm/6in long. Twist two strands together and join the ends to make a circle. Place on the prepared baking sheets and bake for 15–20 minutes, or until golden.

5 To make the topping, stir the icing sugar and liqueur together. Dip the top of each cookie into the topping and sprinkle with angelica.

> **Variation**
> If you are baking these cookies for children, use lemon syrup instead of the liqueur.

Festival Shortbreads

This Greek version of shortbread is one of the world's most popular sweet treats.

Makes 24–28
250g/9oz/generous 1 cup unsalted (sweet) butter
65g/2½oz/⅓ cup caster (superfine) sugar
1 large (US extra large) egg yolk
30ml/2 tbsp Greek ouzo, Pernod or brandy
115g/4oz unblanched almonds
65g/2½oz/⅔ cup cornflour (cornstarch)
300g/11oz/2¾ cups plain (all-purpose) flour

For the decoration
about 60ml/4tbsp triple-distilled rose-water
500g/1¼lb/5 cups icing (confectioners') sugar

1 Preheat the oven to 180°C/350°F/Gas 4. Lightly grease two or three baking sheets.

2 In a bowl, beat together the butter and add the sugar until light and fluffy. Add the egg yolk and alcohol and mix well.

3 Grind the almonds in a processor or nut grinder to a coarse texture and mix into the butter mixture. Beat in the cornflour and enough flour to give a firm dough-like mixture.

4 Divide the dough into 24–28 equal portions. Form each into a crescent around a finger. Place on the prepared baking sheets, spaced well apart, and bake in the oven for 20–25 minutes. Check the cookies during baking and lower the oven temperature if they seem to be colouring too much. Loosen with a metal spatula and leave on the baking sheets to cool completely.

5 Pour the rose water into a small bowl and tip the sifted icing sugar into a larger one. Dip a cookie briefly first into the rose water and then into the icing sugar. Repeat until all the cookies are thoroughly coated. Set aside on waxed paper until dry.

6 Place in an airtight container, packing the cookies loosely or they will stick together.

Italian Glazed Lemon Party Rings Energy 125kcal/530kJ; Protein 1.7g; Carbohydrate 23.5g, of which sugars 14g; Fat 3.1g, of which saturates 1.8g; Cholesterol 19mg; Calcium 28mg; Fibre 0.4g; Sodium 25mg. Festival Shortbreads Energy 220kcal/926kJ; Protein 2.1g; Carbohydrate 31.9g, of which sugars 21.5g; Fat 10g, of which saturates 4.9g; Cholesterol 26mg; Calcium 38mg; Fibre 0.6g; Sodium 58mg.

Tiramisù Special Occasion Cookies

These delicate cookies taste like the wonderful Italian dessert with its flavours of coffee, chocolate, rum and rich creamy custard.

Makes 14

50g/2oz/¼ cup butter, at room
   temperature, diced
90g/3½oz/½ cup caster
   (superfine) sugar
1 egg, beaten
50g/2oz/½ cup plain
   (all-purpose) flour

For the filling

15ml/1 tbsp dark rum
2.5ml/½ tsp instant
   coffee powder
150g/5oz/⅔ cup mascarpone
15ml/1 tbsp light muscovado
   (brown) sugar

For the topping

75g/3oz white chocolate
15ml/1 tbsp milk
30ml/2 tbsp crushed
   chocolate flakes

1 To make the filling, in a large bowl, mix together the rum and coffee powder, stirring well until the coffee has dissolved. Add the mascarpone and muscovado sugar and beat well. Cover with clear film (plastic wrap) and chill until required.

2 Preheat the oven to 200°C/400°F/Gas 6. Line two or three baking sheets with baking parchment.

3 To make the cookies, in a bowl, beat together the butter and sugar until light and fluffy. Add the beaten egg and mix well. Stir in the flour and mix thoroughly.

4 Put the mixture into a piping (pastry) bag fitted with a 1.5cm/½in plain nozzle and pipe 28 small heaps on to the baking sheets, spaced slightly apart. Cook for about 6–8 minutes until firm in the centre and just beginning to brown on the edges. Set aside to cool.

5 Spread a little of the filling on to half the cookies and place the other halves on top.

6 Put the chocolate and milk in a heatproof bowl and melt over a pan of hot water. Spread evenly over the cookies, then sprinkle with crushed chocolate flakes to finish.

Party Cookies with Praline

These almond cookies, filled with vanilla cream and coated in praline, are just the thing for an afternoon gathering of friends.

Makes 17–18

150g/5oz/1¼ cups plain
   (all-purpose) flour
75g/3oz/¾ cup ground almonds
75g/3oz/6 tbsp unsalted
   butter, at room
   temperature, diced
1 egg yolk
5ml/1 tsp vanilla extract
icing (confectioners') sugar, sifted,
   for dusting

For the praline

25g/1oz/¼ cup whole blanched
   almonds
50g/2oz/¼ cup caster
   (superfine) sugar

For the filling

150g/5oz/1¼ cups icing
   (confectioners') sugar, sifted
75g/3oz/6 tbsp unsalted
   butter, at room
   temperature, diced
5ml/1 tsp vanilla extract

1 To make the praline, lightly oil a baking sheet and place the almonds on it. Melt the sugar in a non-stick pan over a very low heat until it turns dark golden brown. Pour immediately over the almonds. Set aside to cool. Crush the praline finely.

2 Preheat the oven to 160°C/325°F/Gas 3. Line three baking sheets with baking parchment.

3 Put the flour, ground almonds and butter in a bowl. Rub together. Add the egg and vanilla and work together using your hands to make a soft dough. Roll out to 5mm/¼in thick on baking parchment. Using a 5cm/2in round cookie cutter, stamp out rounds and place them on the prepared baking sheets.

4 Bake for about 15–20 minutes, until golden brown. Leave to stand for 5 minutes to firm up. Transfer to a wire rack to cool.

5 To make the filling, beat together the icing sugar, butter and vanilla until creamy. Use to sandwich the cookies in pairs. Roll the edges of each cookie in the praline until thickly coated. Dust the tops of the cookies with icing sugar.

Tiramisù Special Occasion Cookies Energy 124kcal/519kJ; Protein 2.3g; Carbohydrate 14.1g, of which sugars 11.4g; Fat 6.6g, of which saturates 4g; Cholesterol 26mg; Calcium 27mg; Fibre 0.1g; Sodium 34mg. Party Cookies with Praline Coating Energy 172kcal/717kJ; Protein 2.2g; Carbohydrate 18.5g, of which sugars 12g; Fat 10.4g, of which saturates 4.7g; Cholesterol 29mg; Calcium 34mg; Fibre 0.7g; Sodium 53mg.

Summer Shortcakes

Irresistibly pretty, these delicious cookies are the perfect treat for a special summer occasion.

Makes 6
75g/3oz/³⁄₄ cup plain
   (all-purpose) flour
50g/2oz/4 tbsp butter, diced
25g/1oz/2 tbsp caster
   (superfine) sugar
grated rind of ¹⁄₂ orange
extra sugar, for sprinkling

For the filling
175g/6oz Greek (US strained
   plain) yogurt
15ml/1 tbsp icing (confectioners')
   sugar
250g/9oz/2¹⁄₄ cups strawberries
5ml/1 tsp Cointreau (optional)
2 sprigs of fresh mint, to decorate

1 Preheat the oven to 180°C/350°F/Gas 4.

2 Place the flour and butter in a bowl, and rub the fat into the flour until the mixture resembles fine breadcrumbs. Stir in the sugar and orange rind and mix to a dough.

3 Knead the dough lightly, then roll out on a floured surface to 5mm/¹⁄₄in thick. Stamp out 9cm/3¹⁄₂in fluted rounds with a cookie cutter.

4 Place the shapes on a baking sheet, prick with a fork and sprinkle with a little extra sugar. Bake for 10–12 minutes, until pale golden, then leave to cool on the baking sheet.

5 For the filling, blend the yogurt with the sugar. Reserve eight strawberries and process the rest in a blender, then press through a sieve (strainer).

6 Put 45ml/3 tbsp of the yogurt in a bowl and stir in the Cointreau, if using. Slice four strawberries and halve two, place on a plate and cover.

7 Spoon purée over the plates to cover completely. Put one cookie on each plate, spoon the reserved yogurt on top, then add the sliced strawberries. Top with the remaining cookies. Decorate with the yogurt mixed with Cointreau, strawberry halves and mint sprigs.

Raspberry and Rose Petal Shortcakes

Rose water-scented cream and fresh raspberries form the filling for this delectable cookie dessert.

Makes 6
115g/4oz/¹⁄₂ cup unsalted
   butter, softened
50g/2oz/¹⁄₄ cup caster
   (superfine) sugar
¹⁄₂ vanilla pod (bean), split and
   seeds reserved
115g/4oz/1 cup plain
   (all-purpose) flour, plus extra
   for dusting
50g/2oz/¹⁄₃ cup semolina
icing (confectioners') sugar,
   for dusting

For the filling
300ml/¹⁄₂ pint/1¹⁄₄ cups double
   (heavy) cream
15ml/1 tbsp icing (confectioners')
   sugar
2.5ml/¹⁄₂ tsp rose water
450g/1lb/2²⁄₃ cups raspberries

For the decoration
12 miniature roses, unsprayed
6 fresh mint sprigs
1 egg white, beaten
caster (superfine) sugar,
   for dusting

1 In a bowl, beat the butter, caster sugar and vanilla seeds until pale and fluffy. Sift in the flour and semolina and mix to a dough. Knead gently on a lightly dusted surface, then roll out thinly and prick with a fork. Stamp out 12 rounds with a 7.5cm/3in cookie cutter. Place on a lightly greased baking sheet and chill for 30 minutes.

2 To make the filling, whisk the cream with the sugar until soft peaks form. Fold in the rose water and chill until required.

3 Preheat the oven to 180°C/350°F/Gas 4. To make the decoration, paint the roses and leaves with the egg white. Dust with sugar, then dry on a wire rack.

4 Bake the cookies until lightly golden, about 15 minutes. Transfer to a wire rack and allow to cool.

5 Cover half the cookies with the filling, add the raspberries and top with a second cookie. Dust with icing sugar and decorate with the roses and mint.

Summer Shortcakes Energy 175kcal/734kJ; Protein 34.6g; Carbohydrate 198.1g, of which sugars 61.7g; Fat 10g, of which saturates 5.9g; Cholesterol 17.8mg; Calcium 73mg; Fibre 0.9g; Sodium 74.5mg.
Raspberry and Rose Petal Shortcakes Energy 547kcal/2273kJ; Protein 4.7g; Carbohydrate 37.1g, of which sugars 16g; Fat 43.2g, of which saturates 26.8g; Cholesterol 109mg; Calcium 81mg; Fibre 2.7g; Sodium 132mg.

Brandy Snaps with Cream

Brandy snaps were once considered a special treat for high days and holidays.

Makes about 12
50g/2oz/4 tbsp butter
50g/2oz/¼ cup caster (superfine) sugar
30ml/2 tbsp golden (light corn) syrup
50g/2oz/½ cup plain (all-purpose) flour
2.5ml/½ tsp ground ginger
5ml/1 tsp brandy
150ml/¼ pint/⅔ cup double (heavy) or whipping cream

1 Preheat the oven to 180°C/350°F/Gas 4. Line two or three baking sheets with baking parchment.

2 Gently heat the butter, sugar and golden syrup in a pan until the butter has melted and the sugar has dissolved. Remove the pan from the heat.

3 Sift the flour and ginger and stir into the butter mixture with the brandy.

4 Put small spoonfuls of the mixture on the lined baking sheets, spacing them about 10cm/4in apart to allow for spreading. Bake for 7–8 minutes, or until bubbling. Meanwhile, grease the handles of several wooden spoons.

5 Allow the cookies to cool on the baking sheet for 1 minute, then loosen with a metal spatula and quickly roll around the spoon handles. Leave to set for 1 minute, before sliding them off the handles and cooling completely on a wire rack.

6 Whip the cream until soft peaks form, spoon into a piping (pastry) bag and pipe into both ends of each brandy snap.

> **Cook's Tip**
> *Store unfilled brandy snaps in an airtight container for up to 1 week. Fill with cream just before serving.*

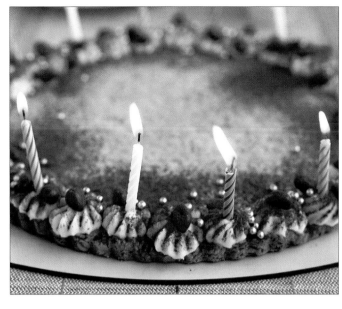

Giant Birthday Cookie

This enormous cookie is one for cookie-lovers of any age. Complete with candles and a personalized icing message, if you like, it makes the perfect centrepiece.

Makes one 28cm/11in cookie
175g/6oz/ ¾ cup unsalted butter, at room temperature, diced
125g/4¼oz/⅔ cup light muscovado (brown) sugar
1 egg yolk
175g/6oz/1½ cups plain (all-purpose) flour
5ml/1 tsp bicarbonate of soda (baking soda)
finely grated rind of 1 orange or lemon
75g/3oz/scant 1 cup rolled oats

For the decoration
125g/4¼oz/generous ½ cup cream cheese
225g/8oz/2 cups icing (confectioners') sugar
5–10ml/1–2 tsp lemon juice
birthday candles
white and milk chocolate-coated raisins or peanuts
unsweetened cocoa powder, for dusting
gold or silver balls, for sprinkling

1 Preheat the oven to 190°C/375°F/Gas 5. Lightly grease a 28cm/11in metal flan tin (tart pan) and place on a large baking sheet.

2 In a bowl, beat the butter and sugar together until pale and creamy. Stir in the egg yolk. Add the flour, bicarbonate of soda, grated rind and oats and beat well.

3 Turn the mixture into the tin and flatten. Bake for 15–20 minutes, until golden. Leave to cool in the tin. Slide the cookie from the tin on to a large serving plate.

4 To decorate, beat the cream cheese in a bowl, then add the icing sugar and 5ml/1 tsp of the lemon juice. Beat until smooth and peaking, adding more juice if required.

5 Spoon the mixture into a piping (pastry) bag and pipe swirls around the edge of the cookie. Press the candles into the frosting. Sprinkle with chocolate raisins or peanuts and dust with cocoa powder. Finish by sprinkling with gold or silver balls.

Brandy Snaps with Cream Energy 121kcal/505kJ; Protein 0.6g; Carbohydrate 11.7g, of which sugars 10g; Fat 7.9g, of which saturates 5g; Cholesterol 21mg; Calcium 16mg; Fibre 0.1g; Sodium 24mg.
Giant Birthday Cookie Energy 4188kcal/17559kJ; Protein 35.3g; Carbohydrate 557.4g, of which sugars 369.4g; Fat 217.5g, of which saturates 130.2g; Cholesterol 694mg; Calcium 649mg; Fibre 10.5g; Sodium 1496mg.

Mini Party Pizzas

These cute confections look amazingly realistic and older children will love them. They're fun to make and are simply a basic cookie topped with icing, marzipan and dark cherries.

Makes 16
90g/3¹/₂oz/7 tbsp unsalted
   butter, at room
   temperature, diced
90g/3¹/₂oz/¹/₂ cup golden caster
   (superfine) sugar
15ml/1 tbsp golden (light
   corn) syrup

175g/6oz/1¹/₂ cups self-raising
   (self-rising) flour, plus extra
   for dusting

For the topping
150g/5oz/1¹/₄ cups icing
   (confectioners') sugar
20–25ml/4–5 tsp lemon juice
red food colouring
90g/3¹/₂oz yellow marzipan,
   grated
8 dark glacé (candied)
   cherries, halved
a small piece of angelica,
   finely chopped

1 Preheat the oven to 180°C/350°F/Gas 4. Lightly grease two baking sheets.

2 In a bowl, beat together the butter and sugar until light and creamy. Beat in the syrup and then the flour.

3 Turn the mixture on to a lightly floured surface and cut into 16 even-size pieces. Roll each piece into a ball, then space well apart on the baking sheets, slightly flattening each one.

4 Bake for about 12 minutes, or until pale golden. Leave on the baking sheets for 3 minutes, then transfer to a wire rack to cool.

5 To make the topping, put the icing sugar in a bowl and stir in enough lemon juice to make a fairly thick, spreadable paste. Mix in enough food colouring to make the paste a deep red colour.

6 Spread the icing to within 5mm/¹/₄ in of the edges of the cookies. Sprinkle with the grated marzipan and place a halved cherry in the centre. Arrange a few pieces of chopped angelica on top so that the cookies resemble little cheese and tomato pizzas.

Chocolate Crispy Cookies

These little chocolate-coated cornflake cookies are always a hit with kids. They couldn't be easier to make – and are great for young aspiring cooks who want to get involved in the kitchen. The challenge is giving the cookies time to set before they're gobbled up by hungry helpers.

Makes 10
90g/3¹/₂oz milk chocolate
15ml/1 tbsp golden (light
   corn) syrup
90g/3¹/₂oz/3¹/₂ cups cornflakes
icing (confectioners') sugar,
   for dusting

1 Break the chocolate into a heatproof bowl and add the syrup. Set the bowl over a pan of gently simmering water and leave until melted, stirring frequently.

2 Put the cornflakes in a plastic bag and, using a rolling pin, lightly crush them, breaking the cornflakes into fairly small pieces.

3 Remove the bowl from the heat and add the cornflakes. Mix well until the cornflakes are thoroughly coated in the chocolate mixture.

4 Using paper muffin cases, put a spoonful of the chocolate mixture in the centre. Pack down firmly with the back of the spoon to make a thick cookie.

5 Continue making cookies in this way until all the mixture has been used up. Chill for 1 hour.

6 Put a little icing sugar in a small bowl. Lift each cookie from the paper and roll the edges in the icing sugar to finish.

Variation
You can also use other breakfast cereals, such as rice crispies or puffed rice. These may not need breaking up.

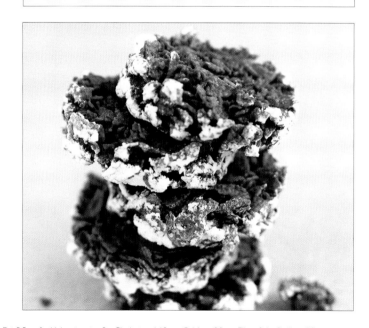

Mini Party Pizzas Energy 163kcal/687kJ; Protein 1.4g; Carbohydrate 28.8g, of which sugars 20.4g; Fat 5.5g, of which saturates 3g; Cholesterol 12mg; Calcium 28mg; Fibre 0.4g; Sodium 39mg.
Chocolate Crispy Cookies Energy 84kcal/355kJ; Protein 1.4g; Carbohydrate 14.2g, of which sugars 7.2g; Fat 2.8g, of which saturates 1.7g; Cholesterol 2mg; Calcium 21mg; Fibre 0.2g; Sodium 112mg.

Silly Faces

Silly faces are great fun for kids to decorate as they can experiment with different hairstyles and features.

Makes 14
115g/4oz/½ cup unsalted
    butter, at room
    temperature, diced
115g/4oz/generous ½ cup golden
    caster (superfine) sugar
1 egg
115g/4oz/scant ⅓ cup golden
    (light corn) syrup
400g/14oz/3½ cups self-raising
    (self-rising) flour, plus extra
    for dusting

For the decoration
75g/3oz/6 tbsp unsalted
    butter, at room
    temperature, diced
150g/5oz/1¼ cups icing
    (confectioners') sugar
strawberry, apple or
    liquorice strands
glacé (candied) cherries, halved
tubes red and black writing icing
small multi-coloured
    sweets (candies)

1 In a large bowl, beat together the butter and sugar until pale and creamy. Beat in the egg and golden syrup, then the flour.

2 Turn the mixture on to a lightly floured surface and knead until smooth. Wrap in clear film (plastic wrap) and chill.

3 Preheat the oven to 180°C/350°F/Gas 4. Lightly grease two baking sheets.

4 Roll out the dough on a floured surface and stamp out rounds using a 9cm/3½in cookie cutter. Transfer to the baking sheets. Bake for 10–12 minutes until turning golden around the edges. Transfer to a wire rack to cool.

5 To decorate, beat together the butter and icing sugar in a bowl until smooth and creamy. Spread a little buttercream along the top edge of each cookie, then secure the strawberry, apple or liquorice strands for hair. Use a dot of buttercream to secure a cherry for a nose. Pipe eyes and mouths using the icing, then add halved sweets, attached with buttercream, for the centres of the eyes.

Gingerbread House Cookies

For a party of young children, these gingerbread house cookies provide plenty of entertainment. You could incorporate a house decorating session as one of the party games, allowing the children to design their own house and take it home after the party.

Makes 10
115g/4oz/½ cup unsalted
    butter, at room
    temperature, diced
115g/4oz/½ cup light muscovado
    (brown) sugar

1 egg
115g/4oz/scant ⅓ cup black
    treacle (molasses) or golden
    (light corn) syrup
400g/14oz/3½ cups self-raising
    (self-rising) flour, plus extra
    for dusting
5ml/1tsp ground ginger (optional)

For the decoration
1 tube white decorating icing
1 tube pastel-coloured
    decorating icing
selection of small multi-coloured
    sweets (candies), sugar flowers
    and silver balls

1 In a large bowl, beat together the butter and sugar until pale and creamy. Beat in the egg and treacle or syrup, then add the flour and ginger, if using. Mix together to make a thick paste.

2 Turn the mixture on to a floured surface and knead until smooth. Wrap in clear film (plastic wrap) and chill.

3 Preheat the oven to 180°C/350°F/Gas 4. Lightly grease three baking sheets. On a piece of cardboard, draw an 11 × 8cm/ 4½ × 3¼in rectangle. Add a triangle to the top for the roof. Cut out the shape to use as a template.

4 Roll out the dough on a lightly floured surface. Using the template, cut out the houses. Transfer to the baking sheets. Bake for 12–15 minutes, until risen and golden. Transfer the cookies to a wire rack to cool.

5 Use the icing in the tubes to pipe roof tiles, window and door frames and other decorative touches. Secure sweets and decorations to finish, cutting them into smaller pieces if necessary.

Silly Faces Energy 300kcal/1261kJ; Protein 3.2g; Carbohydrate 48g, of which sugars 26.7g; Fat 11.9g, of which saturates 7.2g; Cholesterol 43mg; Calcium 116mg; Fibre 0.9g; Sodium 213mg.
Gingerbread House Cookies Energy 275kcal/1156kJ; Protein 4.5g; Carbohydrate 43.2g, of which sugars 12.7g; Fat 10.5g, of which saturates 6.2g; Cholesterol 44mg; Calcium 67mg; Fibre 1.2g; Sodium 79mg.

Jelly Bean Cones

Chocolate-dipped cookie cones filled with jelly beans make great treats for kids of all ages. The filled cones look very pretty arranged in glasses to keep them upright. This way they can double as a tasty treat and a delightful table decoration.

Makes 10
3 egg whites
90g/3½oz/½ cup caster (superfine) sugar
25g/1oz/2 tbsp unsalted butter, melted
40g/1½oz/⅓ cup plain (all-purpose) flour
30ml/2 tbsp single (light) cream
90g/3½oz plain (semisweet) chocolate
jelly beans or other small sweets (candies)

1 Preheat the oven to 190°C/375°F/Gas 5. Line two baking sheets with baking parchment and lightly grease them.

2 Put the egg whites and sugar in a bowl and whisk lightly until the egg whites are broken up. Add the melted butter, flour and cream and stir well to make a smooth batter.

3 Using a 15ml/1 tbsp measure, place a rounded tablespoon of the mixture on one side of a baking sheet. Spread to a 9cm/3½in round with the back of the spoon. Spoon more mixture on to the other side of the baking sheet and spread out to make another round.

4 Repeat with the cookie mixture on the second baking sheet.

5 Bake both sheets of cookies for about 8–10 minutes, until the edges are golden.

6 Peel away the paper from the baked cookies and roll them into cones. Leave to set. Continue until you have 10 cones.

7 Break the chocolate into a heatproof bowl set over a pan of simmering water and stir until melted. Dip the wide ends of the cookies in the chocolate and prop them inside narrow glasses to set, then fill with jelly beans or other sweets.

Secret Message Cookies

These fortune cookies are light and wafer-like, and what they lack in substance, they make up for in their fun capacity. These are great for older kids who can prepare birthday messages, jokes or predictions to tuck into the cookies as soon as they're baked.

Makes 18
3 egg whites
50g/2oz/½ cup icing (confectioners') sugar
40g/1½oz/3 tbsp unsalted butter, melted
50g/2oz/½ cup plain (all-purpose) flour

1 Preheat the oven to 200°C/400°F/Gas 6. Line and lightly grease two baking sheets with baking parchment. Cut a piece of paper into 18 small strips, measuring 6 × 2cm/2½ × ¾in. Write a message on each one.

2 Lightly whisk the egg whites and icing sugar until the whites are broken up. Add the melted butter and flour and beat until smooth.

3 Using a 10ml/2 tsp measure, spoon a little of the paste on to one baking sheet and spread to a 7.5cm/3in round with the back of a spoon. Add two more spoonfuls of mixture to the baking sheet and shape in the same way.

4 Bake for 6 minutes, until the cookies are golden. Meanwhile, prepare three more cookies on the second baking sheet. Remove the first batch of cookies from the oven and replace with the second batch.

5 Working quickly, peel a hot cookie from the paper and fold it in half, tucking a message inside the fold. Rest the cookie over the rim of a glass or bowl and, very gently, fold again. (It probably won't fold over completely.) Fold the remaining two cookies in the same way.

6 Continue to bake and shape the remaining cookies in the same way, one baking sheet at a time, until all the batter and messages have been used.

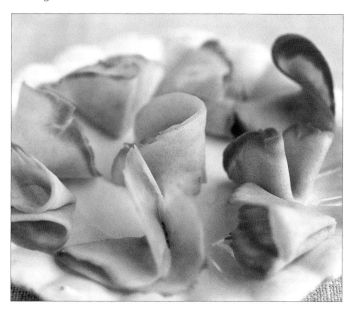

Jelly Bean Cones Energy 160kcal/670kJ; Protein 1.9g; Carbohydrate 18.3g, of which sugars 15.2g; Fat 9.3g, of which saturates 5.8g; Cholesterol 18mg; Calcium 18mg; Fibre 0.4g; Sodium 66mg.
Secret Message Cookies Energy 38kcal/160kJ; Protein 0.6g; Carbohydrate 5.1g, of which sugars 3g; Fat 1.9g, of which saturates 1.2g; Cholesterol 5mg; Calcium 6mg; Fibre 0.1g; Sodium 19mg.

Train Cookies

These cookies are so effective, especially if you let them trail across the party table. The quantity makes enough for two trains.

Makes 2 trains
150g/5oz/1¼ cups plain
   (all-purpose) flour
90g/3½oz/7 tbsp unsalted
   butter, chilled, diced
50g/2oz/½ cup golden icing
   (confectioners') sugar
1 egg yolk
5ml/1 tsp vanilla extract

For the decoration
40g/1½oz/3 tbsp butter, softened
75g/3oz/¾ cup golden icing
   (confectioners') sugar
blue food colouring
large bag of liquorice allsorts

1 Put the flour and butter in a food processor. Process until the mixture resembles fine breadcrumbs. Add the sugar, egg yolk and vanilla extract and blend to a smooth dough. Wrap in clear film (plastic wrap) and chill for 30 minutes.

2 Preheat the oven to 200°C/400°F/Gas 6. Lightly grease a large baking sheet.

3 Roll out the dough and cut 7.5 × 4cm/3 × 1½ in rectangles. Cut two 3 × 2cm/1¼ × ¾ in rectangles and secure to the top of the larger rectangles for the engines (locomotives).

4 Place on the baking sheet and bake for about 10 minutes, until pale golden around the edges. Leave for 2 minutes on the baking sheet, then transfer to a wire rack to cool completely.

5 To make butter icing, put the butter and icing sugar in a bowl with a dash of blue food colouring and beat until smooth and creamy.

6 Chop plenty of the liquorice allsorts into small dice.

7 Spread a little buttercream along one long side of all the cookies except the engines and press the chopped sweets (candies) into it. Halve some square sweets and secure to the engines for windows and another piece on the front of the engine for the funnel. Secure two wheels on all the cookies.

Cornflake Caramel Slice

A wickedly decadent caramel layer nestles between the base and the crispy cornflake topping. These cookies are simply irresistible – and fun to make too.

Makes 12
175g/6oz/¾ cup butter
150g/5oz/¾ cup caster
   (superfine) sugar
300g/10oz/2½ cups plain
   (all-purpose) flour
1 egg, beaten

For the topping
30ml/2 tbsp golden (light
   corn) syrup
400g/14oz can sweetened
   condensed milk
50g/2oz/¼ cup butter
90ml/6 tbsp sour cream
about 40g/1½oz/1½ cups
   cornflakes
icing (confectioners') sugar
   (optional), for sprinkling

1 Preheat the oven to 190°C/375°F/Gas 5. Lightly grease and line a 28 × 18cm/11 × 7in shallow cake tin (pan) with baking parchment.

2 Put the butter in a pan and melt over a low heat, and set aside.

3 Put the sugar and flour in a bowl. Add the beaten egg and melted butter and mix well. Press the mixture evenly into the base of the prepared tin.

4 Bake for about 20 minutes, until golden brown. Leave the base to cool completely in the tin.

5 For the topping, put the syrup, condensed milk and butter in a pan over a low heat for 10–15 minutes, stirring occasionally, until the mixture is thick and turns a golden caramel colour.

6 Remove the pan from the heat and stir in the sour cream. Spread the caramel topping evenly over the base. Sprinkle over the cornflakes and leave to set. Sprinkle lightly with icing sugar, if using, and cut into bars.

Train Cookies Energy 174kcal/728kJ; Protein 1.8g; Carbohydrate 24.8g, of which sugars 13.3g; Fat 8.1g, of which saturates 4.9g; Cholesterol 39mg; Calcium 32mg; Fibre 0.5g; Sodium 57mg.
Cornflake Caramel Slice Energy 397kcal/1667kJ; Protein 6.5g; Carbohydrate 56.3g, of which sugars 34.6g; Fat 17.8g, of which saturates 10.8g; Cholesterol 67mg; Calcium 151mg; Fibre 0.8g; Sodium 187mg.

Gold Medals

These cookies are great for kids' parties. You can present each child with a huge cookie medal when they sit down at the table or hand them out to winners of party games. Alternatively, they make great going-home gifts when children leave.

Makes 10

50g/2oz/¼ cup unsalted
   butter, at room
   temperature, diced

115g/4oz/generous ½ cup caster
   (superfine) sugar
1 egg
150g/5oz/1¼ cups self-raising
   (self rising) flour
1.5ml/¼ tsp bicarbonate of soda
   (baking soda)

For the decoration
1 egg white
200g/7oz/1¾ cups icing
   (confectioners') sugar
small brightly coloured
   sweets (candies)

1 Preheat the oven to 180°C/350°F/Gas 4. Lightly grease two baking sheets with a little butter.

2 In a bowl, beat together the butter and sugar until smooth and creamy, then beat in the egg. Add the flour and bicarbonate of soda and mix well to combine.

3 Place large spoonfuls of the mixture on the baking sheets, spacing them well apart to allow room for spreading. Bake for about 15 minutes, or until pale golden and slightly risen.

4 Using a skewer, make quite a large hole in each cookie, 1cm/½ in from the edge. Transfer to a wire rack and leave to cool.

5 To make the icing, beat the egg white in a bowl using a wooden spoon. Gradually beat in the icing sugar to make a thick paste that just holds its shape. Spoon the icing into a piping (icing) bag and snip off the tip.

6 Write an icing message in the centre of each cookie. Secure a circle of sweets around the edge of each cookie with a little of the icing, then leave to set.

7 Thread each cookie with a piece of ribbon.

Party Bracelets

These tiny cookies are threaded on to fine ribbon along with an assortment of brightly coloured sweets that have a ready-made hole in the middle. Make the cookies a day or two in advance and thread together with the sweets on the day of the party.

Makes 22

50g/2oz/¼ cup unsalted
   butter, at room
   temperature, diced

115g/4oz/generous ½ cup caster
   (superfine) sugar
5ml/1 tsp vanilla extract
pink or green food colouring
1 egg
200g/7oz/1¾ cups self-raising
   (self-rising) flour, plus extra
   for dusting

For the decoration
2 large bags of boiled sweets
   (hard candies) with holes in
   the centre
narrow pastel-coloured ribbon,
   for threading

1 Preheat the oven to 180°C/350°F/Gas 4. Lightly grease two baking sheets.

2 In a bowl, beat together the butter, sugar and vanilla extract until pale and creamy. Add a dash of pink or green food colouring, then beat in the egg. Add the flour and mix well to form a dough.

3 Turn the dough on to a lightly floured surface and roll out under the palms of your hands into two long, thin sausages, each about 40cm/16in long.

4 Slice each roll into 5mm/¼in rounds and space them slightly apart on the baking sheets. Chill for about 30 minutes.

5 Bake the cookies for about 8 minutes, until slightly risen and beginning to colour. Remove from the oven and, using a skewer, immediately make holes for the ribbon to be threaded through. Transfer the cookies to a wire rack to cool.

6 Thread the cookies on to 20cm/8in lengths of ribbon, alternating them with the sweets (about seven cookies on each ribbon). Tie the ends of the ribbons together in bows to finish.

Gold Medals Energy 221kcal/936kJ; Protein 2.5g; Carbohydrate 44.6g, of which sugars 33.2g; Fat 4.9g, of which saturates 2.8g; Cholesterol 30mg; Calcium 42mg; Fibre 0.5g; Sodium 46mg.
Party Bracelets Energy 72kcal/303kJ; Protein 1.2g; Carbohydrate 12.5g, of which sugars 5.6g; Fat 2.2g, of which saturates 1.3g; Cholesterol 13mg; Calcium 17mg; Fibre 0.3g; Sodium 18mg.

Peanut Butter and Jelly Cookies

These cookies are a twist on the original American peanut butter cookie and are a real hit with kids and adults alike. Give them a try – you'll love the crunchy nuts and sweet raspberry centres.

Makes 20–22

227g/8oz jar crunchy peanut butter (with no added sugar)
75g/3oz/6 tbsp unsalted butter, at room temperature, diced
90g/3½oz/½ cup golden caster (superfine) sugar
50g/2oz/¼ cup light muscovado (brown) sugar
1 large (US extra large) egg, beaten
150g/5oz/1¼ cups self-raising (self-rising) flour
250g/9oz/scant 1 cup seedless raspberry jam

1 Preheat the oven to 180°C/350°F/Gas 4. Line three or four baking sheets with baking parchment.

2 Put the peanut butter and unsalted butter in a large bowl and beat together until well combined and creamy.

3 Add the caster and muscovado sugars and beat well. Add the beaten egg and blend well. Sift in the flour and mix to a stiff dough.

4 Roll the dough into 40–44 walnut-size balls between the palms of your hands (make an even number of balls). Place the balls on the prepared baking sheets, spaced well apart, and gently flatten each one with a fork to make a rough-textured cookie with a lightly ridged surface. (Don't worry if the dough cracks slightly.)

5 Bake for 10–12 minutes, or until cooked but not browned. Using a metal spatula, carefully transfer the cookies to a wire rack to cool completely.

6 Spoon a little raspberry jam on to the flat side of one cookie and top with a second. Continue to sandwich the cookies in this way.

Chocolate Birds' Nests

These delightful crispy chocolate nests make a perfect Easter teatime treat and are a real favourite with kids. They're so quick and easy to make and young children can have great fun shaping the chocolate mixture inside the paper cases and tucking the pastel-coloured eggs inside.

Makes 12

200g/7oz milk chocolate
25g/1oz/2 tbsp unsalted butter, diced
90g/3½oz Shredded Wheat cereal
36 small pastel-coloured, sugar-coated chocolate eggs

1 Line the cups of a tartlet tray (muffin pan) with 12 decorative paper cake cases.

2 Break the milk chocolate into pieces and put in a bowl with the butter. Set the bowl over a pan of gently simmering water and stir frequently until the chocolate and butter have melted and the mixture is smooth. Remove from the heat and leave to cool for a few minutes.

3 Using your fingers, crumble the Shredded Wheat into the melted chocolate. Stir well until the cereal is completely coated in chocolate.

4 Divide the mixture among the paper cases, pressing it down gently with the back of a spoon, and make a slight indentation in the centre. Tuck three eggs into each nest and leave to set for about 2 hours.

Cook's Tip
Bags of sugar-coated chocolate eggs are widely available in supermarkets at Easter time. However, if you have trouble finding them out of season, try an old-fashioned sweet store. Often they have large jars of this type of sweet (candy), which they sell all year round. You can also buy small fluffy chicks to decorate the set nests.

Peanut Butter and Jelly Cookies Energy 169kcal/709kJ; Protein 3.4g; Carbohydrate 21g, of which sugars 15.3g; Fat 8.5g, of which saturates 3.2g; Cholesterol 18mg; Calcium 35mg; Fibre 0.8g; Sodium 89mg.
Chocolate Birds' Nests Energy 214kcal/896kJ; Protein 3.4g; Carbohydrate 24.4g, of which sugars 19g; Fat 12.1g, of which saturates 7.2g; Cholesterol 12mg; Calcium 77mg; Fibre 1g; Sodium 42mg.

Sweet Peanut Wafers

Delicate wafers filled with a sweet, peanut-flavoured buttercream make a fun, no-bake recipe that kids of any age can help with. Just remember to chill the wafer sandwiches after they have been assembled, otherwise they will be almost impossible to cut.

Makes 12
65g/2½oz/5 tbsp unsalted butter, at room temperature, diced
65g/2½oz/generous ½ cup icing (confectioners') sugar
115g/4oz/½ cup crunchy peanut butter
12 fan-shaped wafers
50g/2oz plain (semisweet) chocolate

1 In a bowl beat together the butter and icing sugar until light and creamy. Beat in the peanut butter until thoroughly combined.

2 Using a metal spatula, spread a thick layer of the mixture on to a wafer and spread to the edges.

3 Place another wafer on top and press it down very gently. Spread the top wafer with more buttercream, then place another wafer on top and press down gently. Be careful not to break the wafers.

4 Use the remaining peanut buttercream and wafers to assemble three more fans in the same way. Spread any remaining buttercream around the sides of the fans. Chill in the refrigerator for at least 30 minutes until firm.

5 Using a serrated knife, carefully slice each fan into three equal wedges and arrange in a single layer on a small tray.

6 Break the chocolate into pieces and put in a heatproof bowl placed over a pan of gently simmering water. Stir frequently until melted. Remove the bowl from the heat and leave to stand for a few minutes to cool slightly.

7 Drizzle lines of chocolate over the wafers, then leave to set in a cool place for at least 1 hour.

Jammie Bodgers

These buttery cookies are an absolute classic. Sandwiched with buttercream and a generous spoonful of strawberry jam, they make a perfect snack served with a glass of milk at teatime, or are equally good in a school lunchbox as a post-sandwich treat.

Makes 20
225g/8oz/2 cups plain (all-purpose) flour, plus extra for dusting
175g/6oz/¾ cup unsalted butter, chilled and diced
130g/4¼oz/⅔ cup caster (superfine) sugar
1 egg yolk

For the filling
50g/2oz/¼ cup unsalted butter, at room temperature, diced
90g/3½oz/scant 1 cup icing (confectioners') sugar
60–75ml/4–5 tbsp strawberry jam

1 Put the flour and butter in a food processor and process until the mixture resembles breadcrumbs. Add the sugar and egg yolk and process until the mixture starts to form a dough.

2 Knead on a floured surface until smooth. Shape into a ball, wrap in clear film (plastic wrap) and chill for 30 minutes.

3 Preheat the oven to 180°C/350°F/Gas 4. Lightly grease two baking sheets.

4 Roll out the dough thinly on a lightly floured surface and cut out 40 rounds using a 6cm/2½in cookie cutter.

5 Place half the cookie rounds on a prepared baking sheet. Using a small heart cutter stamp out the centres of the remaining rounds. Place on the second baking sheet. Bake the cookies for about 12 minutes, until pale golden, then transfer to a wire rack and leave to cool completely.

6 To make the buttercream, beat together the butter and sugar until smooth and creamy. Spread a little buttercream on to each whole cookie. Spoon a little jam on to the buttercream, then gently press the cut-out cookies on top.

Jammie Bodgers Energy 166kcal/695kJ; Protein 1.2g; Carbohydrate 22.4g, of which sugars 13.8g; Fat 8.6g, of which saturates 5.4g; Cholesterol 22mg; Calcium 24mg; Fibre 0.4g; Sodium 65mg.
Sweet Peanut Wafers Energy 184kcal/769kJ; Protein 3.7g; Carbohydrate 19.4g, of which sugars 9.1g; Fat 10.7g, of which saturates 4.8g; Cholesterol 12mg; Calcium 30mg; Fibre 0.6g; Sodium 79mg.

Meringue Squiggles

Free from gluten, wheat and cow's milk, these wiggly wands are great for children's parties. They are fun to shape and eat and kids of all ages love making and decorating them.

Makes 14–16
2 egg whites
90g/3½oz/½ cup caster
   (superfine) sugar
45ml/3 tbsp icing
   (confectioners') sugar
multi-coloured sugar sprinkles,
   to decorate

1 Preheat the oven to 150°C/300°F/Gas 2. Line a large baking sheet with baking parchment.

2 Put the egg whites in a large, clean bowl and whisk with a hand-held electric whisk until they form firm peaks.

3 Add a spoonful of caster sugar to the whisked egg whites and whisk for about 15 seconds to combine. Add another spoonful and whisk again. Continue in this way until all the sugar has been added.

4 Spoon the meringue mixture into a large piping (pastry) bag fitted with a large plain nozzle. Alternatively, spoon the mixture into a plastic bag, gently push it into one corner and snip off the tip so that the meringue can be pushed out in a 2cm/¾ in-thick line.

5 Pipe wavy lines of meringue, about 13cm/5in long, on to the baking sheet and bake for about 1 hour, until dry and crisp.

6 Carefully peel the meringues off the baking parchment and transfer to a wire rack to cool.

7 Put the icing sugar in a small bowl and mix in a few drops of water to make a smooth paste.

8 Using a fine pastry brush, lightly brush the tops of the meringues with a little of the sugar paste, then evenly scatter over the multi-coloured sugar sprinkles to decorate. Leave to set before serving.

Shortbread Ring Cookies

Decorated with colourful chopped sweets, these little cookies make delicious lunchbox fillers or snacks during the day.

Makes 8–10
150g/5oz/1¼ cups plain
   (all-purpose) flour, plus extra
   for dusting
90g/3½oz/½ cup rice flour
finely grated rind of 1 lemon
75g/3oz/6 tbsp butter

50g/2oz/¼ cup caster
   (superfine) sugar
1 egg yolk
10ml/2 tsp water

For the decoration
90g/3½oz/scant 1 cup icing
   (confectioners') sugar
50g/2oz/¼ cup butter
small jellied fruit sweets (candies)

1 Put the flour, rice flour, lemon rind and butter in a food processor and process briefly to combine. Add the sugar, egg yolk and water and mix to a dough.

2 Turn the dough on to a lightly floured surface and knead. Wrap in clear film (plastic wrap) and chill for about 30 minutes.

3 Preheat the oven to 180°C/350°F/Gas 4. Lightly grease a baking sheet.

4 Roll out the dough on a lightly floured surface to a thickness of about 5mm/¼in. Using a 6.5cm/2½in cookie cutter, cut out rounds and place on the baking sheet. Using a 4cm/1½in round cutter, cut out and remove the centre of each round.

5 Bake for about 20 minutes, until beginning to turn pale golden. Leave on the baking sheet for 2 minutes, then transfer to a wire rack to cool.

6 To make the topping, put the icing sugar and butter in a bowl and beat together until creamy.

7 Pipe or spoon the topping on to the ring cookies. Cut the jellied sweets into small pieces with a pair of scissors and gently press them into the cream to decorate.

Meringue Squiggles Energy 35kcal/148kJ; Protein 0.4g; Carbohydrate 8.8g, of which sugars 8.8g; Fat 0g, of which saturates 0g; Cholesterol 0mg; Calcium 5mg; Fibre 0g; Sodium 8mg.
Shortbread Ring Cookies Energy 242kcal/1008kJ; Protein 1.9g; Carbohydrate 34g, of which sugars 14.8g; Fat 10.9g, of which saturates 4.6g; Cholesterol 22mg; Calcium 16mg; Fibre 0.5g; Sodium 103mg.

Marshmallow Toasties

These soft cookie squares topped with a layer of strawberry jam and melted marshmallow make a sweet, sticky treat. When you're toasting the marshmallows, watch them very closely because once they start to colour, they brown extremely quickly.

Makes 12

130g/4¹/₂oz/generous ¹/₂ cup
   unsalted butter, at room
   temperature, diced

75g/3oz/scant ¹/₂ cup caster
   (superfine) sugar
finely grated rind of 1 lemon
10ml/2 tsp vanilla extract
75g/3oz/ ³/₄ cup ground almonds
1 egg
115g/4oz/1 cup self-raising
   (self-rising) flour
150g/5oz/¹/₂ cup strawberry jam
200g/7oz pink and white
   marshmallows
icing (confectioners') sugar,
   for dusting

1 Preheat the oven to 180°C/350°F/Gas 4. Lightly grease the base and sides of a 23cm/9in square baking tin (pan) and line with baking parchment.

2 Put the butter, sugar and lemon rind in a bowl and beat until creamy. Beat in the vanilla extract, ground almonds and egg, then add the flour and stir well.

3 Turn the mixture into the tin and spread in an even layer. Bake for 20 minutes, until pale golden and just firm. Leave to cool in the tin for 10 minutes.

4 Spread the cookie base with jam. Using scissors, cut the marshmallows in half, then arrange them, cut sides down, in an even layer over the jam. Preheat the grill (broiler) to medium.

5 Put the tin under the grill for 2 minutes, until the marshmallows are melted. Remove from the heat and press down each marshmallow to create an even layer. Return to the grill for a minute until the surface is toasted. Leave to cool.

6 Dust lightly with icing sugar, cut into 12 bars or squares and remove from the tin.

Pink Pigs

These are what you could call rainy day cookies. They are fun to make and thoroughly absorbing when the family is stuck indoors.

Makes 10

90g/3¹/₂oz/scant 1 cup icing
   (confectioners') sugar, plus
   extra for dusting

50g/2oz/¹/₄ cup unsalted butter,
   at room temperature, diced
10 rich tea (plain cookies)
   or digestive biscuits
   (graham crackers)
200g/7oz white ready-to-roll icing
pink food colouring
small, pink soft sweets (candies)
tube of black writing icing

1 To make the buttercream, put the icing sugar and butter in a bowl and beat until smooth, pale and creamy.

2 Spread the rich tea or digestive biscuits almost to the edges with the buttercream.

3 Reserve 25g/1oz of the white ready-to-roll icing. Add a few drops of pink food colouring to the remainder. Knead on a surface that has been lightly dusted with icing sugar until the pink colouring is evenly distributed. Reserve about 25g/1oz of the pink icing. Roll out the remaining pink icing thinly.

4 Using a cookie cutter that is just slightly smaller than the rich tea or digestive biscuits, cut out rounds of pink icing. Place a round over each and press it down on to the buttercream.

5 Halve five of the pink sweets. Make two small holes in each one with a wooden skewer to make a nose. Using buttercream, attach a halved sweet to the centre of each cookie.

6 Using the black writing icing, pipe two dots of icing above the nose to resemble eyes, then pipe a small, curved mouth.

7 Thinly roll out the reserved pink icing and the reserved white icing. Dampen the white icing with a little water and press the pink icing gently on top. Cut out triangles for ears. Dampen one edge of the ears with water and secure, pink side up, to the cookies. Gently curl the ears out at the ends.

Marshmallow Toasties Energy 269kcal/1131kJ; Protein 3.6g; Carbohydrate 37g, of which sugars 26.4g; Fat 13g, of which saturates 6.1g; Cholesterol 39mg; Calcium 38mg; Fibre 0.8g; Sodium 82mg.
Pink Pigs Energy 188kcal/794kJ; Protein 1g; Carbohydrate 33g, of which sugars 25.8g; Fat 6.8g, of which saturates 3.8g; Cholesterol 16mg; Calcium 25mg; Fibre 0.3g; Sodium 110mg.

Chocolate Cookies on Sticks

Let your imagination run riot when decorating these fun chocolate cookies. Use plenty of brightly coloured sweets or create a real chocolate feast by only using chocolate decorations. Whichever you choose, these cookies are very sweet so should be kept as a real treat for extra special occasions.

Makes 12
125g/4¼oz milk chocolate
75g/3oz white chocolate
50g/2oz chocolate-coated
  digestive biscuits (graham
  crackers), crumbled
  into chunks
a selection of small
  coloured sweets (candies),
  chocolate chips or chocolate-
  coated raisins
12 wooden ice lolly (popsicle)
  sticks

1 Break the milk and white chocolate into pieces and put in separate heatproof bowls. Place each bowl in turn over a pan of simmering water and heat, stirring frequently, until melted.

2 Meanwhile, draw six 7cm/2¾in rounds on baking parchment and six 9 × 7cm/3½ × 2¾in rectangles. Invert the parchment on to a large tray.

3 Spoon the milk chocolate into the outlines on the paper, reserving one or two spoonfuls of chocolate. Using the back of a spoon, carefully spread the chocolate to the edges to make neat shapes.

4 Press the end of a wooden ice lolly stick into each of the shapes, and spoon over a little more melted milk chocolate to cover the stick. Sprinkle the chocolate shapes with the crumbled cookies.

5 Pipe or drizzle the cookies with the melted white chocolate, then sprinkle the cookies with the coloured sweets, chocolate chips or chocolate-coated raisins, pressing them gently to make sure they stick.

6 Chill for about 1 hour until set, then carefully peel away the baking parchment.

Chocolate Wands

Shaping these long, wafery chocolate cookies is fun, but you need to work quickly. Only bake two cookies at a time; any more and they will become brittle before you have time to shape them into wands.

Makes 10–12
3 egg whites
90g/3½oz/½ cup caster
  (superfine) sugar

25g/1oz/2 tbsp unsalted
  butter, melted
30ml/2 tbsp plain
  (all-purpose) flour
15ml/1 tbsp unsweetened
  cocoa powder
30ml/2 tbsp single (light) cream
90g/3½oz milk chocolate and
  multi-coloured sprinkles,
  to decorate

1 Preheat the oven to 180°C/350°F/Gas 4. Line two large baking sheets with baking parchment and grease the paper well.

2 In a bowl, briefly beat together the egg whites and sugar until the whites are broken up. Add the melted butter, flour, cocoa powder and cream to the egg whites and beat with a wooden spoon until smooth.

3 Place 2 teaspoons of the mixture to one side of a baking sheet and spread the mixture into an oval, about 15cm/6in long. Spoon more mixture on to the other side of the baking sheet and shape in the same way. Bake for 7–8 minutes, until the edges begin to darken.

4 After 30 seconds lift one off the paper and wrap it around a wooden spoon handle. As soon as it holds its shape ease it off the spoon and shape the second cookie in the same way.

5 Prepare more cookies on the second baking sheet. Repeat until all the mixture has been used up.

6 Melt the chocolate in a heatproof bowl set over a pan of gently simmering water. Dip the ends of the cookies in the chocolate, then in coloured sprinkles and place on a sheet of baking parchment. Leave for about 1 hour, until set.

Chocolate Cookies on Sticks Energy 107kcal/448kJ; Protein 1.5g; Carbohydrate 12.3g, of which sugars 10.9g; Fat 6.1g, of which saturates 3.5g; Cholesterol 2mg; Calcium 43mg; Fibre 0.2g; Sodium 30mg.
Chocolate Wands Energy 103kcal/432kJ; Protein 1.6g; Carbohydrate 14.3g, of which sugars 12.2g; Fat 4.8g, of which saturates 2.9g; Cholesterol 8mg; Calcium 28mg; Fibre 0.3g; Sodium 41mg.

Flake "99s"

You don't need a special cutter to make these party cookies. They're shaped using an ordinary round cutter to which you add a V-shaped cone when cutting them out.

Makes 15
150g/5oz/1¼ cups self-raising (self-rising) flour, plus extra for dusting
90g/3½oz/7 tbsp unsalted butter, diced
50g/2oz/¼ cup light muscovado (brown) sugar
1 egg yolk
5ml/1 tsp vanilla extract

For the decoration
75g/3oz/6 tbsp unsalted butter, softened
5ml/1 tsp vanilla extract
115g/4oz/1 cup icing (confectioners') sugar
2 chocolate flakes

1 Put the flour and butter in a food processor and process until the mixture resembles fine breadcrumbs. Add the sugar, egg yolk and vanilla and blend to a smooth dough. Wrap in clear film (plastic wrap) and chill for 30 minutes.

2 Preheat the oven to 200°C/400°F/Gas 6. Grease a large baking sheet.

3 Roll the dough out thinly on a floured surface. Stamp out 5cm/2in rounds using a cookie cutter. Trim two sides off to make cornets. Repeat to use up the dough. Using a sharp knife, make a pattern on each cookie.

4 Bake for 8–10 minutes until pale golden. Leave for 2 minutes, then transfer to a wire rack to cool.

5 For the buttercream, beat together the butter, vanilla and icing sugar until smooth. Add 5ml/1 tsp hot water and beat again until the mixture is light and airy. Place in a piping (pastry) bag fitted with a large plain nozzle. Pipe swirls on to the tops of the cookies so that they look like swirls of ice cream. Cut the chocolate flakes across into 5cm/2in lengths. Carefully cut each piece lengthways into four small lengths. Push a flake piece into each cookie.

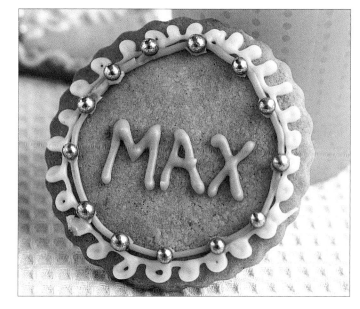

Name Cookies

You could decorate these cookies for children coming to a birthday party. It can be a fun idea to prop a name cookie up against the glass at each place setting around the tea table and let the children find their own seats.

Makes 20
200g/7oz/scant 1 cup unsalted butter, chilled and diced
finely grated rind of 1 orange
300g/10oz/2½ cups plain (all-purpose) flour, plus extra for dusting
90g/3½oz/scant 1 cup icing (confectioners') sugar
2 egg yolks

For the decoration
1 egg white
200g/7oz/1¾ cups icing (confectioners') sugar
2 different food colourings
silver balls

1 Put the butter, orange rind and flour in a food processor and process until the mixture resembles fine breadcrumbs. Add the icing sugar and egg yolks and blend until smooth. Wrap in clear film (plastic wrap) and chill for 30 minutes.

2 Preheat the oven to 200°C/400°F/Gas 6. Lightly grease two baking sheets.

3 Roll out the dough on a floured surface and stamp out cookies in a variety of shapes at least 7.5cm/3in across. Transfer to the baking sheets, spacing them slightly apart, and bake for 10–12 minutes, until pale golden around the edges.

4 Leave the cookies on the baking sheet for about 2 minutes to firm up, then transfer to a wire rack to cool completely.

5 To make the icing, put the egg white and icing sugar in a bowl and beat together until smooth and the icing just holds its shape. Divide the icing into two, then mix a few drops of food colouring into each to make two different colours.

6 Spoon the two different icings into piping (icing) bags fitted with a writing nozzle. Write the names of party guests on the cookies. Decorate as desired with icing and silver balls.

Flake "99s" Energy 198kcal/828kJ; Protein 1.8g; Carbohydrate 23.1g, of which sugars 15.5g; Fat 11.6g, of which saturates 7.1g; Cholesterol 38mg; Calcium 38mg; Fibre 0.4g; Sodium 74mg.
Name Cookies Energy 189kcal/795kJ; Protein 2g; Carbohydrate 26.9g, of which sugars 15.4g; Fat 9g, of which saturates 5.4g; Cholesterol 41mg; Calcium 33mg; Fibre 0.5g; Sodium 66mg.

Butter Gems

These tiny shortbread-based cookies are topped with rosettes of soft buttercream and a pretty sprinkling of brightly coloured sugar. They make a great treat for even the smallest of mouths.

Makes about 40

115g/4oz/½ cup unsalted butter, at room temperature, diced
50g/2oz/¼ cup caster (superfine) sugar
175g/6oz/1½ cups plain (all-purpose) flour, plus extra for dusting

For the decoration
50g/2oz/4 tbsp unsalted (sweet) butter, at room temperature, diced
5ml/1 tsp vanilla extract
90g/3½oz/scant 1 cup icing (confectioners') sugar
25g/1oz/2 tbsp sugar
green, lilac or pink food colourings

1 Put the diced butter and the sugar in a large bowl and beat together until smooth and creamy. Add the flour to the creamed butter and mix well to form a thick paste.

2 Turn the dough on to a lightly floured surface and knead until smooth. Wrap the dough in clear film (plastic wrap) and chill for at least 30 minutes.

3 Preheat the oven to 180°C/350°F/Gas 4. Lightly grease two baking sheets.

4 Roll out the dough on a lightly floured surface and cut out rounds using a 3.5cm/1¼in cookie cutter. Space slightly apart on the baking sheets and bake for 10 minutes, or until pale golden. Transfer to a wire rack to cool completely.

5 To decorate the cookies, beat the butter with the vanilla extract and icing sugar until smooth and creamy. Spoon the buttercream into a piping (pastry) bag fitted with a star-shaped nozzle, then pipe a rosette on to each cookie.

6 Put the sugar into a small bowl and add several drops of the food colouring. Mix the colouring into the sugar. Sprinkle a little of the sugar over the cookies.

Alphabetinis

These funny little letters are great for kids – and might even be a good way to encourage them to practise their spelling. They are great fun to make and even better to eat.

Makes about 30

2 egg whites
15ml/1 tbsp cornflour (cornstarch)
50g/2oz/½ cup plain (all-purpose) flour
150g/5oz/¾ cup caster (superfine) sugar
10ml/2 tsp vanilla extract
90g/3½oz milk chocolate

1 Preheat the oven to 180°C/350°F/Gas 4. Line two large baking sheets with baking parchment.

2 In a clean glass bowl, whisk the egg whites until they form soft peaks when the whisk is lifted. Sift the cornflour and plain flour over the egg whites. Add the sugar and vanilla extract. Fold in using a large metal spoon.

3 Spoon half the mixture into a plastic bag and gently squeeze it into a corner of the bag. Snip off the corner so that the cookie mixture can be squeezed out in a 1cm/½in-wide line.

4 Pipe letters on to one of the lined baking sheets, making each letter about 6cm/2½in tall. Repeat with the remaining cookie mixture.

5 Bake the cookies for 12 minutes, or until crisp and golden. Transfer to a wire rack to cool.

6 Melt the chocolate in a heatproof bowl set over a pan of simmering water.

7 Spoon the melted chocolate into a small paper piping (icing) bag fitted with a plain nozzle (or use a smaller plastic bag and snip off the merest tip).

8 Pipe the chocolate in lines over the cookies to highlight the shape of each letter. Leave to set for at least 1 hour.

Butter Gems Energy 57kcal/238kJ; Protein 0.5g; Carbohydrate 6.4g, of which sugars 3.1g; Fat 3.4g, of which saturates 2.2g; Cholesterol 9mg; Calcium 8mg; Fibre 0.1g; Sodium 25mg.
Alphabetinis Energy 42kcal/178kJ; Protein 0.5g; Carbohydrate 8.5g, of which sugars 6.9g; Fat 0.9g, of which saturates 0.6g; Cholesterol 1mg; Calcium 10mg; Fibre 0g; Sodium 8mg.

Flower Power Cookies

Look for little piped sugar flower decorations in the supermarket. Some are pretty pale colours, while others are much brighter and more vibrant.

finely grated rind of 1 orange
130g/4¼ oz/generous ½ cup
    light muscovado (brown) sugar
1 egg yolk

Makes 28
225g/8oz/2 cups plain
    (all-purpose) flour, plus extra
    for dusting
175g/6oz/¾ cup unsalted butter,
    chilled and diced

For the decoration
30ml/2 tbsp orange juice
200g/7oz/1¾ cups icing
    (confectioners') sugar
green, yellow and orange
    food colourings
multi-coloured sugared flowers

1 Put the flour, butter and orange rind into a food processor. Process until the mixture resembles fine breadcrumbs. Add the sugar and egg yolk and process until the mixture binds together.

2 Turn the mixture out on to a lightly floured surface and knead until it forms a dough. Shape the dough into a ball, wrap tightly in clear film (plastic wrap) and chill for 30 minutes.

3 Preheat the oven to 180°C/350°F/Gas 4. Lightly grease two or three baking sheets.

4 Roll out the dough thinly on a floured surface and cut out rounds using a cookie cutter about 6cm/2½in in diameter.

5 Transfer the cookies to the baking sheets, spacing them slightly apart. Bake for 12–15 minutes, until pale golden, then transfer to a wire rack to cool completely.

6 For the icing, put the orange juice in a bowl and gradually stir in the icing sugar until the mixture has the consistency of thick pouring cream. Make the icing different colours.

7 Spoon a little icing on to the cookies, spreading it to within 1cm/½in of the cookie edges. Top each one with a sugared flower. Leave to set for about 1 hour.

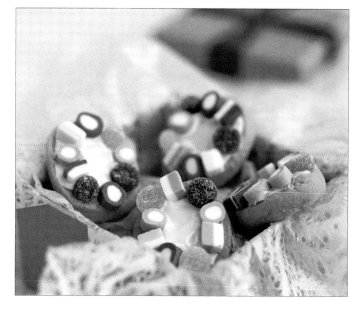

Dolly Cookies

These pretty cookies look like they belong at a doll's tea party. The cookies are made by simply chilling a roll of dough, then slicing off pieces on to a baking sheet. Baking doesn't get much easier than this.

50g/2oz/¼ cup caster
    (superfine) sugar
pink food colouring
5ml/1 tsp vanilla extract
175g/6oz/1½ cups plain
    (all-purpose) flour, plus extra
    for dusting
90g/3½oz white chocolate
75g/3oz multi-coloured
    sweets (candies)

Makes 14
115g/4oz/½ cup unsalted
    butter, at room
    temperature, diced

1 Put the butter and sugar in a bowl with a dash of pink food colouring and the vanilla extract. Beat together until smooth and creamy.

2 Add the flour to the butter and sugar mixture and stir well until thoroughly combined. Turn the dough out on to a lightly floured surface and knead until smooth.

3 Using your hands, roll the dough into a thick sausage, about 12cm/4½ in long and 5cm/2in in diameter. Wrap the dough in clear film (plastic wrap) and chill for at least 30 minutes.

4 Preheat the oven to 180°C/350°F/Gas 4. Lightly grease two baking sheets.

5 Cut the dough into 5mm/¼in slices and space them slightly apart on the baking sheets. Bake for 15–18 minutes, or until the cookies begin to colour. Transfer to a wire rack to cool completely.

6 Break up the chocolate and melt it in a heatproof bowl set over a pan of gently simmering water. Using a sharp knife, cut the sweets in half.

7 Using a knife swirl a little chocolate on to each cookie and decorate with a ring of sweets. Leave to set.

Flower Power Cookies Energy 123kcal/516kJ; Protein 1g; Carbohydrate 18.7g, of which sugars 12.5g; Fat 5.4g, of which saturates 3.3g; Cholesterol 21mg; Calcium 20mg; Fibre 0.3g; Sodium 39mg.
Dolly Cookies Energy 169kcal/709kJ; Protein 1.8g; Carbohydrate 21.9g, of which sugars 12.4g; Fat 8.9g, of which saturates 5.5g; Cholesterol 18mg; Calcium 39mg; Fibre 0.4g; Sodium 59mg.

Puppy Faces

These little pups are so appealing it seems a shame to eat them. Fortunately, they taste great.

Makes 10

100g/3½oz/scant 1 cup plain (all-purpose) flour, plus extra for dusting
50g/2oz/½ cup rolled oats
2.5ml/½ tsp mixed (apple pie) spice
50g/2oz/¼ cup unsalted butter, chilled and diced
100g/3½oz/½ cup caster (superfine) sugar
1 egg yolk

For the decoration

60ml/4 tbsp apricot jam
250g/9oz white ready-to-roll icing
10 round coloured sweets (candies)
black and red writing icing tubes
icing (confectioners') sugar, for dusting

1 Put the flour, oats and spice in a bowl. Rub in the butter until the mixture resemble breadcrumbs. Stir in the sugar, egg yolk and 5ml/1 tsp water until the mixture forms a ball.

2 Turn the dough out on to a lightly floured surface and knead until smooth. Wrap and chill for 30 minutes.

3 Preheat the oven to 200°C/400°F/Gas 6. Lightly grease a large baking sheet.

4 Roll out the dough on a floured surface and cut out rounds using a 6cm/2½in cutter. Bake for 12 minutes. Leave to cool.

5 Brush the cookies with jam. Roll out half of the icing. Stamp out 10 rounds with a 6cm/2½in cutter and place on the cookies. Halve the sweets, brush the icing with water and press on the sweets for eyes.

6 Use the writing tubes to pipe the noses and mouths, finishing with little red tongues.

7 To make the ears, divide the remaining icing into 20 pieces. Roll each piece into a ball and flatten at one end to make a flat pear shape. Brush the icing with water and secure the ears.

Gingerbread Family

You can have great fun with these cookies by creating characters with different features. By using an assortment of different gingerbread cutters you can make a gingerbread family.

Makes about 12

350g/12oz/3 cups plain (all-purpose) flour, plus extra for dusting
5ml/1 tsp bicarbonate of soda (baking soda)
5ml/1 tsp ground ginger
115g/4oz/½ cup unsalted butter, chilled and diced
175g/6oz/¾ cup light muscovado (brown) sugar
1 egg
30ml/2 tbsp black treacle (molasses) or golden (light corn) syrup
50g/2oz each plain (semisweet), milk and white chocolate, to decorate

1 Preheat the oven to 180°C/350°F/Gas 4. Lightly grease two large baking sheets.

2 Put the flour, bicarbonate of soda, ginger and diced butter into the food processor. Process until the mixture begins to resemble fine breadcrumbs.

3 Add the sugar, egg and black treacle or golden syrup to the food processor and process the mixture until it begins to form into a ball.

4 Turn the dough out on to a lightly floured surface and knead until smooth and pliable. Roll out the dough on a lightly floured surface. Cut out figures using people-shaped cutters, then transfer to the baking sheets.

5 Bake for 15 minutes until slightly risen and starting to colour around the edges. Leave for 5 minutes, then transfer to a wire rack to cool.

6 To decorate the cookies, melt each type of chocolate in a separate bowl set over a pan of simmering water. Spoon the melted chocolate into piping (pastry) bags fitted with a plain tip, then pipe faces and clothes on to the cookies. Leave to set.

Puppy Faces Energy 251kcal/1063kJ; Protein 2.1g; Carbohydrate 52.2g, of which sugars 40.9g; Fat 5.2g, of which saturates 2.8g; Cholesterol 31mg; Calcium 37mg; Fibre 0.7g; Sodium 38mg.
Gingerbread Family Energy 305kcal/1281kJ; Protein 4.1g; Carbohydrate 47.6g, of which sugars 25.2g; Fat 12.2g, of which saturates 7.3g; Cholesterol 37mg; Calcium 71mg; Fibre 1.2g; Sodium 71mg.

Tree Cookies

These cookies look really effective with their chocolate cookie "trunks" and brightly coloured "fruits". Arrange the cookies in a line on the tea table.

Makes 10
50g/2oz/¼ cup unsalted butter, at room temperature, diced
115g/4oz/½ cup light muscovado (brown) sugar
1 egg

150g/5oz/1¼ cups self-raising (self-rising) flour
2.5ml/½ tsp bicarbonate of soda (baking soda)
finely grated rind of 1 lemon

For the decoration
50g/2oz/½ cup icing (confectioners') sugar
10ml/2 tsp lemon juice
10 milk chocolate fingers
brightly coloured sweets (candies), such as M&Ms

1 Preheat the oven to 180°C/350°F/Gas 4. Lightly grease two baking sheets.

2 In a large bowl, beat together the butter and sugar until smooth and creamy. Beat in the egg. Add the flour, bicarbonate of soda and lemon rind and mix until smooth.

3 Place 5 large spoonfuls of the mixture on to each baking sheet, spacing them well apart. Bake for 15 minutes, until the cookies have risen. Leave on the baking sheet for 5 minutes to firm up, then transfer to a wire rack to cool.

4 To decorate the cookies, mix together the icing sugar and lemon juice to make a thick paste. Use a little paste to secure one end of a chocolate finger to each cookie.

5 Attach the coloured sweets in the same way, securing each one with a little paste. Leave the cookies to set for 1 hour.

> **Variation**
> To create pretty blossoming trees, attach pastel-coloured sugar flowers to the cookies instead of coloured sweets (candies).

Marshmallow Crispie Cakes

Easy to make and guaranteed to be demolished in no time at all, these little cakes can easily be made by very young children, who like to help in the kitchen.

Makes 45
250g/9oz bag of toffees
50g/2oz/4 tbsp butter
45ml/3 tbsp milk
115g/4oz/1 cup marshmallows
175g/6oz/6 cups crisped rice cereal

1 Lightly grease a 20 x 33cm/8 x 13in roasting pan.

2 Put the toffees, butter and milk in a pan and heat gently, stirring until the toffees have melted.

3 Add the marshmallows and cereal and stir until well mixed and the marshmallows have melted.

4 Spoon the mixture into the prepared pan, level the surface and leave to set. When cool and hard, cut into squares, remove from the tin and put into paper cases to serve.

Fruit and Nut Clusters

This fun, no cook recipe will be loved by children and adults alike.

Makes 24
225g/8oz white chocolate
50g/2oz/⅓ cup sunflower seeds
50g/2oz/⅓ cup almond slivers
50g/2oz/⅓ cup sesame seeds
50g/2oz/⅓ cup seedless raisins
5ml/1 tsp ground cinnamon

1 Break the white chocolate into small pieces. Put the chocolate into a heatproof bowl set over a pan of gently simmering water and melt. Remove from the heat.

2 Mix the sunflower seeds, almond slivers, sesame seeds, raisins and ground cinnamon into the chocolate and stir well. Using a teaspoon, spoon the mixture into paper cases and leave to set.

Tree Cookies Energy 162kcal/681kJ; Protein 1.3g; Carbohydrate 24g, of which sugars 21.6g; Fat 7.2g, of which saturates 2.8g; Cholesterol 30mg; Calcium 24mg; Fibre 0.2g; Sodium 54mg.
Marshmallow Crispie Cakes Energy 56kcal/235kJ; Protein 0.7g; Carbohydrate 9g, of which sugars 4.4g; Fat 2.2g, of which saturates 1.1g; Cholesterol 3mg; Calcium 39mg; Fibre 0g; Sodium 28mg.
Fruit and Nut Clusters Energy 93kcal/386kJ; Protein 2g; Carbohydrate 7.5g, of which sugars 7g; Fat 6.3g, of which saturates 2.1g; Cholesterol 0mg; Calcium 48mg; Fibre 0.5g; Sodium 12mg.

Traditional Sugar Cookies

Sweet and sugary, these delightful cookies can be decorated with different colours of sugar to make a pretty party spread.

Makes 36
12oz/350g/ cups plain
(all-purpose) flour, plus extra
for dusting
5ml/1 tsp bicarbonate of soda
(baking soda)
10ml/2 tsp baking powder
pinch of grated nutmeg

115g/4oz/cups butter, softened
225g/8oz/ cups caster (superfine)
sugar
2.5ml/½ tsp vanilla extract
1 egg
125ml/4fl oz milk
coloured or demerara sugar,
for sprinkling

1 Sift the flour, bicarbonate of soda, baking powder and nutmeg into a bowl. Set aside.

2 In a bowl beat together the butter, caster sugar and vanilla extract until the mixture is light and fluffy. Add the egg and beat well to mix.

3 Add the flour to the butter and sugar mixture in batches, beating well after each addition, and alternating the flour with the milk. Stir to make a soft dough. Wrap the dough in cling film (plastic wrap) and chill in the refrigerator for at least 30 minutes, or overnight.

4 Preheat the oven to 350°F/180°C/Gas 4.

5 Roll out the dough on a lightly floured surface to a thickness of 3mm/⅛in. Stamp out rounds using a cookie cutter. Gather together the trimmings and roll and stamp out cookies until the dough has been used up.

6 Transfer the cookies to ungreased baking sheets. Sprinkle each with sugar. Bake for 10–12 minutes, until golden brown. With a metal spatula transfer the cookies to a wire rack and leave to cool completely.

Pink Sugared Hearts

Pretty and pink, these delightful cookies are always a hit. Rolling the edges in coloured sugar to accentuate their shape really adds to the decoration.

Makes 32
225g/8oz/2 cups plain
(all-purpose) flour, plus extra
for dusting
175g/6oz/¾ cup unsalted butter,
chilled and diced

130g/4¼oz/⅔ cup caster
(superfine) sugar
1 egg yolk

For the decoration
50g/2oz/¼ cup sugar
pink food colouring
225g/8oz/2 cups icing
(confectioners') sugar
30–45ml/2–3 tbsp lemon juice

1 Preheat the oven to 180°C/350°F/Gas 4. Lightly grease two baking sheets.

2 Put the flour and butter into a food processor, then process until the mixture resembles breadcrumbs. Add the sugar and egg yolk and process until the mixture begins to form a ball.

3 Turn the dough out on to a lightly floured surface and knead until smooth. Shape the dough into a ball, wrap in clear film (plastic wrap) and chill for at least 30 minutes.

4 Working in batches, roll out the dough thinly on a lightly floured surface and cut out heart shapes using a cookie cutter. Transfer to the baking sheets, spacing them slightly apart. Bake for 10 minutes, or until pale golden. Transfer to a wire rack to cool.

5 To decorate, put the sugar in a bowl and add a dot of pink food colouring. Mix until the sugar is pink.

6 Put the icing sugar in a separate bowl and add 30ml/2 tbsp of the lemon juice, stirring until smooth. Spread a little icing on to each cookie to within 5mm/¼ in of the edge.

7 Turn each iced cookie on its side and gently roll in the coloured sugar. Leave to set for 1 hour.

Traditional Sugar Cookies Energy 85kcal/359kJ; Protein 1.2g; Carbohydrate 14.3g, of which sugars 6.9g; Fat 3g, of which saturates 1.8g; Cholesterol 12mg; Calcium 22mg; Fibre 0.3g; Sodium 23mg.
Pink Sugared Hearts Energy 265kcal/1126kJ; Protein 1g; Carbohydrate 58.2g, of which sugars 52.9g; Fat 4.8g, of which saturates 2.9g; Cholesterol 18mg; Calcium 38mg; Fibre 0.2g; Sodium 37mg.

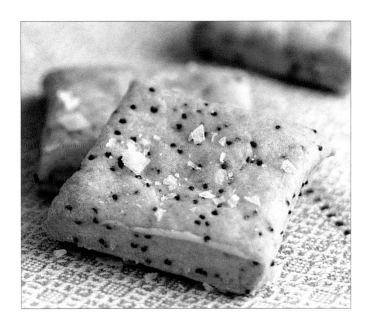

Poppy Seed and Sea Salt Crackers

These attractive little crackers are ideal to use as the base of drinks party canapés, or they can be served plain as tasty snacks in their own right.

Makes 20
115g/4oz/1 cup plain
　(all-purpose) flour, plus extra
　for dusting
pinch of salt
5ml/1 tsp caster (superfine) sugar
15g/½oz/1 tbsp butter
15ml/1 tbsp poppy seeds
about 90ml/6 tbsp single
　(light) cream

1 Preheat the oven to 150°C/300°F/Gas Mark 2.

2 Sift together the flour, salt and sugar into a bowl. Add the butter and rub in with your fingertips until the mixture resembles fine breadcrumbs. Stir in the poppy seeds. Add just enough cream to mix to a stiff dough.

3 Turn the dough on to a lightly floured surface and roll out to a 20 x 25cm/8 x 10in rectangle. Cut into 20 squares with a sharp knife.

4 Put the crackers on to one or two ungreased baking sheets and brush lightly with milk. Sprinkle a few flakes of sea salt over each cracker.

5 Bake for about 30 minutes, until crisp but still quite pale. Using a metal spatula, carefully transfer the crackers to a wire rack to cool completely.

> **Variations**
> • You can substitute white poppy seeds for the black ones used here or use a mixture of the two.
> • Vary the flavour of these crackers by using other small seeds: for example, celery seeds for sharpness, caraway for piquancy or sesame for a slight sweetness.

Festive Cheese Nibbles

Shape these spicy cheese snacks in any way you wish – stars, crescent moons, triangles, squares, hearts, fingers or rounds. Serve them with drinks from ice-cold cocktails to hot and spicy mulled wines.

Makes 60
115g/4oz/1 cup plain
　(all-purpose) flour, plus extra
　for dusting
5ml/1 tsp mustard powder
pinch of salt
115g/4oz/½ cup butter
75g/3oz/¾ cup Cheddar
　cheese, grated
pinch of cayenne pepper
30ml/2 tbsp water
1 egg, beaten
poppy seeds, sunflower seeds or
　sesame seeds, to decorate

1 Preheat the oven to 200°C/400°F/Gas 6. Lightly grease two baking sheets.

2 Sift the flour, mustard powder and salt into a bowl and rub in the butter until the mixture resembles fine breadcrumbs.

3 Stir in the cheese and cayenne pepper and sprinkle on the water. Add half the beaten egg, mix to a firm dough and knead lightly until smooth.

4 Roll out the dough on a lightly floured surface and cut out a variety of shapes. Re-roll the trimmings and cut more shapes until all the dough has been used up.

5 Place the shapes on the prepared baking sheets and brush with the remaining egg. Sprinkle on the seeds. Bake for 8–10 minutes until puffed and golden. Leave to cool on the baking tray for a few minutes before carefully removing to a wire rack with a metal spatula.

> **Cook's Tip**
> Serve these nibbles as they are with pre-dinner drinks, or add them to the cheeseboard at the end of a meal.

Classic Oatcakes

These are very simple to make and are an excellent addition to a cheeseboard.

Makes 24
225g/8oz/1²/₃ cups medium
    oatmeal, plus extra
    for sprinkling
75g/3oz/³/₄ cup plain
    (all-purpose) flour
pinch of bicarbonate of soda
    (baking soda)
pinch of salt
25g/1oz/2 tbsp hard white
    vegetable fat (shortening)
25g/1oz/2 tbsp butter
60–90ml/4–6 tbsp boiling water

1 Preheat the oven to 220°C/425°F/Gas Mark 7.

2 Put the oatmeal in a large bowl. Sift together the flour, bicarbonate of soda and salt into the bowl and mix well.

3 Put the vegetable fat and butter into a small pan and melt over a low heat, stirring occasionally.

4 Add the mixture of melted fats to the dry ingredients, stirring well to combine. Stir in enough boiling water to mix to a soft, but not sticky dough.

5 Sprinkle a work surface with a little oatmeal and turn out the dough. Knead lightly, then roll out thinly. Stamp out 24 rounds with a 5cm/2in plain cookie cutter and place them on ungreased baking sheets.

6 Bake for about 15 minutes, until light golden brown and crisp. Leave to cool on the baking sheets, then using a metal spatula, remove them carefully.

> **Cook's Tips**
> • *You can store these oatcakes in an airtight container in a cool place for up to 1 week.*
> • *Oatcakes are traditionally made with lard so if you want an authentic flavour, use this instead of vegetable fat (shortening).*

Oatcake Triangles

These oatcakes are delicious served as a snack with grapes and wedges of cheese. They are also good topped with thick honey for breakfast.

Makes 8
175g/6oz/1 cup medium
    oatmeal, plus extra
    for sprinkling
pinch of salt
pinch of bicarbonate of soda
    (baking soda)
15ml/1 tbsp pure vegetable
    margarine
75ml/5 tbsp water

1 Preheat the oven to 150°C/300°F/Gas 2. Put the oatmeal into a large mixing bowl, add the salt and bicarbonate of soda and mix well.

2 Melt the margarine with the water in a small pan over a low heat. Bring to the boil, then add to the oatmeal mixture and mix to a moist dough.

3 Turn the dough on to a surface sprinkled with extra oatmeal and knead to a smooth ball. Turn a large baking sheet upside-down, grease it, sprinkle it lightly with oatmeal and place the ball of dough on top. Sprinkle the dough with oatmeal, then roll out to a 25cm/10in round.

4 Using a sharp knife, cut the round into eight equal triangular sections, ease them apart slightly and bake for about 50–60 minutes until crisp.

5 Leave to cool on the baking sheet, then carefully remove the oatcakes with a metal spatula.

> **Cook's Tip**
> *To achieve a neat round, place a 25cm/10in plate upside down on top of the oatcake dough. Cut away any excess dough with a knife, then gently remove the plate.*

Herby Seeded Oatcakes

The addition of thyme and sunflower seeds to this traditional recipe makes these oatcakes an especially good accompaniment to cheese – try them spread with goat's cheese or ripe Brie or Camembert.

Makes 32

rolled oats, for sprinkling
175g/6oz/1¹/₂ cups plain
  wholemeal (all-purpose
  whole-wheat) flour, plus extra
  for dusting
175g/6oz/1¹/₂ cups fine oatmeal
pinch of salt
1.5ml/¹/₄ tsp bicarbonate of soda
  (baking soda)
75g/3oz/6 tbsp white vegetable
  fat (shortening)
15ml/1 tbsp fresh thyme
  leaves, chopped
30ml/2 tbsp sunflower seeds

1 Preheat the oven to 150°C/300°F/Gas 2. Sprinkle two ungreased, non-stick baking sheets with rolled oats. Set aside.

2 Put the flour, oatmeal, salt and bicarbonate of soda in a bowl and rub in the fat until the mixture resembles fine breadcrumbs. Stir in the thyme.

3 Add just enough cold water (about 90–105ml/6–7 tbsp) to the dry ingredients to mix to a stiff, but not sticky dough.

4 Gently knead the dough on a lightly floured surface until smooth, then cut roughly in half and roll out one piece on a lightly floured surface to make a 23–25cm/9–10in round.

5 Sprinkle sunflower seeds over the dough and press them in with the rolling pin. Cut into triangles and arrange on one of the baking sheets. Repeat with the remaining dough. Bake for 45–60 minutes until crisp but not brown. Cool on wire racks.

> **Variation**
> These oatcakes are also great sprinkled with sesame seeds.

Oatmeal Crackers

Although not as neat as bought ones, these home-made oatmeal crackers make up in flavour and interest anything they might lose in presentation – and they make the ideal partner for many cheeses, especially with some fresh fruit to accompany them.

Makes about 18

75g/3oz/³/₄ cup plain
  (all-purpose) flour
pinch of salt
1.5ml/¹/₄ tsp baking powder
115g/4oz/1 cup fine pinhead
  oatmeal, plus extra
  for sprinkling
65g/2¹/₂oz/generous ¹/₄ cup white
  vegetable fat (shortening)

1 Preheat the oven to 200°C/400°F/Gas 6. Lightly grease one or two baking sheets.

2 Sift together the flour, salt and baking powder into a mixing bowl. Add the oatmeal and mix well. Add the white vegetable fat and rub it in with your fingertips until the mixture is crumbly.

3 Blend in just enough water to work the mixture into a stiff dough.

4 Turn out the dough on a work surface sprinkled with a little fine oatmeal and knead lightly until smooth and manageable. Roll out to about 3mm/¹/₈in thick and cut into rounds, squares or triangles with a plain cookie cutter or a sharp knife. Transfer to the prepared baking sheets.

5 Bake in the preheated oven for about 15 minutes, until crisp. Using a metal spatula, carefully transfer the crackers to a wire rack and leave to cool completely.

> **Cook's Tip**
> Store the crackers when absolutely cold in an airtight container lined with baking parchment. Check for crispness before serving; reheat for 4–5 minutes in a preheated oven at 200°C/400°F/ Gas 6 to crisp up if necessary.

Herby Seeded Oatcakes Energy 62kcal/259kJ; Protein 1.6g; Carbohydrate 7.7g, of which sugars 0.2g; Fat 3g, of which saturates 0.9g; Cholesterol 0mg; Calcium 6mg; Fibre 0.9g; Sodium 21mg.
Oatmeal Crackers Energy 72kcal/301kJ; Protein 1.2g; Carbohydrate 7.9g, of which sugars 0.1g; Fat 4.2g, of which saturates 1.8g; Cholesterol 3mg; Calcium 9mg; Fibre 0.6g; Sodium 57mg.

Rosemary Crackers

Here rosemary flowers are used to flavour and garnish the top of savoury rosemary crackers, which are really delicious either on their own or with a mild-flavoured cheese. Use freshly-picked rosemary leaves for the best flavour in these crackers.

Makes about 25
225g/8oz/2 cups plain
   (all-purpose) flour, plus extra
   for dusting
2.5ml/¹/₂tsp baking powder
good pinch of salt
2.5ml/¹/₂tsp curry powder
75g/3oz/6 tbsp butter
30ml/2tbsp finely chopped young
   rosemary leaves
1 egg yolk
milk, to glaze

To decorate
30ml/2tbsp cream cheese
rosemary flowers

1 Put the flour, baking powder, salt and curry powder in a food processor. Add the butter, cut into small pieces, and blend until the mixture resembles fine breadcrumbs.

2 Add the rosemary, egg yolk and 30–45ml/2–3 tbsp cold water and mix to a firm dough. (Alternatively, sift the flour, baking powder, salt and curry powder together into a bowl, add the butter and rub in with your fingertips until the mixture resembles fine breadcrumbs. Stir in the rosemary, egg yolk and water and mix to a firm dough.) Chill for 30 minutes.

3 Thinly roll out the dough on a lightly floured surface and stamp out about 25 crackers using a 5cm/2in plain or fluted round cookie cutter.

4 Transfer to a large baking sheet and prick with a fork. Brush with milk to glaze and bake for about 10 minutes, until pale golden. Transfer to a wire rack and leave to cool.

5 Spread a little cream cheese on to each cracker and secure a few rosemary flowers on top, using tweezers to position the flowers, if that makes it easier.

Wheat Thins

These classic wheat crackers are especially delicious with rich-tasting creamy cheeses, and also make a quick snack simply spread with butter when you are in a hurry.

Makes 18
175g/6oz/1¹/₂ cups fine
   stoneground wholemeal
   (whole-wheat) flour, plus extra
   for dusting
pinch of salt
5ml/1 tsp baking powder
50g/2oz/¹/₂ cup coarse oatmeal
40g/1¹/₂oz/3 tbsp sugar
115g/4oz/¹/₂ cup unsalted butter,
   chilled and diced

1 Preheat the oven to 190°C/375°F/Gas 5.

2 Put all the ingredients into a food processor and process until the mixture starts to clump.

3 (Alternatively, sift the flour, salt and baking powder into a bowl. Tip in the bran remaining in the sieve (strainer) and stir in the oatmeal and sugar. Add the butter and rub in with your fingertips until the mixture resembles breadcrumbs.)

4 Tip out on to a lightly floured surface, gather the dough together with your hands and roll out.

5 Stamp out 18 rounds with a 7.5cm/3in cookie cutter. Place on an ungreased baking sheet.

6 Bake for 12 minutes until just beginning to colour at the edges. Leave to cool slightly, then transfer to a wire rack to cool completely.

Cook's Tip
These cookies are perfect for serving with a cheeseboard and look very pretty cut into different shapes. You could make star-shaped cookies for Christmas, or heart-shaped ones for Valentine's Day.

Rosemary Crackers Energy 61kcal/254kJ; Protein 1g; Carbohydrate 7g, of which sugars 0.2g; Fat 3.4g, of which saturates 2g; Cholesterol 16mg; Calcium 15mg; Fibre 0.3g; Sodium 22mg.
Wheat Thins Energy 98kcal/408kJ; Protein 1.6g; Carbohydrate 10.6g, of which sugars 2.6g; Fat 5.7g, of which saturates 3.4g; Cholesterol 14mg; Calcium 8mg; Fibre 1.1g; Sodium 73mg.

Thyme and Mustard Crackers

These aromatic crackers are delicious served with herbed cheese as a light, savoury last course. Alternatively, wrap them in cellophane and tie with string for a pretty gift.

Makes 40
175g/6oz/1½ cups wholemeal (whole-wheat) flour, plus extra for dusting
50g/2oz/⅔ cup rolled oats
25g/1oz/2 tbsp caster (superfine) sugar
10ml/2 tsp baking powder
30ml/2 tbsp fresh thyme leaves
pinch of salt
50g/2oz/¼ cup butter, diced
25g/1oz/2 tbsp white vegetable fat (shortening), diced
45ml/3 tbsp milk
10ml/2 tsp Dijon mustard
30ml/2 tbsp sesame seeds
ground black pepper

1 Preheat the oven to 200°C/400°F/Gas 6. Lightly grease two or three baking sheets.

2 Put the flour, oats, sugar, baking powder and thyme leaves into a bowl, season with salt and pepper and mix together. Add the butter and white vegetable fat and rub in with your fingertips until the mixture resembles breadcrumbs.

3 Pour the milk into a small bowl, add the mustard and whisk lightly with a fork until combined. Add to the dry ingredients and stir well to make a soft dough.

4 Turn out the dough on to a lightly floured surface and knead briefly. Roll out to a thickness of 5mm/¼in. Stamp out rounds with a 5cm/2in fluted round cookie cutter. Place them, spaced slightly apart to allow room for spreading, on the prepared baking sheets. Gather up the scraps, knead together lightly and re-roll. Stamp out more rounds until all the dough is used up.

5 Prick the biscuits with a fork and sprinkle them evenly with the sesame seeds. Bake for 10–12 minutes, until golden.

6 Leave to cool completely on the baking sheets. Store in a cool place in an airtight container for up to 5 days.

Blue Cheese and Chive Crisps

Advance preparation is the key with these crisps. You need to begin the day before you want to serve them. They are perfect for serving after a special festive meal.

Makes 48
225g/8oz/2 cups blue cheese, crumbled
115g/4oz/½ cup unsalted butter
1 egg
1 egg yolk
30ml/2 tsp chopped fresh chives
black pepper
225g/8oz/2 cups plain (all-purpose) flour, sifted

1 In a large bowl, beat together the blue cheese and butter until well blended using an electric mixer. Add the egg, egg yolk, chopped chives and a little pepper, and beat until just blended.

2 Add the flour in three batches, folding in well with a metal spoon between each addition.

3 Divide the dough into two and roll each half into a log about 5cm/2in in diameter. Tightly wrap each log in baking parchment and chill overnight in the refrigerator.

4 Preheat the oven to 190°C/375°F/Gas 5. Light grease two or three baking sheets.

5 Cut the dough logs into slices about 3mm/⅛in thick. Place the slices on the prepared baking sheets. Bake in the oven for about 10 minutes, until just golden around the edges.

6 Leave to firm up slightly on the baking sheets for a few minutes. Using a metal spatula, transfer the crisps to a wire rack and leave to cool completely.

> **Cook's Tip**
> *The cheese crisps will keep for up to 10 days in an airtight container.*

Thyme and Mustard Crackers Energy 40kcal/168kJ; Protein 0.9g; Carbohydrate 4.5g, of which sugars 0.8g; Fat 2.2g, of which saturates 1g; Cholesterol 3mg; Calcium 9mg; Fibre 0.5g; Sodium 21mg.
Blue Cheese and Chive Crisps Energy 55kcal/229kJ; Protein 1.7g; Carbohydrate 3.8g, of which sugars 0.1g; Fat 3.8g, of which saturates 2.3g; Cholesterol 18mg; Calcium 32mg; Fibre 0.2g; Sodium 77mg.

Savoury Cocktail Crackers

Serve these savoury snacks at a party or with pre-dinner drinks. Each of the spice seeds contributes to the flavour.

Makes 20–30

150g/5oz/1¼ cups plain (all-purpose) flour, plus extra for dusting
10ml/2 tsp curry powder
115g/4oz/½ cup butter, chopped
75g/3oz/¾ cup grated Cheddar cheese
10ml/2 tsp poppy seeds
5ml/1 tsp black onion seeds
1 egg yolk
cumin seeds, to garnish

1 Lightly grease two baking sheets. Sift the flour and curry powder into a large mixing bowl.

2 Add the butter and rub in with your fingertips until the mixture resembles breadcrumbs.

3 Stir in the cheese, poppy seeds, black onion seeds and egg yolk and mix to a firm dough. Wrap in clear film (plastic wrap) and chill for 30 minutes.

4 Dust a rolling pin and roll out the dough on a floured surface to a thickness of about 3mm/⅛in.

5 Stamp out 20–30 rounds with a floured plain cookie cutter. Arrange the rounds on the prepared baking sheets, spaced slightly apart, and sprinkle with the cumin seeds. Chill in the refrigerator for 15 minutes.

6 Preheat the oven to 190°C/375°F/Gas 5. Bake for 20 minutes, until the cookies are crisp and golden. Cool slightly and serve warm or cold.

> **Variation**
> *Try using caraway or sesame seeds in place of the poppy seeds, if you wish.*

Sunflower and Almond Sesame Crackers

You might be surprised to learn that crackers aren't always based on flour. Here, ground nuts and seeds are the basis for crisp crackers that are just as tasty with cheese or pâté as their more usual counterparts.

Makes about 24

130g/4½ oz/1 cup ground sunflower seeds
90g/3½ oz/generous ¾ cup ground almonds
5ml/1 tsp baking powder
30ml/2 tbsp milk
1 egg yolk
25g/1oz/2 tbsp butter, melted
25g/1oz/¼ cup sesame seeds

1 Preheat the oven to 190°C/375°F/Gas 5.

2 Reserve 25g/1oz/¼ cup of the ground sunflower seeds for rolling out, and mix the remaining ground seeds with the ground almonds and baking powder in a bowl.

3 Blend together the milk and egg yolk and stir into the ground seed and almond mixture with the melted butter, mixing well. Gently work the mixture with your hands to form a moist dough.

4 Roll out the dough to 5mm/¼in thickness on a cool surface, lightly dusted with a little of the reserved ground sunflower seeds, with a little more sprinkled on top to prevent sticking.

5 Sprinkle the dough with sesame seeds and cut into rounds using a 5cm/2in cookie cutter. Place on a non-stick baking sheet.

6 Bake for about 10 minutes, until lightly browned. Remove from the oven and leave for a minute or two. Transfer to a wire rack and leave to cool.

> **Variation**
> *Sprinkle some poppy seeds on top of a few of the crackers.*

Savoury Cocktail Crackers Energy 62kcal/257kJ; Protein 1.3g; Carbohydrate 4g, of which sugars 0.1g; Fat 4.5g, of which saturates 2.6g; Cholesterol 17mg; Calcium 32mg; Fibre 0.3g; Sodium 43mg.
Sunflower and Almond Sesame Crackers Energy 72kcal/296kJ; Protein 2.2g; Carbohydrate 1.3g, of which sugars 0.3g; Fat 6.4g, of which saturates 1.1g; Cholesterol 11mg; Calcium 25mg; Fibre 0.7g; Sodium 8mg.

Swedish Crispbread

This is a very traditional Swedish crispbread with a lovely rye flavour. The texture is crunchy. Pile with pâté, spread or cream cheese-type toppings, then add fruit or chopped raw vegetables.

Makes 8

450g/1lb/4 cups rye flour, plus extra for dusting
pinch of salt
50g/2oz/1/4 cup butter
20g/3/4 oz fresh yeast
275ml/9fl oz/generous 1 cup lukewarm water
75g/3oz/2 cups wheat bran

1 Preheat the oven to 230°C/450°F/Gas 8. Lightly grease two baking sheets. Mix the rye flour and salt in a large bowl. Add the butter and rub in with your fingertips until the mixture resembles breadcrumbs. Make a well in the centre.

2 Cream the yeast with a little water until smooth, then stir in the remaining lukewarm water. Pour into the well in the centre of the flour, mix to a dough, then mix in the bran. Knead on a lightly floured surface for 5 minutes until smooth and elastic.

3 Divide the dough into 8 equal pieces and roll each one out on a lightly floured surface, to a 20cm/8in round.

4 Place 2 rounds on the prepared baking sheets and prick all over with a fork. Cut a hole in the centre of each round, using a 4cm/1½in cutter.

5 Bake for 15–20 minutes, or until the crispbreads are golden and crisp. Transfer to a wire rack to cool. Repeat with the remaining crispbreads.

Cook's Tip
The hole in the centre of these crispbreads is a reminder of the days when breads were strung on a pole, which was hung across the rafters to dry. Make smaller crispbreads, if you like, and tie them together with bright red ribbon for an unusual Christmas gift.

Malted Wheat and Mixed Seed Crackers

These large crackers have plenty of crunch and flavour provided by the selection of different seeds that are used. They taste simply fabulous with robust farmhouse cheeses.

Makes 12–14

250g/9oz/2¼ cups Granary (whole-wheat) or malted wheat flour, plus extra for dusting
pinch of salt
2.5ml/½ tsp baking powder
115g/4oz/½ cup butter, chilled and diced
1 egg, beaten
30ml/2 tbsp milk, plus extra for brushing
15ml/1 tbsp pumpkin seeds
15ml/1 tbsp sunflower seeds
15ml/1 tbsp sesame seeds
2.5ml/½ tsp celery salt

1 Preheat the oven to 180°C/350°F/Gas 4. Put the flour, salt, baking powder and butter in a bowl. Rub together.

2 Add the egg and milk and mix to a stiff dough. Roll out on a floured surface to about 5mm/¼in thick.

3 Using a pastry brush, brush a little milk over the dough. Sprinkle all the pumpkin, sunflower and sesame seeds over the top in an even layer, then sprinkle the celery salt over the top.

4 Very gently, roll the rolling pin back and forth over the seeds to press them into the dough.

5 Stamp out rounds using a 10cm/4in cookie cutter and place on a non-stick baking sheet, spacing them slightly apart.

6 Bake the crackers for about 15 minutes, or until just beginning to brown. Transfer to a wire rack to cool completely.

Cook's Tip
To make celery salt, grind five parts lightly toasted celery seeds with one part sea salt.

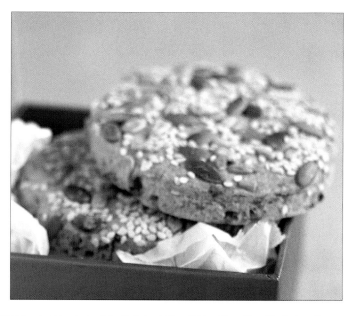

Swedish Crispbread Energy 253kcal/1070kJ; Protein 6.1g; Carbohydrate 44.9g, of which sugars 0.3g; Fat 6.7g, of which saturates 3.5g; Cholesterol 13mg; Calcium 29mg; Fibre 9.5g; Sodium 41mg.
Malted Wheat and Mixed Seed Crackers Energy 140kcal/586kJ; Protein 3.4g; Carbohydrate 12.1g, of which sugars 0.5g; Fat 9.1g, of which saturates 4.6g; Cholesterol 31mg; Calcium 14mg; Fibre 1.8g; Sodium 126mg.

Rye and Caraway Seed Sticks

Wonderful with cocktails or pre-dinner drinks and a great addition to the cheeseboard, these long sticks are made with rye flour and have crunchy caraway seeds inside and out.

Makes 18–20
90g/3¹/₂oz/generous ¾ cup plain (all-purpose) flour
75g/3oz/¾ cup rye flour
pinch of salt
2.5ml/¹/₂ tsp baking powder
90g/3¹/₂oz/7 tbsp unsalted butter, diced
10ml/2 tsp caraway seeds
60ml/4 tbsp boiling water

1 Preheat the oven to 180°C/350°F/Gas 4. Put the flours, salt and baking powder in a bowl and mix together. Add the butter and rub in gently with your fingertips until the mixture resembles fine breadcrumbs.

2 Stir in 5ml/1 tsp of the caraway seeds. Add the water and mix well to form a soft dough.

3 Divide the dough into about 18 even-size pieces and, using your fingers, gently roll each one out to a long thin stick about 25cm/10in long. Do not use any flour when rolling out the sticks unless the mixture is a little too moist. Try to make the sticks as uniform as possible.

4 Place the sticks on a non-stick baking sheet. Sprinkle over the remaining caraway seeds, rolling the sticks in any spilled seeds.

5 Bake the sticks in the oven for about 20 minutes, until crisp. Remove from the oven and transfer carefully to a wire rack. Leave to cool completely.

> **Cook's Tip**
> Rye flour has a rich and distinctive flavour that complements smoked fish. Try serving these sticks with a dip, such as taramasalata or smoked fish pâté, as part of a party buffet table. They are also delicious served with a seafood soup.

Parmesan Tuiles

These lacy tuiles look very impressive, but they couldn't be easier to make. Believe it or not, they use only a single ingredient – grated Parmesan cheese.

Makes 8–10
115g/4oz Parmesan cheese

1 Preheat the oven to 200°C/400°F/Gas 6. Line two baking sheets with baking parchment.

2 Grate the cheese using a fine grater, pulling it down slowly to make long strands.

3 Spread the grated cheese out in 7.5–9cm/3–3¹/₂in rounds. Do not spread the cheese too thickly; it should only just cover the parchment. Bake for 5–7 minutes, until bubbling and golden brown.

4 Leave the tuiles on the baking sheet for about 30 seconds, and then carefully transfer them, using a metal spatula, to a wire rack to cool and set. Alternatively, drape them over a rolling pin while they are still warm so that they set in a curved shape.

> **Cook's Tip**
> Parmesan cheese will keep for months if stored properly. Wrap it in foil and store in a plastic box in the least cold part of the refrigerator, such as the salad drawer or one of the compartments in the door.

> **Variation**
> Tuiles can be made into little cup shapes by draping over an upturned egg cup. These little cups can be filled to make tasty treats to serve with drinks. Try a little cream cheese flavoured with herbs.

Rye and Caraway Seed Sticks Energy 64kcal/269kJ; Protein 0.9g; Carbohydrate 6.4g, of which sugars 0.1g; Fat 4.1g, of which saturates 2.4g; Cholesterol 10mg; Calcium 12mg; Fibre 0.6g; Sodium 77mg.
Parmesan Tuiles Energy 52kcal/216kJ; Protein 4.5g; Carbohydrate 0g, of which sugars 0g; Fat 3.8g, of which saturates 2.4g; Cholesterol 12mg; Calcium 138mg; Fibre 0g; Sodium 125mg.

Sun-dried Tomato Butter Crackers

These buttery crackers have all the flavours of classic pizza – cheese, tomato, oregano and olives.

Makes about 25
175g/6oz/1½ cups plain (all-purpose) flour
150g/5oz/⅔ cup unsalted butter, chilled and diced
150g/5oz/1¼ cups grated mature (sharp) Cheddar cheese
15ml/1 tbsp sun-dried tomato paste
25g/1oz semi-dried sun-dried tomatoes, coarsely chopped
15ml/1 tbsp oregano
15g/½oz/2 tbsp pitted black olives, drained
15–30ml/1–2 tbsp cold water
50g/2oz sesame seeds

1 Put all the ingredients, except the water and sesame seeds, into a food processor. Process until the mixture forms fine crumbs.

2 Add enough water to mix to a soft dough, then shape it into a neat log about 25cm/10in long.

3 Spread out the sesame seeds over a sheet of baking parchment or on a large plate. Roll the dough log in the seeds until the sides are thoroughly coated. Wrap in clear film (plastic wrap) and chill for about 2 hours.

4 Preheat the oven to 180°C/350°F/Gas 4. Using a long, sharp knife, slice the unwrapped log into 1cm/½in slices and place on non-stick baking sheets, spaced slightly apart. Bake for 15–20 minutes, or until golden brown. Transfer the cookies to a wire rack to cool.

> **Variations**
> • If you don't like olives, you can still retain the pizza theme by substituting the same quantity of drained, chopped capers or caper berries.
> • If you prefer, roll the dough log in chopped pine nuts instead of sesame seeds.

Three-cheese Crumble Crackers

A delicious combination of mozzarella, Red Leicester and Parmesan cheese and the fresh taste of pesto make these cookies totally irresistible. Make mini ones to serve with drinks.

Makes 10
225g/8oz/2 cups self-raising (self-rising) flour
50g/2oz/¼ cup butter, diced
50g/2oz mozzarella cheese, diced
50g/2oz Red Leicester cheese, diced
15ml/1 tbsp fresh pesto
1 egg
60ml/4 tbsp milk
15g/½oz/2 tbsp Parmesan cheese, grated
15ml/1 tbsp mixed chopped nuts

1 Preheat the oven to 200°C/400°F/Gas 6.

2 Put the flour in a large mixing bowl, add the butter and rub in with your fingertips until the mixture resembles fine breadcrumbs.

3 Add the diced mozzarella and Red Leicester cheeses to the bowl and stir to mix well. In a separate bowl, beat together the pesto, egg and milk, then pour into the flour and cheese mixture. Stir together quickly until well combined.

4 Using a tablespoon, place in rocky piles on non-stick baking sheets, spaced slightly apart. Sprinkle over the Parmesan cheese and chopped nuts. Bake for 12–15 minutes, until well risen and golden brown. Using a metal spatula carefully transfer to a wire rack to cool.

> **Variations**
> You can vary any or all of the cheeses in this recipe according to taste, but it is best to keep to the same types. Try feta or curd (farmer's) cheese instead of mozzarella, or substitute a creamy blue cheese, such as Bleu d'Auvergne or Gorgonzola. Other semi-hard cheeses, such as Provolone, sage Derby or Cantal could replace the Red Leicester, and pecorino is a good substitute for Parmesan.

Sun-dried Tomato Butter Crackers Energy 107kcal/442kJ; Protein 2.6g; Carbohydrate 5.6g, of which sugars 0.2g; Fat 8.2g, of which saturates 4.6g; Cholesterol 19mg; Calcium 69mg; Fibre 0.4g; Sodium 95mg. **Three-cheese Crumble Crackers** Energy 182kcal/760kJ; Protein 6.6g; Carbohydrate 17.9g, of which sugars 0.7g; Fat 9.7g, of which saturates 5.3g; Cholesterol 41mg; Calcium 135mg; Fibre 0.8g; Sodium 129mg.

Polenta Dippers

These tasty Parmesan-flavoured batons are best served warm from the oven with a spicy, tangy dip such as Thai chilli dipping sauce or creamy guacamole.

Makes about 80

1.5 litres/2½ pints/6¼ cups water
10ml/2 tsp salt
375g/13oz/3¼ cups instant polenta
150g/5oz/1½ cups freshly grated Parmesan cheese
90g/3½oz/scant ½ cup butter
10ml/2 tsp cracked black pepper
olive oil, for brushing

1 Put the water in a large heavy pan and bring to the boil over a high heat. Reduce the heat, add the salt and pour in the polenta in a steady stream, stirring constantly with a wooden spoon. Cook over a low heat, stirring constantly, until the mixture thickens and comes away from the sides of the pan – about 5 minutes.

2 Remove from the heat and add the cheese, butter and pepper and salt to taste. Stir until the butter melts and the mixture is smooth.

3 Pour on to a smooth surface, such as a baking sheet. Spread the polenta to a thickness of 2cm/¾in and shape into a rectangle. Leave for at least 30 minutes to become quite cold.

4 Preheat the oven to 200°C/400°F/Gas 6. Lightly oil two or three baking sheets with some olive oil.

5 Cut the polenta slab in half, then cut into even-size strips. Bake for about 40–50 minutes, until dark golden brown and crunchy. Turn the strips over from time to time during cooking. Serve warm.

Cook's Tip
The dough can be made a day ahead, then wrapped in clear film (plastic wrap) and kept chilled until ready to bake.

Fennel and Chilli Ring Crackers

Based on an Italian recipe, these cookies are made with yeast and are dry and crumbly. Try them with drinks, dips or with a selection of antipasti.

Makes about 30

500g/1lb 2oz/4½ cups type 00 flour, plus extra for dusting
115g/4oz/½ cup white vegetable fat (shortening)
5ml/1 tsp easy-blend (rapid-rise) dried yeast
15ml/1 tbsp fennel seeds
10ml/2 tsp crushed chilli flakes
15ml/1 tbsp olive oil
400–550ml/14–18fl oz/ 1⅔–2½ cups lukewarm water
olive oil, for brushing

1 Put the flour in a bowl and rub in the fat until the mixture resembles fine breadcrumbs. Add the yeast, fennel and chilli and mix well. Add the oil and enough water to make a soft but not sticky dough. Turn out on to a floured surface and knead lightly.

2 Take small pieces of dough and shape into sausages about 15cm/6in long. Shape into rings and pinch the ends together.

3 Place the rings on a non-stick baking sheet and brush lightly with olive oil. Cover with a dish towel and set aside at room temperature for 1 hour to rise slightly.

4 Meanwhile, preheat the oven to 150°C/300°F/Gas 2.

5 Bake the cookies for 1 hour, until they are dry and only slightly browned. Leave on the baking sheet to cool completely.

Cook's Tip
Type 00 is an Italian grade of flour used for pasta. It is milled from the centre part of the endosperm so that the resulting flour is much whiter than plain (all-purpose) flour. It contains 70 per cent of the wheat grain. It is available from Italian delicatessens and some large supermarkets. If you cannot find it, try using strong white bread flour instead.

Polenta Dippers Energy 34kcal/142kJ; Protein 1.2g; Carbohydrate 3.4g, of which sugars 0g; Fat 1.7g, of which saturates 1g; Cholesterol 4mg; Calcium 23mg; Fibre 0.1g; Sodium 27mg.
Fennel and Chilli Ring Crackers Energy 92kcal/385kJ; Protein 1.6g; Carbohydrate 13g, of which sugars 0.3g; Fat 4.1g, of which saturates 1.5g; Cholesterol 1mg; Calcium 24mg; Fibre 0.5g; Sodium 31mg.

Curry Crackers

Crisp curry-flavoured crackers are very good with creamy cheese or yogurt dips and make an unusual nibble with pre-dinner drinks. Add a pinch of cayenne pepper for an extra kick.

Makes about 30

175g/6oz/1½ cups self-raising (self-rising) flour, plus extra for dusting

pinch of salt
10ml/2 tsp garam masala
75g/3oz/6 tbsp butter, diced
5ml/1 tsp finely chopped fresh coriander (cilantro)
1 egg, beaten

For the topping
beaten egg
black onion seeds
garam masala

1 Preheat the oven to 200°C/400°F/Gas 6. Put the flour, salt and garam masala into a bowl. Rub in the butter until the mixture resembles fine breadcrumbs. Stir in the coriander, add the egg and mix to a soft dough.

2 Turn out on to a lightly floured surface and knead gently until smooth. Roll out to a thickness of about 3mm/⅛in.

3 Cut the dough into neat rectangles measuring about 7.5 × 2.5cm/3 × 1in. Brush with a little beaten egg and sprinkle each cracker with a few black onion seeds. Place on non-stick baking sheets and bake in the oven for about 12 minutes, until the crackers are light golden brown all over.

4 Remove from the oven and transfer to a wire rack using a metal spatula. Put a little garam masala in a saucer and, using a dry pastry brush, dust each cracker with a little of the spice mixture. Leave to cool before serving.

> **Cook's Tip**
> *Garam masala is a mixture of Indian spices that usually contains a blend of cinnamon, cloves, peppercorns, cardamom seeds and cumin seeds. You can buy it ready-made or make your own.*

Low-fat Curry Thins

These spicy, crisp little crackers are very low fat and are ideal for serving with drinks.

Makes 12

50g/2oz/1½ cups plain (all-purpose) flour, plus extra for dusting
pinch of salt
5ml/1 tsp curry powder
1.5ml/¼ tsp chilli powder
15ml/1 tbsp chopped fresh coriander (cilantro)
30ml/2 tbsp water

1 Preheat the oven to 180°C/350°F/Gas 4.

2 Sift the flour and salt into a mixing bowl. Add the curry powder and the chilli powder. Make a well in the centre and add the coriander and water. Gradually incorporate the flour and mix to a firm dough.

3 Turn out on to a lightly floured surface, knead until smooth and leave to rest for 5 minutes.

4 Cut the dough into 12 equal pieces and knead each into a small ball. Roll out each ball very thinly to a 10cm/4in round, sprinkling more flour over the dough if necessary to prevent it from sticking to the rolling pin.

5 Arrange the rounds on two ungreased baking sheets, spaced apart, then bake for 15 minutes, turning them over once during cooking. Using a metal spatula, carefully transfer the crackers to a wire rack to cool.

> **Cook's Tip**
> *Commercial curry powders vary enormously in flavour and their degree of heat, depending on the specific spices used and their proportions. The best-quality ones tend to be more expensive, but this is not invariably the case. Try different brands until you find one that you like.*

Curry Crackers Energy 39kcal/164kJ; Protein 0.6g; Carbohydrate 4.6g, of which sugars 0.1g; Fat 2.2g, of which saturates 1.3g; Cholesterol 5mg; Calcium 11mg; Fibre 0.3g; Sodium 17mg.
Low-fat Curry Thins Energy 17kcal/73kJ; Protein 0.5g; Carbohydrate 3.6g, of which sugars 0.1g; Fat 0.2g, of which saturates 0g; Cholesterol 0mg; Calcium 14mg; Fibre 0.4g; Sodium 6mg.